D1391302

NO
MEAN
SOLDIER

NO MEAN SOLDIER

The Autobiography of
a Professional Fighting Man

Peter McAleese
with Mark Bles

ORION

Copyright © 1993 Peter McAleese and Mark Bles

All rights reserved

The rights of Peter McAleese and Mark Bles to be identified
as the authors of this work has been asserted by them in accordance
with the Copyright, Designs and Patents Act 1988

First published in Great Britain in 1993 by
Orion
An imprint of Orion Books Ltd
Orion House, 5 Upper St Martin's Lane, London WC2H 9EA

A CIP catalogue record for this book
is available from the British Library

ISBN 1 85797 250 3

Filmset by Selwood Systems, Midsomer Norton

Printed in Great Britain by Butler & Tanner Ltd, Frome and London

It is not the critic who counts, not the man who points out how the strong man stumbled, or where the doer of the deed could have done better.

The credit belongs to the man who is actually in the arena, whose face is marred by dust and sweat and blood, who strives valiantly, who errs and comes short again and again, because there is no effort without error and shortcoming, who does actually strive to do the deeds, who knows the great enthusiasms and spends himself in a worthy cause, who at best, knows in the end the triumph of high achievement, and at worst, if he fails, at least fails while daring greatly.

His place shall never be with those cold and timid souls who knew neither victory nor defeat.

Theodore Roosevelt

Contents

Acknowledgements

I am very much in the debt of the following people who offered help, advice, and encouragement during the making of this book: Rose and Jeff Brewer for looking after us during the writing of it, Ken Connor, Hortense Daman-Clews for translations from Afrikaans, Murray Davies for background research on Angola, Major Tom Duffy for detail on the Parachute Regiment, Molly Hassall, Dave Tompkins, Al Venter and Joe Lock for photos, Steve Kluzniak, my family, Catherine McAleese, Peter McAleese, Billy McAleese and my wife Jane McAleese, Gill Smith, Tim Spicer, Colonel Jap Swart (SADF), Danny West and Mark Whitcombe.

Also, I want to thank all those people who prefer their names not to appear in print, for one reason or another. They may remain nameless, but their contribution has been none the less considerable and is much appreciated.

Special thanks go to all those people who work in various government departments, libraries and newspaper offices who have been so generous with their time and assistance during the research for this book. They have been unstinting in answering a host of detailed and obscure questions.

Finally, I am particularly grateful to Mark Bles, without whose editorial and moral support this book would not have emerged saying the things I wanted it to say.

Preface

Before you start, I want to clear up a couple of points.

I've always been a professional operational soldier and not, repeat not, a 'career' soldier of the sort who wants only to keep his nose clean and worries about his promotion and pension prospects.

In fact, I don't think I made a bad depot soldier when necessary, and maybe my turnout has been smarter than most. I wonder how many soldiers nowadays bother to iron creases into their combat uniforms?

I've never soldiered just for profit. During all my service in three regular armies, my pay was unimpressive by modern standards. I went from one fighting zone to another but I receive no pension. Nor do I have funds from any other source. I've done it for the adventure, because I have always been a professional soldier, and because I love a fight. I've never been happier than in action.

A British infantry officer said to me, 'Staff McAleese, you are an extreme man. Your obsessions are your strong points, your qualities and your character. You have experience, you have drive, use it.'

I think I have.

The press love extremes. You might think there is enough exciting material in my life to satisfy the most news-hungry of journalists, but there have been some terrible lies written about me and this book puts the record straight.

It's true that I've been a mercenary for a few months of my life, in northern Angola in 1976 and in Colombia. But Gurkhas are mercenaries too, and so are all the British officers and men who served in the Sultan of Oman's Armed Forces.

I am proud to have served for years as a regular soldier in the world's finest airborne regiments in three armies: in the Parachute Regiment and 22 Special Air Service in Britain, in 1 Special Air Service Regiment in what was then Rhodesia, and in the Pathfinders of 44 Parachute Brigade in the South African Defence Force.

You, as the reader, must make up your own mind. Do not be

1

manipulated by the press or second-hand stories you have heard. See what I've done and decide for yourself.

This, then, is my story.

Peter McAleese
Telford, 1993.

First Principles

O Thou, who Man of baser Earth didst make
And who with Eden didst devise the Snake
For all the Sin wherewith the Face of Man
Is blackened, Man's forgiveness give – and take.

EDWARD FITZGERALD,
Rubaiyat of Omar Khayyam

I could not describe the first person I killed, nor the last. There is nothing personal in that. I have never felt any personal animosity towards the enemies I have fought. It was just the way it happened, in the darkness and the chaos of fighting, but the first time was important to me, as I suppose it must be for anyone.

We were in the Aden Protectorate, about four hours' uncomfortable driving in a truck from Aden Port over a rough graded road into the interior which was an arid desert land of harsh rocky mountains. We lived in Habilayn, a dusty camp of tents, barbed wire and sandbags which the British Army had pegged out in neat military lines in the middle of a flat plain circled by hills, where our enemy lived. Every evening as the sun went down, the gunners fired the 105s into the mouths of wadis from which they thought the enemy would emerge to attack us. A group of us waited to go out on night patrol and I felt like a soldier on the Northwest Frontier, listening to the roar of the guns and watching the orange explosions far out on the darkening hillsides while the sky faded to deep blue. Stars appeared in the east and away across the guy ropes and poles of Habilayn Camp, I could faintly hear the garrison bugler sounding the Retreat.

When the guns fell silent after nightfall, we walked out, in two half-squadron groups, in single file, through the barbed wire and pickets towards the dark jagged ridges to the west under a black sky hanging with stars. The ground was brutal, rocky, like a moonscape and we humped heavy rucksacks, old Para-type, with canvas sacks and A-frames. We carried SLRs (Self Loading Rifles) and wore 'trousers and shirts OG' (olive green) and Clarke's desert shoes because they were light and cooler than boots.

Our enemy were Arab tribesmen, the National Liberation Front, the NLF, and their rivals the Federation for the Liberation of South Yemen, FLOSY. They were hard men with dark faces, fine looking, with long hair and dirty robes. They lived like the Saracens of centuries ago but they had twentieth-century weapons, from the huge Second World War arms dumps which the British Army had left behind in Egypt when we were booted out after Suez in 1956, only nine years before.

The thing I remember most about the march that night was being literally soaked with sweat. I followed Sergeant Dave Haley, our patrol commander, or rather the huge rucksack on legs in front of me which is all he seemed to be. He stopped us every hour for a break. When I sat down, I shivered as the sweat cooled on me in the night air and I worried about the amount of water I would need. I was carrying two one-gallon heavy-duty plastic water containers in my rucksack and had two more water bottles on my belt kit. With that and ammunition, seven magazines and extra link for the gunner carrying the GPMG (General Purpose Machine Gun), and food, which was last in order of priority, our rucksacks weighed nearly 70 lbs, excluding what we carried in pouches on our belts. It was tiring work and we needed to replace all the fluid lost.

In darkness, we crossed a small range of hills about four miles from Habilayn and then the moon came up. Six miles later, somewhere after midnight, we started to climb up the side of the Jebel Barash, which was very distinct, a sharp ridge with two lumps on it like a camel's hump. We slogged upwards, each one of us exhausted, drenched with sweat and almost mindlessly following the dark shape of the man ahead until we finally breasted the top and moved into a saddle, on a reverse slope. We collected loose rocks lying about, of which there was no shortage, to make sangars with low protective walls, and then set up our shade for the day ahead. I stretched four netted face veils sewed together across the sangar, from wall to wall, held with rocks and supported in the middle with bits of stick I always brought with me. There weren't any trees in those mountains, not that we would have been allowed to go out and cut them. We settled down to rest, sleep and lie up for the day.

The heat was really intense. And the Jebel was bare, like the moon. You could see for miles. Any movement in the open would have been seen by the enemy tribesmen who kept lookouts sitting about on the tops of the mountains. So before first light we always ran a piece of string out between the sangars tied to a rock which could be moved to attract the attention of people in other sangars. This meant sentry duty was done sangar by sangar, in pairs so one person could not fall asleep on his own, and the sangars were mutually supporting. We used binos, with the objective lenses covered with a piece of face veil, in case the enemy saw a glint of reflected sunlight.

The year before, a nine-man patrol from 3 Troop of 'A' Squadron had marched into the centre of the Radfan mountains and a goatherd had stumbled across them by chance. The enemy had gathered fast, pinned them down all day and killed two and wounded another two before the patrol could make a fighting withdrawal to safety. We were sixteen and we had plenty of support, A41 radios to call up the 105 mm artillery and Sarbe radios to bring in RAF ground-attack Hunter jets, and I could even see Habilayn Camp in heat haze far below us on the valley floor, but all that seemed a long way off and we kept very still in our sangars.

In the heat of the afternoon, we ate our meal, curry and rice, had a brew of tea, and then packed our rucksacks ready to go. As the sun faded, we had stand-down, a fine British military tradition. We crouched in our sangars, weapons ready, peering over the rocky hillside for about three-quarters of an hour while the sun set. This marked the transition from day routine to night routine. After dark, we took down the face veils, stowed them away and set about taking down the sangars, scattering the rocks about.

Then we started walking down the western side of the Jebel Barash into a small wadi which connected with the Wadi Mishwarrah. Halfway through the night after about four hours' walking, Dave Haley stopped us at some muddy water and we filled our water bottles. It was filthy and brackish, but we were gasping. I filled my bottles without a second's thought and added the blue and white sterilisation tablets.

Suddenly I smelled a scented sweetness on the still night air and next moment a goatherd appeared. 'Shep' Shepherd was leading scout and Dave called me forward to speak to the goatherd. I had done an Arabic course in Aden three years before and was on the patrol to act as his interpreter.

'Salaam alikum,' I said softly; greetings to you.

'Wa'alikum salaam!' And to you! he replied, shouting. When I asked him if he had seen any other British soldiers, he shouted, 'Aywa!' Yes! About half an hour before.

5

'*Uskat, uskat!*' Be calm, I said, warning him to make less noise, and translated for Dave Haley. The goatherd talked as if he had seen the other half-squadron which we knew was ahead of us and which sounded as if it had turned back up the Wadi Mishwarrah, while the goatherd had come into our tributary wadi behind them.

We assumed everything was going according to plan, and moved on, carefully. The moon was not up yet and it was so dark in the narrow wadi I could only just see the rock walls rearing up beside us.

Five minutes later, Dave Haley whispered, 'Pete, come up. There's some more chappies down here.' I padded up to Dave to speak to them and made out the dark shapes of a group of shepherds, lying on the ground ahead. Just as I started to speak, I saw one of them shift on his side. It was probably the way he moved which warned me and I thought, this is never right!

The Arab shot Dave Haley, full in the chest.

He should have shot me, as I was closest, but I was standing to one side, ready to interpret, and the Arab was lying in such a way that, as he sat up, he was restricted.

Dave collapsed, badly wounded, and I shot the Arab. Six times. Then all hell let loose. The wadi walls came in close just there and tracer streamed past, pinning me to the warm rock at the side. The enemy had DPM automatics with big pan-shaped magazines on the top, the darkness echoed with shouting and they started throwing old British 36 grenades.

The others behind me ran to the flanks at once, Mick Seale shouting he was going to one side and Shep to the other, climbing the steep rocks to find a higher position where they poured fire down onto the enemy. Our medic, Jock Phillips, came up to help Dave Haley who had crawled to one side.

I heard a vicious explosive crack at my feet and doubled back from my exposed position in the middle of the wadi to scramble up the rocks and join the flanking movement. As I climbed, I looked up and saw Shep hit in the shoulder. He was standing on a rock firing down into the wadi beyond and cartwheeled off the rock like a movie star in a Wild West film.

Jock Phillips and another of the guys, Dave Abbotts, now had two wounded men to deal with. Jock was well trained, with weeks of experience in a hospital emergency ward back home, but he had none of the kit now issued to SAS patrol medics. What he really needed was plasma drips and giving sets (the needle and tube connecting an emergency plasma drip to the arm), but all he could do was pack on shell dressings to stop the bleeding (the gaping hole in the side of Dave's chest took six), jab in 100 ml units of penicillin and make them comfortable on the sand. Each man carried two syrettes of Omnopon, taped on string round his neck, but morphine can't be used on wounds to the head, chest or stomach, so Dave Haley did without.

I was extremely busy. Taking a position high up at the front once Shep was lifted down, I kept firing at the muzzle flashes of the Arabs' weapons and throwing grenades which the others passed up to me from below. I used white phosphorus grenades to light the wadi ahead and flush the Arabs out of cover, as the phosphorus blown into the air fell back on them behind the rocks where they were hiding, and high explosive American M26s, which were devastating on the hard open ground.

The explosions lit the night and boomed deafeningly in the narrow valley and the exchange of fire went on for a couple of hours. We were never too concerned about counter attack because we held the steep wadi flanks. After the firing died down we lay there alert all night, until dawn at about five o'clock.

Come first light, several of us advanced down the wadi ahead. The Arabs had gone, leaving the fine silver sand and yellow rocks covered with blood. Another group of the guys picked up a trail of bloodstains which they followed up the hill above the wadi till they found an Arab who had somehow crawled up the steep slope and hidden under a rock. He was very badly wounded but refused to give up. He stupidly opened fire and they shot him dead where he lay.

In the wadi bottom, I looked round the scene of the battle. In their haste, the Arabs had left behind shoes, clothes and little bags of their belongings, including money and watches which they used as currency. Needless to say, these were pounced on by the chaps. We worked out there had been about twelve of them.

Behind us, in cover back up the wadi, our patrol signaller had been busy. As soon as early morning atmospheric conditions allowed, just before dawn, he had tapped out a signal to our base calling for helicopter casevac and just as it was light we heard the beating din of a navy Wessex from the Royal Navy carrier standing off Aden port. Someone talked the pilot down on a Sarbe ground-to-air radio but the wadi was too narrow for the helicopter's big rotors. The pilot pulled off to circle round while we carried Dave and Shep as carefully as we could up the steep sides of the wadi. The sweat poured off us. The Wessex tried again, but was still unable to land. Finally the pilot hovered about fifty feet up, his rotor blades terribly close to the rocks, the loadmaster winched them in and the Wessex pulled away en route for the hospital.

While all this was going on, the other half of our patrol picketed the heights above the wadi, just like the British Army had done high above the Khyber Pass. When we prepared to move on, I found the place where I had shot the first Arab. Typically, the others had dragged him off. The Arabs hated leaving their dead and I was certain I had killed him. The rock slab which had been behind him was covered in blood and there were six holes, in a good group, chipped deep into the stone. I also discovered that the sharp explosion at my feet the night before had been a British 36 grenade which had failed to explode. The detonator had fired, blowing the casing apart, but failed to set off the main charge. I had been lucky. I had survived.

I felt good, I felt fit, I felt hard. This was the first time I had been in a contact and killed anyone. This euphoria was nothing to do with ending another person's life. I felt good because I had not panicked, I had not let down my friends, I had reacted as a professional soldier trained by professional soldiers, and the excitement of the firefight had been nothing short of fantastic. I've never taken drugs but I can't believe there's anything which can equal the thrill of a battle. I loved it.

This was no surprise. I was a very aggressive young man.

***

I've been told that there is a balance in everyone between what we learn from our families and what we are born with. If that's so, I think I was given more than my fair share of extremes in both cases. I'm making no excuses for myself, but you need to understand my background.

I was born on 7 September 1942, at Number 15 Kenmore Street, Shettleston, in Glasgow. My father and grandfather were miners and life in Glasgow was rough. We had moved twice by the time I was five. First to Number 290 Carntyne Road in Carntyne, where three familes shared our 'house', and then to Number 15 Lethamhill Road, Riddrie. This was a block of brick-built Victorian tenements which belonged to Barlinnie Prison and had been built as living quarters for prison warders. In 1947 they were empty and derelict and because life was so cramped in Carntyne Road, a number of families moved in to Lethamhill Road as squatters. There was no caring DHSS then and the council had nowhere else for us to go. Lethamhill Road was in sight of the prison so it was not long before the prison authorities called the police to evict us. My father was away, either in the army or in prison (or both) but my mother gathered up her family, me, my elder brother Billy, Molly who was only three and her youngest, Rose, who was only just born, and the police took us all off to the prison. They gave up with us soon enough, and let us stay in Lethamhill Road, but there aren't many, even in Scotland, who have the dubious claim to have been locked up in Barlinnie Gaol at five years old.

I idolised my father, but it was not till later that I understood his life. He was a typical Glaswegian mixture of Catholic Scottish and Irish, and a miner. In the war, he was called up for the army which promptly sent him to a Welsh regiment. As a result, he hated the Welsh and was constantly in trouble. He was in the army until 1953, so I saw little of him till I was ten. He was either away from home in the barracks in Brecon, or in prison, sometimes in Barlinnie which had a military wing in those days. He had a cell overlooking Lethamhill Road which I could see from the street. He hung things out of his window as signals, like socks or a shirt of different colours, to show my mother what sort of mood he was in. They had known each other since he was six and she was four and they adored each other. She must have loved him to have stayed with him and, in spite of all he did, there was never any doubt about the strength of feeling between them.

I grew up thinking that having a good time was getting blind drunk on Friday and Saturday nights and fighting. I remember when I was very young spying through the keyhole at my father and my uncle Billy shouting and battering each other with their fists in the front room. My uncle Billy was a vicious fighter. He would grab anything to hand to win, but my father got the better of him. He was a clean fighter, well respected as such in the neighbourhood, and Shettleston was as rough a part of Glasgow as any. The men in our area said the boys from the Gorbals came to Shettleston to learn how to scrap.

My father was leader of an illegal gambling school which he ran on rough ground under a railway bridge near Carntyne dog track. It was well sited. They could carry on even if it rained, and if the police came, they had several routes to run away. He liked to wear smart suits, wide silk ties and had a fine pair of yellow shoes. He was the referee, or toller, nicknamed 'Kiter' as he flicked the pennies and he took a portion of the money bet on the pitch and toss. Other men tried from time to time to beat him up and take his place. I remember the terrible shock when he came home one day and I could see in his eyes that he had been beaten. John Doran, a big man from another strong mining family in the area, had beaten him up. I hated to see how disgusted he was with himself and to see his sense of failure. He knew he had been knocked down because he had been in bad shape and he went to my grandfather for advice.

Old Miles, as we all called my grandfather, was sixty years old then. He had been welter-weight champion of Scotland and was feared in his day. By then he was a steady man of experience, a fund of good sense, the sort of person who walked round all day in the house with his braces round his legs, and hoisted them matter-of-fact over his shoulders to go out. He put my father through a punishing six-week training session, just as he had done himself at the boxing gym and in the army. The lesson was not lost on me for the future. I watched my father running, working out with weights and the two sparring together. Then the challenge was issued to John Doran and all the men met on top of a slag heap, which we called a bing, to witness the fight.

I went and hung around on the edge of the crowd. I had to see what happened. There must have been two hundred miners there, all our family and the Dorans in large numbers. My father, Kiter, and John squared up stripped to the waist and their seconds finalised the details. I watched them put up their bare fists and the fight started. Old Miles's training paid off. In moments, Kiter had battered John Doran to the ground. He stayed down. In the pause, one of the Doran family remarked that the fight had been rigged. This was fuel to the fire. Without a second's delay, my uncle Billy drew a long bayonet from under his coat and stabbed the Doran man in the chest. At once, everyone started fighting. Maybe at first some were merely trying to separate the two, but in minutes the bing was covered with miners all wrestling and beating each other. But Kiter won.

He liked to keep ahead of the game. Someone came to tell him that a local villain called Crosby was coming for him, to move him off his tossing school pitch. And, they said, Crosby had a gun.

'Fine,' said my father casually and did nothing more about it.

In the early 1950s few people, even where I came from, had guns and everyone waited, hanging out of the windows, to see what would happen. Hanging out of the windows was everyone's pastime. They could watch the neighbourhood and hear the gossip. Some claimed it was the only way to get fresh air.

Just as he said he would, Crosby walked over the derelict land to Kiter's pitch and toss group under the railway bridge. I was amazed as Crosby produced his gun, a small revolver, grinning fiercely with triumph. The other men backed off, waiting to see what Kiter would do. My father just opened his suit jacket both sides with both hands. Tucked in his belt were two guns, one on each side. Impressed and defeated, Crosby turned and walked off.

In addition to running the local gambling school, my father had other responsibilities. He was in charge of the tenants' association for the building we lived in. The families all put in half a crown a week to pay for repairs, but most people fell behind with their payments, and when a plumber was needed to unblock the one toilet serving sixty people, my father decided to do the job himself. The cause of the blockage was a miscarriage. Such was life in the slums.

My father was a reluctant soldier. While in the Welsh Fusiliers he went absent, got caught and was remanded in custody in the guardroom, pending court martial. But in order to be court-martialled he had to be wearing uniform, and this he refused to do. On his second day of confinement his civilian clothes were stolen while he was having a shower, and he was offered a uniform instead. But he refused to wear it, and for over a week, in mid-winter, this Gandhi-lookalike with shaven head and bare feet walked about the guardroom dressed only in a blanket.

During the Second World War the army could not afford to have people like my father – people who continually questioned the system – but he certainly never lacked moral courage. And in more recent times he might even have been given credit for being an original thinker in his protests.

Unlike my father, my grandfather was a man with genuine military service in action. His stories had a profound effect on me. He too was a miner, a tough man who had joined the Argylls at sixteen and served his time in the trenches in the First World War. He told me that fighting in France was much the same as fighting in Glasgow, only he was allowed to shoot the opposition. He was wounded on three separate occasions, once badly in the thigh during the battle for Loos, in Belgium. He lay down on a bank behind the trenches to wait for a horse-drawn wagon to take him to a field hospital and quietly lit his pipe. An officer passed by and when Old Miles did not move the officer began shouting at him to stand up and salute, and accused him of malingering. Old Miles merely took out his pipe, lifted his kilt and pointed with his pipe at the bloody hole in the top of his leg. Attitudes to suffering and survival were different then. Old Miles and the others in the First War had no helicopters to swoop down and casevac them to hospital, no penicillin, no handy syrettes of morphine nor any of the modern drugs and well-stocked field surgical units for casualties on the battlefield.

Old Miles told me he respected the Germans. They fought hard and fair, and only once did he let himself go, when he heard that his brother, Alexander 'Sanny' McAleese, had been killed in the fighting round Neuve Chapelle. He got very emotional as he talked, sitting in our kitchen at home, his braces round his legs, and admitted to me that he had gone mad at that and killed some German prisoners. He said, 'It was the only time. When I heard about Sanny, I let the war become personal.'

Looking back, remembering the look in his eyes as he told me the story, I think he knew he was wrong, but there was a time later, in Rhodesia, when I came to understand the same madness.

To his family and friends, Old Miles was a people's person with a strong sense of justice and one story of his stuck firmly in my mind. He said there were trench police, like military police, whose job was to prevent desertion and they were hated by the troops. One day, the Argylls had come through a town on their way up to the front and my grandfather and his mates found a wine cellar in an empty house. There was no time to take any wine then, but one of them nipped back from the billet they took over that night nearer the front. He was caught going back by the trench police who accused him of deserting. He admitted he was trying to steal wine, but no one believed him. He was caught in the system and my grandfather's face hardened as he said, 'Desertion, they said it was. Before we knew it, he was ragged, tagged, bagged and shot by the firing squad.' What a price for a drink. Come to think of it, the British trench police don't sound a lot different to the Iraqi special squads which Sadam Hussein used to stop deserters during the Gulf War.

My formal education, as they call it, was short, sharp and very strict. Being of a Catholic family, I was sent to St Thomas's Primary in Riddrie which was run by nuns with a truly Catholic vision of what was right and wrong. We were all terrified of Sister Loyola, a tall stern woman. All us kids reckoned she had been rejected by the Gestapo for being too harsh. When I was only six, Jimmy Dewar peed on me in the toilets so I peed on him. Most young kids have pee fights but we were caught and reported to Sister Loyola who clearly had no idea what we had been doing. She was appalled. For her, this was proof of the degeneration of our minds and souls and by the time I got home after school, she had told my mother that Jimmy Dewar and I had been 'interfering' with each other in the toilets and recommended: 'He should be stripped naked and beaten till he cries.' My mother was a fine woman, a Catholic but a practical woman too. This was too much for her and she preferred to believe my less apocalyptic version of the story.

Most of the people in Riddrie were better off than us. The area was quite posh except for the tenement block slums in Lethamhill Road where we lived, and I was very self-consciously aware at school that all my clothes were handed down to me after they had been used by my older brother Billy. To be fair to my father, he did give us a new rigout once a year, on Easter Sunday for Mass: new trousers, a new shirt with a sleeveless grey pullover and 'sanies', sandshoes. However, most of the year, I went to school in Billy's hand-me-downs, and, as I wasn't very big, I was always flopping about in baggy shorts, a worn jersey hanging off my shoulders and outsize shoes. Maybe this wasn't unique, but most of the other kids were better off, and their fathers had jobs. What really hurt was the meal-ticket system. All us children were given a ticket at the start of the week and a nun would punch a hole in your ticket each lunchtime, five times a week. That was all right, but an awful distinction was made. Children whose parents could pay for their lunches had buff-coloured tickets but if you were were 'on the parish', or your father was in jail, you were given red tickets. I always seemed to have a red ticket. It was like holding up a flashing red light, a beacon of shame, and I would hear people saying in low voices as I queued for meals, 'They say his father's away working in the tunnels at Pitlochry, at the new hydro-electric plant,' which meant they knew perfectly well he was in jail. To make matters worse, with a red card, I was given an old paper bag of rations every Friday to take home for the weekend!

We had hours of religious instruction from the nuns and I used to 'plonk' school to work on a milk float instead. One day, Father Brett, whose reputation was worse than Sister Loyola's, caught me on the milk round and he made me come up on stage in front of the whole school.

'This child here chose to deliver milk,' he shouted out to the entire hall, his Southern Irish accent making two syllables of the word 'milk'. 'He chose to work rather than attend church!'

I cannot remember what else he said, but the mortal danger to my soul by missing religious instruction was nothing compared to the terrible humiliation of standing there feeling very small and exposed to ridicule in my worn clothes, with my hair which was too long and those great big shoes of Billy's banging about on the hollow wooden stage.

We had to go to church every Sunday and of course some of us plonked that too. One Monday morning, Thomas O'Donnell and I were told that Sister Loyola had noticed we'd been missing the day before and was gunning for us. She wanted to see us. That meant we would be subject to one of her famous interrogations and a certain hiding.

Terrified, I was called to her office. 'Good day, Sister Loyola. God bless you, Sister Loyola,' I said, holding my hands balled together on my chest as I walked in, my head bowed. God help us if we didn't always address the nuns and teachers this way.

'Peter McAleese!' she boomed at me sternly in her strong Irish accent. 'You were not in the children's section at church yesterday morning!'

'Yes, Sister Loyola, I was,' I lied, damned if I was going to take a beating without a fight.

The interrogation began. Sister Loyola wanted all the details. 'Who was taking Mass?' She glared at me from behind her plain wood desk.

'Father Courtney, Sister Loyola.'

'What colour were his vestments?'

'Green, Sister Loyola.'

'Who were the altar boys?'

'Tom McGrady and Pat McSweeney, Sister Loyola.'

'Why weren't you on the register of those attending Mass?'

'I got there late, Sister Loyola, just before the consecration.' Missing consecration was a mortal sin but, at that moment, Sister Loyola and her beatings were more terrifying.

She did not let up. She pressed me on details of the epistle, the gospel and Father Courtney's sermon. But I held my own. I had carefully learned all the answers from the other kids at playtime.

'Well done, Peter, you are a good boy,' said Sister Loyola finally. Her bleak face broke into a smile. 'You can have a coconut ice.'

Thomas O'Donnell did not do so well. He told the truth, pleaded guilty and got a sound thrashing.

I don't know what happened exactly at St Thomas's but something went badly wrong there. I went back not long ago and felt the atmosphere of the place creep over me again. Sister Loyola and Father Brett were just names to the nuns there now but they kindly showed me the big ledger with all the McAleese family names written in it. They looked very beautiful there, in that neat calligraphic handwriting, but it was hardly a true record of the reality of Lethamhill Road. Then I walked round the school yard and I was overcome with emotion. I hesitate to say this after all the things I have seen and done since, and some people who know me might find it hard to believe, but I could not stop myself crying. It wasn't just nostalgia or thinking of the one teacher, Miss Crawshaw, who I liked and who treated me as a person, and who was the only one to encourage me. It was the power of the place and the rigid Catholic discipline exerting its influence again. Perhaps Sister Loyola, Father Brett and the others were hard because they faced educating us in a hard, unforgiving society, but the iron rules of their education showed us no spark of freedom or opportunity to find a way out of the likes of Lethamhill Road. I spent seven years there, between five and eleven, terribly formative years, and I think this place was as much a part of me as my family background and my own character.

In 1954, I left St Thomas's and went to St Roche's Junior Secondary school. In between the classroom, my education in violence continued and I became used to running round the streets in gangs. Like my father and uncle Billy, fighting rivals with sticks, iron bars and knives became second nature. I went round 'tooled up' with an axe or knife hidden under my jacket without thinking. I preferred a long bayonet, not for stabbing but whipping the 'enemy' about the head with the thick steel. Not surprisingly, Mr Kelly expelled me from St Roche's for fighting and I went instead to St Mark's for the last two years of schooling which I finished aged fifteen.

To understand my behaviour as a boy, you have to understand the subculture of the slums. Success in that environment was not measured by the usual indicators – a good job, a nice home or a car. It was measured by how tough you were. Could you handle yourself, could you 'go ahead' (fight); were you capable of a 'comeback' (a return fight after you'd been beaten)? One local called Tommy Shaint was obsessed with the Westerns featuring a character called 'Edge', and used to use Edge's favourite weapon, a razor. He had a comeback in Kenmore Street, and I remember Tommy's adversary leaving the scene minus an ear. But after a comeback malice was uncommon. The pecking order was maintained or reshuffled and everyone then carried on as normal.

People hated the system that supported them, and felt it was there to be 'knocked' (abused). After joining the army I came back on leave once and found one of my mates had strapped a vacuum cleaner hose to his gas meter in order to blow the numbers backwards. When I was growing up, a more common method was the potato trick. A small hole was drilled in the electricity meter and a needle inserted with a potato attached to act as a weight and stop the wheel from spinning. A character known as 'Johnny Boo' used to take the bulb from a streetlamp and attach a cable from his house, thereby enjoying the privilege of free electricity during the hours of darkness. Nowadays things are more sophisticated, and professionals instal switches into the system that allow electricity meters to be bypassed at will.

An outsider might be horrified by all this – the violence and the fiddling – but in the slums this was the norm, where the cramped conditions determined the values people lived by. However, my childhood memories are far from being uniformly grim. Easter Sunday was great fun. It meant new clothes and Easter eggs, and seemed to be the beginning of the Catholic social calendar; the weather picked up and school holidays were discussed. For myself I used to work for a farmer called Sanny Mungall. The fresh air and milk which he used to let us have did us the world of good, and while he used to work us hard, deep down we knew he had a soft spot for us. Sadly, his farm was eventually eaten up by the encroaching housing estates.

Courting or 'winching', as it was called, took the following form. The prospective candidate was 'eyed up' and normally approached in the local café owned by an Italian called Johnny Matteo. A date was made and the couple used to go to the pictures. With each visit they moved further back in the rows, and when you reached the back row you were winching. Soon after that the couple would marry and move into a 'single end', a one-bedroom flat with an inset bed. As a rule the marriages used to fare well in the beginning; there was employment for young people in the whisky bonds or the carpet factory. The problems began when the children came along: the income was halved, the single end became cramped and the men would start spending their time in the pub. Once the men reached the age of twenty-one they would lose their jobs, that being the age when employers would have to pay adult wages. The men were then on the 'buroo' (the dole) and the pressure was on. I don't claim that the whole of Glasgow was like this, but it is definitely the way it was in the East End suburbs of Shettleston, Parkhead and Carntyne. There were only two options if you wanted to escape this existence: move to England or join the army. I chose the latter.

I had wanted to be a soldier from an early age. Old Miles was a great influence with his stories of the war and I picked up everything I could about the army, especially about the Parachute Regiment. You might say I was obsessed. I saw the film *The Red Beret* seventeen times! I learned later that this was about the Bruneval Raid, but I can still remember Alan Ladd as Private McKendrick, nicknamed 'Canada', Stanley Baker as the parachute jump despatcher, and Leo Genn as Colonel John Frost, who was called Major Snow in the film.

And I laugh when I think of the day when I was twelve and I saw a Parachute Regiment soldier walking along Lethamhill Road going home on leave, kitbag over his shoulder, and I followed him through the streets. I was fascinated by his smart uniform, his brown and green camouflaged smock, his neatly pressed khaki trousers, his polished boots and immaculately rolled puttees, and most of all the shiny silver parachute badge on his red beret. I followed him for quite a long way and of course finally he lost his temper. He swung round on me and asked in utter amazement, 'What the fuck are you doing?' It's a pity now that the Northern Ireland troubles mean that soldiers proud of their uniforms daren't wear them in public.

I had a few years to kill before I could join up so, in 1957 I went to work in a Teachers' whisky bond (a bonded warehouse) for a while and then started as an apprentice plasterer. However, the following year my elder brother Billy and I left home. We went to work in Aberdeen and I found a job as a fish porter in the docks which I kept for two years, drifting back and forth to Glasgow, before I got sacked. Then Billy quit, went on the dole and was immediately picked up for his National Service. He went into the Ordnance Corps.

I joined the Parachute Regiment. On 1 March 1960, at seventeen, I signed on for nine years and began a crucial grounding in my soldiering career.

I was sent south, to Aldershot, where I was put in intake Number 197. I became very fit, and I must say I loved it. This was the first time I had been out of Scotland and the things that stick in mind are absurd, looking back. The accents from all over the country were utterly confusing to start with, the water was hard compared to the soft waters off the Scottish hills and English bitter tasted foul. However, the training was excellent and I absorbed myself in it totally. In the recruit company were my intake sergeant, George Brown, CSM Tovell, Company Commander Major Maurice Tugwell and my officer was Lieutenant Duke Pirie, the first direct entry officer to the Parachute Regiment who was later 'B' Squadron Commander in the SAS, and quite coincidentally lived next door to Dave Tomkins, of whom more later. I took pride in my uniform and appearance. I was slow, but once I grasped the system I think I did quite well. Lord Mountbatten took my passing out parade in June that year, and the following month I passed my parachute course at Abingdon, near Oxford.

My first posting was to 1 Para in Albuera Barracks in the old Wellington Lines at Aldershot and I was put straight into the Mortar Platoon in Support Company. This was unusual, in that most new soldiers went to a rifle company first, and to begin with I was given a hard time by the older hands. Support Company men were normally the most experienced in any battalion, but I was beginning to learn the army system and settled in.

At the depot, I found out that while the Parachute Regiment is an elite among infantry troops there was another Regiment which demands higher standards of all its soldiers. I applied to join 22 Special Air Service and formed up to speak to WO2 Johnson, the Support Company CSM.

'Permission to speak, Sergeant Major, sir!' I said, standing rigidly to attention in front of him. You could not speak to the CSM any other way.

'Yes?'

'I want to join the Special Air Service, sir.'

He just looked at me, a faint mischievous smile on his face, and replied, 'The SAS? We send all our shit there. All they want to do is go into the jungle and build tents.' Then he just walked away and left me!

However, I applied and took selection in January 1962. There is a lot of rubbish written in the press about the SAS but it is true that selection over the Brecon hills is hard work. There are four hundred miles of tabbing as fast as you can over the mountains, carrying a rifle and increasing weights up to 65 lbs. In a nutshell, people of all shapes and sizes pass simply because they want to, but it's sweaty work. I was in good shape, but I was only nineteen and my map reading was still shaky, so I scraped through on my fitness and determination.

My SAS continuation training was excellent, run by professionals such as Sergeant Tanky Smith, Sergeant Alec Spence and Captain George Morgan. It took seven months. Most of it was based in Hereford though we spent an invaluable six weeks jungle training in Grik in Malaya.

I was posted to 'D' Squadron where I was one of the youngest and we went to train with the United States Special Forces in Fort Bragg, North Carolina. Here, I got into trouble. A group of us were off duty in a bar, an argument started with an American who insisted on pressing me for a fight so I obliged him. A squadron corporal took the American's side and I took him on too, twice, because later he tried to creep up on me in the middle of the night when he thought I was asleep. The squadron officers took a dim view of all this, perhaps because they were embarrassed for our American hosts. I certainly broke the rules, fighting with senior ranks, and I believe I would have done the same as they did faced by a person like me, but it would have been nice if the other side of the story had been aired too. Anyway, I found myself sent back to the Paras. This was bad news, but I make no excuses. We were out on the town, and, as I have said before, I was aggressive. Besides, the American and the corporal both deserved it!

My father had a more severe experience during the war. As I've said, he was posted to a Welsh battalion, and there he hit an officer. I can't remember the reason, but hitting officers is not encouraged, especially not in a national army in wartime. Discipline was not as severe as that practised by Old Miles's trench police, but you can't have soldiers smacking officers and getting away with it. Kiter was sent away for two years. Barlinnie again. Even volunteering to fight in North Africa was no good. They made him serve his two-stretch. So for me, going back to the Paras was not so bad.

At any rate, that's what I thought till I found myself in 'A' Company of 1 Para. The company sergeant major was a famous Parachute Regiment name, Nobby Arnold (later the Regimental Sergeant Major), and the company commander was Major Jack Thorpe. Discipline was manic and our love-hate relationship with these two bound us all together. 'A' Company's reputation was such that, if the men in other companies stepped out of line, they were threatened with being posted to join us. Beau Geste himself would have cracked in 'A' Company!

At least we travelled and I saw something of the world when few people from my background could, and it was good military experience. In December 1962, we went to Bahrain in the Gulf, on standby to reinforce Kuwait in case Iraq attacked. I don't suppose Iraqis have changed much but they were not led by a megalomaniac then. They made a lot of noise but stayed their side of the border, so we spent several hot months over Christmas constructing Hamala Camp, breaking stones for the buildings with pick and sledge under the glaring sun, like prisoners, and we trained in Shajah in the desert. All this was a tough apprenticeship, not much like the plastering I had started in Glasgow, but these years gave me a solid base in soldiering.

I did one trip in a blue beret for the United Nations, right at the start of 1964. All 1 Para was on Christmas leave and I was in Glasgow when a telegram arrived on New Year's Day telling me to report back to Aldershot at once for an emergency deployment. Drinking was forgotten and I took the train south in great excitement. Hasty preparations were made and we were flown out to Cyprus with the

UN. In my ignorance, I hoped for action. Instead, we spent three weeks in Dhekelia sitting about on our backsides in a tented camp wondering why we had been rushed back off Christmas leave. We concluded that the Paras didn't like us having Christmas at home.

Colonel John Woodhouse allowed me back to the SAS in October that year and I suppose I was lucky he never made me do selection over again. However, I was very fit and had learned a lot in the intervening two years. I picked up all my old kit from Drag Rowbottom in the stores where it had been kept in a container and joined 'D' Squadron again on a training trip to South Arabia.

Being in Aden again brings me back to where I started, so I will explain something of the situation. The background is simply that Britain wanted out. This was officially called decolonisation, but on British terms. For this, in February 1959, the Conservative government invented the Federation of South Arabia, roping together a motley crew of sultanates, emirates and sheikhdoms, some of which had been enemies for generations. Aden port was supposed to be an economic jewel which would generate income and tie in the tribesmen of the interior. The British supported the new Federation's Arab leaders – the traditional rulers of these different groups – formed the British-officered Federal Regular Army and the Federal National Guard, and promised to keep troops there in support. This was the crucial part of the arrangement. HQ Middle Eastern Command was established in Aden in 1960, having been chased out of Egypt, Palestine and Cyprus, and Britain was keen to keep naval and air base facilities in Aden which was still seen then as an important staging post to the Far East.

However, the tribes in the interior wanted total independence. I suppose they did not trust either the British or the town Arabs ruling Aden and they were stirred up with revolutionary Marxism by Egypt, where Nasser was top dog and hated the British after the Suez debacle. Russia was behind him. They kept up a stream of anti-British radio broadcasts from Cairo and Sana'a in Yemen and supplied plenty of arms carried over the border on camels.

Anyway, that was what we called 'the big picture'. On the ground, at troopie level, I went every year to Aden from 1964 to 1967 and each year things got worse. In 1964, there were only thirty-six terrorist incidents and thirty-six casualties including two British servicemen killed. Then, while I was busy learning Arabic on a six-week Arabic course in the Command Arabic Language School, Harold Wilson defeated the Conservatives. To start with, the new Labour government followed the existing policy but it made no difference. Figures rose through 1965 to 286 incidents, 239 casualties with 6 servicemen killed and 83 wounded.

It's clear now that people in all the countries which had fallen under control of the British Empire wanted their freedom but even when Labour announced independence for South Arabia and the withdrawal of all British forces matters did not improve. In fact the British announcement had the opposite effect. It completely undermined the existing Arab Federal leaders who depended on the British for their power. The strength of the tribes in the interior grew, and the terrorism increased in the streets of Aden itself, making some areas completely 'no-go' to British troops. The result? Soldiers and civilians died in greater numbers. At minimum, it became common for troops being trucked about the town on mere admin trips to expect to be fired on. So, by 1966 there were 480 incidents with 573 casualties, 5 servicemen killed and 218 wounded, and in 1967, the last year I went there and the year the British pulled out, there were nearly 3,000 incidents, with 1248 casualties, 44 servicemen killed and 325 wounded. It was an ignominious retreat, inevitable for more than two years before it actually happened and a lot of soldiers died for nothing.

Compared with the line infantry, who had the thankless job of policing Aden, the SAS was fortunate in being given jobs with more purpose, based on what intelligence there was, with a reasonable chance of finding the enemy, like our Wadi Mishwarrah operation, and at least we had the opportunity to create a greater impression on the local situation through 'hearts and minds' work. So I was sent to the fort at Ataq, about 200 miles from Aden near the Hadramaut border in the east, where a Federal National Guard battalion was based, to improve my Arabic, report what went on and show British support for the FNG.

We lived in a stone fort like something out of a Foreign Legion film; Beau Geste again, sand, rocks, steep hills, thorny acacia trees round mud huts, and goats. The place was hot and dry as dust. However, my Arabic improved and I began to create a good rapport with the Arab FNG soldiers. They had FN rifles which they loved as they were heavy, looked the part and fired the powerful 7.62mm NATO round. One day on the range, which was just a piece of dry empty hillside near by, they were firing a close quarter combat (CQB) practice and kept pushing me to join in. I had nothing more than a 9mm pistol but I could never resist a challenge. I suddenly drew my pistol, twisted round and fired at the target, a tin on a rock. To their delight and amazement, my first shot sent the tin flying and my second hit it again in mid-air. The Arabs put a great deal of store by good shooting and this really impressed them. They tried to persuade me to fire again but I coolly refused. I was just as amazed as them and I knew perfectly well it had been sheer luck, probably the product of good instinctive shooting, but I had no chance of repeating it and no intention of losing my advantage by trying.

Things did not always go so well. A local Arab came to me one morning with a sick goat. Its eyes were badly infected and seething with maggots. I had done a short medical course and decided to impress the Arabs with my concern for their goat. I explained this and they sat about watching in awe as I pulled out a syringe, drew off some penicillin and jabbed the goat. To these people, the height of good doctoring was to slap camel dung over a burn or a cut. Injections were 'white man's magic'. They watched fascinated as I cleaned up the wretched goat's eyes with swabs and antiseptic, until suddenly the goat leapt out of my hands and started jumping about like a dervish. The circle of Arabs backed off in alarm as the goat flung itself on the dusty ground, kicked its legs in the air and died. I had given it too much penicillin and the poor thing was allergic. It had gone into anaphylactic shock followed quickly by a total collapse of blood pressure and death. The Arabs moved off in stunned silence, their confidence in white man's magic severely dented.

However, I got on well with them. They loved having their photograph taken and I often sent films of various characters in Fort Ataq down to base in Habilayn Camp for developing. Perhaps because I could use a camera, which they had never seen, they called me 'jaasoos', and for a long time I translated this as 'the elite' and felt rather pleased with myself. Then I discovered they actually meant I was a 'spy', mainly because these people tended to call any outsider a spy, but that was not how I saw myself at all.

However, even spies had their uses and when a dissident blew up the Khalifah's house in Ataq village, the FNG asked me to go on a patrol with them to level the score. The man had run away to a village called Bihan, a cluster of mud-brick flat-roofed houses some miles away in the hills. We drove there in Land Rovers over the bumpy desert and while the FNG picketed the high ground with water-cooled Vickers machine guns, I was taken by a squad of Arab soldiers into Bihan and shown the culprit's house. At that time, I had never blown up a real target before, and I was conscious this was not the time to foul up. Recalling my demolitions instruction, my plan was to set off a fuel-air petrol bomb; vaporise the petrol all round the room and then ignite it. The ensuing conflagration uses up all the oxygen at once, creates a vacuum and implosion brings down the house. The FNG soldiers watched closely while I set up a charge attached to a petrol bomb dead centre in the main room of the mud-brick house. I ignited the safety fuse and shoved the curious Arabs out of the house or I am sure they would have stayed to see what happened next. In seconds the charge blew, the walls and roof lifted slightly and then totally collapsed inwards. This gave me a lot of satisfaction, seeing the theory work in practice. Frankly, I doubt it did much good for the cause of the Federation, but blowing up suspects' houses was the way it went then. Indeed, the Israelis still do it to Palestinians in Gaza.

Weakness was almost a sin for these Arabs. Perhaps it was the harsh arid environment, but those who didn't measure up were rejected by their society. Outside the fort in Ataq, on the edge of the few drab village houses, the Arabs kept a man chained to a rock. There were no padlocks, the chains were just tied and knotted round him in thick coils. He was plainly a real villain, but when I asked what he had done, the FNG officers wagged their fingers and said warningly, '*Majnoon! Majnoon!*' He was mad.

In amazement, they agreed to let me take him for walks but on no account to untie his chains. So, every day, I got them to loosen him from his rock, I gave him water and took him for walks in the desert on a length of chain, like a dog. Nick Angus was with me at the time and I suppose we made a bizarre sight, brown soldiers in shorts and Clarke's desert shoes either side of this lunatic festooned in chains, but we practised our Arabic and he enjoyed the break from the awful monotony of his life.

I came back to Aden in February 1966. We did our build-up training at Sennybridge after Christmas and our troop commander was Captain Robin Letts. He had difficulty understanding that rifles zeroed in freezing damp conditions in mid-winter in Wales are not likely to keep on target in the blazing dry heat of Aden, but he was a good troop officer and took us on an operation in the Wadi Bila that year. The problem was always that the tribesmen seemed to know exactly what was going on in their areas, and we were always breaking new ground to keep ahead of them. Just creeping into the mountains by night was no longer any good in 1966. The Arabs had their own pickets on the tops of hills and every goatherd and small boy tending the animals was part of their lookout system. So, our squadron commander, Major Glyn Williams, known to us all as 'Punchy', devised a new scheme for the Wadi Bila operation which included a cunning deception plan.

The Wadi Bila was a deep and wide valley surrounded by steep arid mountains. Two troops, 16 and 19 Troops, walked in at night, as we had on the Wadi Mishwarrah Op, and we hid on the tops of the mountains in rocky sangars on the reverse side of the slope out of sight of the wadi. In 16 Troop, my patrol was led by Corporal Mick Welsh. Sergeant Don 'Lofty' Large, who was a veteran of Korea, hid 18 Troop out of sight to the north.

We went into a typical day and night routine. Every night, just after evening stand-down, we left our hilltop position and crept down into the wadi to ambush tracks used by dissidents moving under cover of darkness. In the small hours before dawn, we sweated back uphill to our sangars where we lay up and rested, keeping a watch through the heat haze on the surrounding hills. Inevitably, very early one morning, an ambush position was compromised by a goatherd, who scuttled off to tell the dissidents.

At once our deception plan was put into effect. Captain Letts called in the Scout helicopters to lift out all 16 Troop and, using one of our Tokai hand-held radios (which the SAS bought on the civilian market because the Army had nothing suitable), he deliberately gathered us on open ground in full view of the whole of Wadi Bila. When four Scout helicopters came in to pick us up, all Arabia must have heard and seen what was going on. We were flown back to Almeila Camp where we dumped our rucksacks in our billets, washed up, cleaned our weapons and sat about ready for the expected call out.

In the wadi, the dissident Arabs thought they had flushed out all the British soldiers and happily emerged from their hiding places, but 18 Troop were waiting for them and Don Large radioed back to our operations officer that he could see twelve dissidents approaching in line, Mark IV .303 rifles casually slung over their shoulders. The reply was, 'Can you be sure they are enemy?'

Don Large was not certain. Most Arabs in the region carried rifles, especially old British Army .303s, and there was no way of saying whether these men had been responsible for recent attacks on Habilayn Camp.

'Then report only and do not open fire,' ordered the ops officer, conscious that shooting innocent locals could do nothing but harm to the British position. However, just in case, he ordered us to deploy at once.

Crossly, Don Large watched the twelve Arabs walk freely through the killing ground right in the centre of his ambush, while in Almeila, we all sprinted back to the helicopters.

Most SAS operations involve carrying ludicrously heavy rucksacks and it was a real treat to be going out with just belt kit and weapon. It was exciting too: the beat of the chopper blades, seeing the other three choppers flying with us, hugging the contours, cutting over the mountain tops, and the certainty of action. As we approached the Wadi Bila, Punchy's Scout heli climbed high into orbit so he could see the whole area and place the rest of us in the wadi as cut-off groups, so 18 Troop could sweep through. These were the same tactics used by the Rhodesians ten years later, and should have been used more often in Southern Arabia and Dhofar. The British Army doesn't seem to have picked up the real usefulness of helicopters in combat as fast as other armies. There is nothing better than good air support, especially helis, against dissidents hiding in difficult country.

The fly-in was exciting. The enemy in the Wadi Bila were well stirred up by 18 Troop and I could hear bullets cracking round us as our Scout came in. I noticed our pilot was blissfully unaware of the danger. He was blocked off from reality by headphones and Punchy's voice ordering him where to land. He dropped us on top of a hill overlooking the wadi, then he pulled away in a steep curling climb to avoid enemy fire and by the time he had turned through 360 degrees above us, he had lost his sense of direction. He glanced down, mistook us for a group of dissidents, and plunged back onto us, firing the GPMGs mounted underneath the belly of his helicopter. It was a good thing these Scouts, early gunships by anyone's definition, were not so well set up as the US Huey Cobras later on in Vietnam, with Mini-guns firing thousands of rounds a minute. We scattered for cover behind the tiniest rocks. I dived into a pouch on my belt kit for my red picket panel which I waved frantically. Thankfully, he recognised this piece of red cloth, an identifying air-marker panel, and he immediately pulled away with no damage done.

'Blue on blue' incidents, as they are called now, are more common than people think. An SAS vehicle patrol in Western Iraq during the Gulf War was bombed by US A-10 pilots, fortunately without casualties, and of course fourteen British infantrymen were killed by US 'friendly fire' some weeks later in the land battle for Kuwait. In Rhodesia, we got round this problem when sweeping through the bush by putting coloured patches on top of our hats. There can be terrible mistakes but no one could accuse the pilots of doing it deliberately. I see it as part of the risk of war which can be minimised but not eliminated.

The last three of 16 Troop, with Sergeant 'Smudge' Smith and Dusty Gray, flew suddenly over a ridge to find the twelve Arabs walking coolly in single file across a wide flat area. As the Scout turned over their heads, the Arabs opened fire on the chopper which pulled round in a tight circle and dropped them in cover under the ridge. The three ran back to see where the Arabs had got to.

Far above them, I lay in cover behind rocks and watched the tiny figures moving in the wadi below. We fired on the Arabs as they ran away, but it was frustrating being well out of the actual fighting. I could see Smudge Smith's group and Captain Letts's group moving carefully along the floor of the valley, flushing out the enemy, and the sound of firing carried distantly. I saw one of the three fall, and minutes later I heard on the Tokai hand radio that Smudge had been badly wounded. At considerable risk of being shot down, one of the Scout pilots landed to take Smudge to hospital. On the way, he noticed blood spattering all over the instruments, blown about by the slipstream through the open doors, and realised it was his. He was lucky to survive.

I could also hear Punchy Williams high above in the Scout talking on the Tokai net, saying he had seen a group of enemy down one side of the steep spur I was on. I could see them with my binos and confirmed the sighting on my Tokai radio. Directed by Punchy above, Robin Letts's group gradually moved up the wadi and cornered several enemy at an impassable wall where they killed two and wounded another four in close fighting with grenades. Trooper Dodds was awarded the Military Medal for his part in this engagement.

The fighting went on all day, with outbreaks of shooting and skirmishes and we returned to Almeila Camp by helicopter in the afternoon, in time for a shower and the evening meal. For me, it was a good day, and unusual: in and out by chopper, showers and eating in the cookhouse. What a great way to soldier! The squadron had done well. By British standards of the time, and compared with most British counter insurgency operations, two dead and four wounded was a great success. Don Large was cross he had not been allowed to shoot all twelve when he had them dead to rights in his ambush, which would have meant Smudge would not have been wounded too, but the ops officer had probably been right. I saw plenty of 'shoot first, ask questions later' in Africa and I do not think it helps any campaign.

The abiding recollection of Aden was the terrain, which was appalling, in its way quite as bad as the jungle, and the whole episode illustrates the amount of sheer hard work, commitment, cost, resources and the professional techniques necessary to flush out and kill a very small number of the enemy.

Don't go away thinking that soldiers in the SAS are nothing but formidable fighting machines. I should mention an incident that occurred during my Arabic course, which illustrates a sense of the ludicrous to balance the fierce image of terrible firefights in the mountains. Much of our language training was done in laboratories wearing headsets with tape machines and repeating 'Bill wa John' lessons into black mesh-covered microphones. This was new, at the leading edge of technology in language training in those days and the instructor, hard-bitten though he was, would have been appalled to see us adapting his shiny electronics to settle the winner of a farting competition. Ken Connor and Jake Allsop spent days eating nothing but peas and cabbage, and then one night, quite sober, we gathered round a microphone in the language lab to hear, and witness, the winning effort. The decibel level was registered on the tape-machine dial as, bare-arsed, Ken made a splendid contribution to science. These were real professionals. Jake was not to be outdone. He dropped his trousers, strained to swing the needle further, and shat all over the microphone.

Disgusting, I can hear you saying, but it amused us a lot, probably because we were living at the extremes. Hot dusty days on hard, sweaty, dangerous patrols in unfriendly mountains, followed by more hot dusty days in tented camps where there was little to do after all the necessary weapon cleaning and admin had been done, except rest, play sport and drink beer. That's army life. Certainly, SAS ops at best are a mixture of extreme excitement and action followed by long periods of boredom. At the worst, it's all boredom and no action. I enjoy operations. I love the challenge and the commitment. I actually feel happy in action. But I am not so good with the boredom! I recall one afternoon in Habilayn Camp when Ken Connor and I had nothing to do and went to the Naafi Club, a large tent with folding tables and chairs on dusty coir matting. Much later, after dark, I said, as one does on these occasions, 'D'ye want anither beer?'

Ken checked his watch and shook his head. 'I've got to go to the Ops Room.' He marched unsteadily out of the Naafi into the hot dark night.

Two Guardsmen watched him leave. They were buying their first beer. One said to the other, 'I been looking forward to this all day.'

The other wiped his sweating red face and nodded, gazing fondly at the beer being pushed across the counter at him.

Their dream was interrupted by a distant whistling noise and a loud explosion on the far side of the camp, shaking the ground.

'Incomers!' I shouted, leaping to my feet and knocking over my chair behind me. 'Mortars!'

'Fer fuck's sake!' muttered the Guardsmen as I ran outside. 'I swear them fucking wogs saw us come in 'ere.'

I burst out of the lighted Naafi tent into the black night and saw the flash of explosions silhouetting the tents around. Enemy mortar rounds were landing inside the camp and the din increased as our 105s opened up on the hillsides where they thought the enemy were positioned. I blinked furiously to get my night vision and ran on. Only, instead of running straight down the path to the main avenue between the tents, I veered blindly sideways, tripped over a taut guy-rope, and plunged head first into a deep slit trench. Most tents had trenches dug beside them, to shelter the occupants in such times of enemy attack, so maybe this was the safest place to be, but I landed on my head, split it open and passed out.

I came to with bright torchlight shining in my eyes. ''Ere, Sarge! Wounded man!'

To my horror, I was lifted gently out of the trench by an immaculately dressed Irish Guards stretcher party, wearing highly polished steel helmets and shirts 'Khaki Drill' with shiny brass buttons, and laid on the stretcher on the ground.

'Let me up,' I shouted, struggling.

'Hold 'im down, lads,' the sergeant boomed, shining his torch over my bloody head. To me he said in a kindly voice, 'The camp was mortared, lad. D'you remember? You've been hit. Nasty wound, by the look of it.'

'No, I fucking well haven't!'

There was no arguing. The Guards had made up their minds. 'You're concussed,' said the sergeant knowledgeably. 'That's common with 'ead wounds.'

And before I knew it, I was lying on an operating table in the full glare of the theatre lights and being inspected by a thoroughly outraged army surgeon in bloodied green overalls and rubber gloves, scalpel poised.

'This man is drunk!' he shouted. 'Get out!'

I scrambled off the table and scurried off. I'm glad his training hadn't been entirely wasted, but what humiliation!

In 1967 during my last trip to Aden, 16 Troop did the British Army's first operational free-fall jump. I think it was also the first operational parachute jump of any kind since Suez in 1956, so you can imagine our excitement when the 'Sky God' free-fallers' talk actually turned into training for a real job. Robin Letts pushed for this op as a means of covert infiltration as, once again, we were trying to find new ways of getting patrols into the difficult terrain of the high mountains occupied by our enemy. Dropping silently out of the sky from 10,000 feet seemed worth a try. I presume staff officers with no experience of the desert picked the name: Operation Snowgoose.

I had been promoted by this time to corporal and the troop gathered for parachute training at Falaise Camp in Little Aden. For a change we lived in wriggly tin huts rather than tents. Para training is totally dependent on aircraft and the weather and we were lucky. Headquarters authorised us full clearance to use Scout helicopters and a Beaver light aircraft flown by the Army Air Corps (AAC) and in nearly three weeks, we managed thirty-three training jumps. Modern free-fallers will not be impressed by this low number, but things were not very advanced then. First, we could only jump in the early morning and evening as the winds picked up in the middle of the day. So, we rolled out of our pits at 5 a.m. for a couple of jumps before breakfast, finishing usually about 8 a.m. Then we had to pack our 'chutes. Not for us the quick ten-minute field shake out and stuff back into the pack which is all that is required for a modern square parachute. We jumped American T-10s, a parabolic-shaped 'chute which took over an hour to pack, with masses of complicated folds and rigging-line checks to make, all vital or you will pack in an automatic malfunction. So, after packing the morning 'chutes, we had lunch and a sleep before driving over to the aircraft for another couple of jumps between 4 and 6 p.m. Later, we jumped with our rucksacks made up to a realistic weight and there is really nothing like a heavy bergen to spoil the pleasure of free-fall. Always at the end of the day there was more 'chute packing to be ready for the next morning. These were long tiring days, but frankly I didn't care. I was too wound up with the chance of a real operational jump.

Captain Robin Letts gave the detailed operation orders in a stuffy tent in Habilayn Camp to a much smaller group than had started the build-up training. From a full troop, we had lost men through injuries, mostly twisted ankles and knees, so that by the time we were ready, there were only six of us left and I was acting troop sergeant. The team were Captain Robin Letts, Corporal Peter McAleese acting Troop Sergeant, Tony Ball, Dave Gregory, Woody Woodford and Tony Dicker. A Royal Marine sergeant gave us the intelligence background. Our aim was to ambush a track junction and kill Mohammad al Maghrebi al Haushabi, a bandit leader whose most recent atrocity had been to attack the beer resupply wagon. We spent the rest of the day preparing and rehearsing; how we would group in free-fall, how to meet up on the ground after landing, and all the immediate action drills for every possible eventuality.

At one o'clock in the morning, a full moon lit the airfield and we walked out to the waiting Scout helicopters. Actually we waddled, like penguins, weighted down with rucksacks hanging off our harnesses behind our legs. I could hardly walk and we all had to be helped into the Scouts. Most unusually for the time, the pilots had willingly agreed to break new ground, toss the book of regulations aside, and had removed the back doors. The AAC flight officer Captain 'Low-level' Greville Edgecombe gave us every support throughout.

I sat wedged in the back, behind the pilots' seats, helmeted and trussed like a turkey, my main parachute on my back, the reserve on my front, my rifle strapped inside my harness at my side, and sitting on my bulging rucksack which was tied to the webbing under my legs, and sweating like a pig. I couldn't wait to get going. The blades started turning. We took off and climbed north over the moonlit desert hills which rose in line after line towards the high mountain range on the border with Yemen. The flight was short, maybe twenty minutes and almost at once it seemed the pilot turned round and shouted, 'Action Stations!'

Time! I struggled out of the back of the heli, let myself down to stand on the skids and held on to the floor rings as the slipstream whipped past. I looked across at the second helicopter and saw the other three clambering out, dark shapes bulky with gear from head to foot, their goggles gleaming in the moonlight. The seconds flashed past as we glided towards the invisible release point high over the target. Above were the rotor blades, the huge full moon and the stars. Below, in clear night air 10,000 feet down between my legs was the pattern of moonlit ridges interlaced with wadis in deep shadow. And our target.

Nearly there. I glanced across at the other heli again, at the two men on the other side of my heli. Thumbs up. Ready.

I stared into the cockpit at the pilot waiting for his signal. It was vital we all left both aircraft at the same time, to fall together, to land together, or we would be scattered over the jebel one by one and terribly vulnerable on our own.

The co-pilot raised his gloved hand, twisting briefly to look at me. I tensed, ready, adrenalin rushing.

The hand chopped down, and 'Go!'

I shoved myself off backwards and fell rapidly away from the beating noise of the heli. What a relief! To be weightless in free-fall after the sweating struggle strapped up with kit like a parcel. I had a quick glimpse round at others falling with me, face down, spread-eagled, like frogs, their helmets glistening in the moonlight. My relief was short lived. As I reached terminal velocity after ten seconds, my rucksack began a mad gyration in the air rushing past, and I had to fight to keep stable and face down, throwing my arms from one side to the other to prevent the rucksack whipping me into a violent spin. We had no automatic BODs, barometric opening devices, to release our parachutes at a pre-set height, so it was vital I stopped the spin catching hold or I might lose consciousness. Grimly, I fought on as the seconds passed, rode it down to 4,000 feet above the ground and pulled.

The T-10 parachute had a fearsome opening shock. The harness straps ripped into my groin and I thought my eyes would pop out of their sockets into my goggles. But it opened and that is all that ever matters. I looked up. The parabolic canopy billowed satisfyingly above me, all the rigging lines in place. I relaxed a bit and checked the sky all round for the others. One, two, three, four, me, five. Fuck. One missing. There was no sign of the sixth. I guessed he had had the same problem as me, spun like a top and piled in.

The ground was coming up. Below, the track junction was exactly where we expected it. Smack on target. The AAC pilots and Green Archer radar had done an excellent job. I dropped my rucksack on its thirty-foot line, put my feet and knees tight together for a good parachute-landing position and hit the earth. I dusted myself off and felt good. You never mind what happens to you in the air as long as you can land and walk away. I would remember that years later, but now I was fine. The other four landed close by, no more than sixty yards away. A quick roll call showed the missing man was Woody.

We looked up into the sky and I spotted a lone parachute, small in the distance. Several thousand feet above us, Woody was drifting off down the wadi. He appeared to be trying to drive against the wind rather than pull handfuls of brake lines down and spiral his parachute out of the sky before the upper winds could carry him away. Robin Letts was not very happy. He agreed to my suggestion that we put out a couple of two-man groups to search out from our position to try and find him. Two hours later, Woody turned up tired and drenched in sweat. Needless to say, our relief that he was still alive was tempered by more tactical concerns.

I snapped, 'You seen any Arabs?'

'No.'

'Where's your parachute?'

'I hid it under a bush,' he admitted.

'A fucking bush!' I hissed at him. 'I hope the goatherds and Arab boys don't find it.'

There was no time to go looking for Woody's parachute then. Faint signs of dawn lightened the eastern sky, so we hoisted our heavy bergens and marched down into our ambush position in the wadi where we remained for two days as planned. The euphoria of the jump quickly wore off. We were back on the ground in the same old sweltering hot routine of ops in Aden and, typically, Mohammad al Maghrebi al Haushabi failed to turn up. We wondered if drinking the spoils off the beer wagon had anything to do with it.

Of course when it was time to pull out, we had to fly in all of 17 Troop to picket the high ground while we searched for Woody's parachute. They thought that was a huge joke and there was much talk of useless 'Sky Gods'. Needless to say, when we started looking for Woody's bush, we saw the wadi was covered in bushes, millions of them. But the quartermaster was emphatic. The T-10 parachute was American, on loan, and had to be returned.

There has been only one other British operational free-fall jump since Op Snowgoose, also by the SAS. In 1970, 24 Troop of 'G' Squadron jumped into the Musandam Peninsula in northern Muscat and they lost a man. Trooper Rip Reddy, who exited the aircraft a fraction later than the others, missed the wadi they were supposed to jump into and plummeted into the side of a mountain before his BOD (Borometric Opening Device) height-finder operated or he could pull his parachute. He was found and his body returned to England.

I love free-fall but I have doubts about free-fall operations. How many jumps actually go right? How many are cost-effective in time, manpower and resources? So much time is needed to train the free-fallers for that one method of entry when there are all the other techniques to train for in preparation for whatever they have to do when they have landed. Free-fall operations are dangerous, with the chance of injury ever-present, and they take up valuable and usually scarce aircraft resources. Good parachute equipment is not always available where you actually need it, and no one has yet produced any workable anti-radar suits – increasingly necessary when even 'Third World' countries operate quite sophisticated radar systems to spot intruder aircraft passing in or near their airspace. I wonder if the effort is really worth it. In my opinion free-fall should only ever be used for certain very specific applications.

However, there is a spin-off. All these technical difficulties, the danger and exhilaration of jumping out of an aircraft at night have established an exclusive club of free-fallers in Special Forces units everywhere. But the benefit is more sexual than operational! The 'Triple Diver's Badge' is coveted more for its success in pulling women (it stands for 'Sky Diving, Skin Diving and Muff Diving') than for giving the holder any special skill in war.

Properly set up, free-fall is ideal for the covert entry of small groups, in direct contrast to static-line parachuting which delivers large groups into action, like the famous drops at Arnhem and Suez. I think I strike a note of sympathy with most Paras when I say we have all grown bored of listening to the veterans of Arnhem and Suez who retell their few seconds of glory over and over, but the fact is there are very few, if any, British soldiers left who have jumped any operational para jumps, especially onto drop zones defended by the enemy. For me, Op Snowgoose was the first of several 'hot' para jumps, but a vastly more technical and complicated way of going into action compared to operations in the jungle.

2

Planning and Preparation

Who knows not toyle can never skill of rest.
Who always walks on carpet soft and gay
Knows not hard hills, nor likes the mountain way.

THOMAS CHURCHYARD

I went to Borneo in February 1965 as a young trooper in 'D' Squadron, in between trips to Aden, and I quickly learned that jungle operations are relentless hard work.

During the Malayan Emergency, military statisticians worked out that a soldier might expect to be on patrol for 1,800 man-hours of slogging through the forests before even seeing the enemy, let alone being quick enough to shoot him before he disappeared into the gloom. When you think that the British Army took twelve long years to kill 6,710 communists in Malaya, you begin to get some idea of the sheer effort (1,378 man-years!) required to defeat an insurgent terrorist enemy in the jungle.

The war in Malaya ended in 1960, though terrorism continued sporadically on the Thai border, and only two years later the British Army was committed again to fight in the jungle, this time in Borneo. At first, on 8 December 1962, insurgents tried to overthrow the Sultan of Brunei and were defeated by prompt action, flying troops from Singapore where the British still boasted a 'Headquarters Far East'.

Next, in early 1963, President Sukarno of Indonesia decided to prevent the formation of Malaysia by destabilising Borneo in a campaign of confrontation. He applied a harsh mix of international political pressure, subversion inside Borneo by the local Clandestine Communist Organisation (CCO), and cross-border attacks through the jungles using his own regular Indonesian troops or CCO terrorists trained and supported by Indonesia. His ultimate aim was nothing short of conquering Borneo.

Borneo, in complete contrast to Malaya, was very vulnerable to such attacks. Borneo has a jagged 1,500-mile-long coastline and a 1,000-mile land border with Indonesia which runs through dense, remote mountainous jungles. Administratively, the country was divided into penny packets, five Divisions in Sarawak, and four Residencies in Sabah. People in the small coastal towns were poor and liable to subversion by the communists' CCO, while the aboriginal tribes in the interior lived in settlements on rivers, which are the arteries of travel in tropical forests, where they were easily terrorised and hard to visit, let alone protect. Lastly, the enemy were regular Indonesian troops, properly trained and equipped and supported by an outside power, advantages the Malayan communists never had.

There was really nothing to stop the enemy crossing the border under the jungle canopy, and it was hard to know if he was there at all. That was how the SAS fitted into the tri-service strategy used to counter Sukarno's aggression. In the first years, SAS patrols worked inside Borneo in the remote border areas, winning the hearts and minds of the tribes, establishing a network of information on enemy movements, and mapping uncharted areas of jungle.

Then in August 1964, Sukarno made a terrible error of judgement, sending a special force of his soldiers to attack targets in Johore Province in Malaya. Thoroughly alarmed, the Malayan Government in Kuala Lumpur gave their support for secret cross-border operations, initially to recce, then later to attack regular Indonesian troops in their camps inside Indonesia, eventually up to 20,000 yards across the border. The strategy behind this was similar to that employed by the South Africans when I was fighting with them in southern Angola years later. The aim was to push the enemy back from the border and harass them inside their country before they could cross and cause trouble in ours. These operations, codenamed Claret, were politically most sensitive, as Britain never actually declared war on Indonesia, and they were classifed 'Secret'.

The conditions of patrolling secretly in the jungle imposed a very strict code of professionalism on the SAS, and it was here that I really learned what the SAS means by absolute attention to detail.

First, I joined a jungle training course run by 'B' Squadron, under the excellent tuition of experienced Malayan hands like Sergeant Geordie Tyndale and Corporal Anthony Hallan, who was a Malay interpreter, and Lance-Corporal Chuck Hinde who had just done a

Borneo tour in Tyndale's patrol. They set up a jungle shooting range camp, a tactics camp and a recce camp, and we moved round all three in sequence, learning how to move silently through the shadowy green foliage, eat and sleep without leaving sign of our presence, and read the enemy's tracks. We spent hours moving slowly and noise-lessly in four-man patrols, learning how to navigate in the forest and tested our skills against each other, playing games of 'ducks and drakes' in our four-man groups through small areas of jungle to see who could spot the other patrol first and react quickest, to hone our contact drills against a 'live' enemy with blank ammunition. For a month we lived in these camps as if we were actually on operations, under the harsh tactical disciplines of no noise, whispering all the time, and living on 'SAS hard routine' with no lights, no smoking and no hot food. We became very lean, very pale from not seeing the sun under the canopy and very fit. Our numbers were made up with men from Patrol Company of 2 Para and the majority were very good men well capable of being in the SAS.

I went back to 'D' Squadron in Kuching, where Major Roger Woodiwiss was about to hand over command of the squadron to Major Glyn 'Punchy' Williams, and joined Sergeant 'Smudge' Smith's four-man patrol. The other two were Trooper Derek Gorman and Trooper Terry Falcon-Wilson who was later killed in the Yemen working for David Stirling's civilian company called Watchguard. Smudge had learned the art of SAS soldiering in the jungle in Malaya. He was fair-haired, well built, strong and he had endless patience. He had come from the Somerset and Cornwall Light Infantry, he never took shortcuts in his work, he rarely swore, indeed I never saw him lose his temper or drink, and he was always at tremendous pains to explain things, even when he was correcting the stupidities of us young troopers. In short, he was an excellent jungle soldier, typical of the older SAS NCOs in Borneo whose professional attention of detail, no matter how tired you felt, was impeccable. I was wild and aggressive but these formative years in the SAS showed me there is no substitute for the seven Ps: proper planning and preparation prevents piss-poor performance!

My first recce patrol was in the Sarawak First Division in the area of Sidut where the squadron set about gathering all available intelligence on the enemy, in particular paths used by the Indonesians to infiltrate across the border. Two years before, Captain Ray England had reported that the Indonesians had established a regular army camp at Sidut for about 100 troops and they had forced the local people to cut infiltration routes for them through the jungle.

The day before going into the trees, Smudge made us practise all our immediate action drills in case we bumped into the enemy, we test-fired our 7.62mm SLRs and packed our bergens, keeping the weight down as much as we could. We tried all sorts of tricks for this, taking low-weight foods with high-fat and high-protein content, like peanuts or sardines, to limit our bergens to a target of 35 lbs, but with fourteen days' rations to carry it was always a real struggle to bring them under 50 lbs. The heavier the bergen, the more tired, sweaty and drained you become, which gives the enemy advantages you cannot afford. At least the weight went down day by day as we ate our rations but I still lost an average of one pound of body-weight per day on patrol.

We came up to the border by Wessex helicopter and crossed the border on foot. Smudge always worked on the principle that the enemy might just be the other side of the next tree, so we moved very cautiously, usually only ten kilometres a day, stepping softly on the dead leaves of the jungle floor, our eyes constantly probing through the gloom for danger signs hidden in the thick undergrowth. We were conscious all the time that we were only a small recce patrol of four men while our Indonesian enemy were trained regular troops familiar with jungle conditions and usually moved in large groups of ten or more.

Although the chance of meeting the enemy was slight, the risks if we did were high. The squadron had lost Sergeant Bexton and Trooper Condon killed in a previous tour and the new tour had started badly with Sergeant Lillico and Trooper Thompson being seriously wounded and lucky to escape with their lives from an enemy ambush just over the border opposite Plaman Mapu, about twenty-two miles from Sidut. The SAS standard tactics at the time were for us to shoot and scoot, leaving a wounded man if necessary to save others being wounded or killed. None of us agreed with this at all. In fact, Smudge, Terry, Derek and I thrashed over the details of the Lillico/Thompson mishap and decided to ignore that particular SOP completely. We were determined that we would never leave anyone. We were all in the shit together and either we all came out or we all stayed, but we would never split up and never leave a wounded man.

The jungle across the border looked the same as our side, but as soon as we slipped over the border ridge, we felt vulnerable. We depended wholly on every detail of our routine to survive, to avoid being ambushed by the Indonesian patrols.

Every morning, at five o'clock, in total darkness, we slipped out of our hammocks and packed up ready to go. First, I took off my dry lightweight para smock and wriggled into my clammy, freezing, wet shirt and trousers which had been hanging on the end of the hammock from the day before. This was bloody miserable, but there's no better place than the jungle for a really good night's rest on operations, because no one can see a damn thing to creep up on you in the utter dark, and it's spoiled if you have to wear clothes soaking with sweat and rain from the day's march. Then I strapped on my webbing belt kit, with the pouches which contained my water bottle, escape rations and four spare magazines of ammunition. I quickly packed away my hammock and shelter sheet in my rucksack and finally I sat down on top of it, my rifle across my knees, to wait for first light.

As soon as we could see each other in the grey shadows of dawn, we silently hoisted our rucksacks onto our backs and moved off on a bearing Smudge had selected the night before. We had to get away from our sleeping position in case the enemy had located us at last light the evening before. After an hour, he led us round in a loop and we halted for a brew and to send the morning radio message back to squadron headquarters. The loop brought us back near the track we had made coming in so that we could hear anyone tracking us, and we could either ambush them or slide away into the green shadows. By the time they could track us round the loop to our position, we would be long gone.

Exercising great caution, we continued on our day's march through the endless green gloom, every hour looping back for a five-minute break. Not being able to see more than a few yards in any direction meant we had to constantly check our position. We judged it against the map, which gave so little topographical information in this area that we recorded the ridges and streams we had crossed for future patrols, comparing the time we had spent moving against our distance travelled, and we took it in turns to count every single pace and step of the way as a final measurement of where we were. At 4 p.m. we looped again and stopped for the afternoon radio schedule to send the daily SITREP and eat our main meal of the day. We worked in pairs. Two cooked the inevitable SAS 'all-in' curry, Derek Gorman, the signaller, tapped out the Morse code on his PRC 128 radio, and the fourth man lay on guard, facing down the track we had made into our position.

These stops were the only breaks during the day, but we never relaxed. Even going for a shit, we always kept our belt kit on, or right to hand. We buried the shit, as a bonus for the dung beetles, but we carried out all our other rubbish. Discarded paper and tins give away a great deal about a soldier's morale, feeding and habits.

After this main stop, we marched for another hour before looping for the last time, at last light, into our night lying-up position. I constantly wondered what the Indo soldiers from Sidut were doing, whether we might bump into them creeping through the jungle to cross the border themselves. I tried to imagine their own routine in their company base in Sidut. Did they have patrols out looking for us? The tension of never being able to see any distance, of always imagining the enemy were so close, never let up. It's a part of jungle operations. I constantly hoped we might meet the enemy, but the days passed frustratingly with nothing to change our slow, dogged, sweaty, wet, tiring routine. Day followed day of inflexible sameness, so we all knew each other so well we hardly had to whisper even to explain what we were doing, but we never saw the enemy. After fourteen days, we marched back over the border.

A few weeks later, Captain Ragman had more success in Sidut. Supported by 9 Company, 1st Battalion Scots Guards who were placed in ambush positions on the border, he combined his own and Sgt Alex Spence's patrol to make a stronger party of eight, and they crept five kilometres over the border through the jungle to ambush an enemy courier in his wood and atap-leaf hut on the edge of Sidut. After a short skirmish, throwing No 36 grenades and firing at the hut, they seized the courier and some important documents which created an impressive stir in Headquarters. The whole essence of this success was that the operation was based on precise intelligence provided to Major Woodiwiss by 'certain persons' who were probably Special Branch acting on source information. The lesson was not lost on me. It was all very well for us to patrol about the jungle in the hope of finding the enemy, but, no matter how highly trained and motivated your best troops may be, there is no substitute for good intelligence. The point has been proved in every campaign I've fought in.

I met other Commonwealth troops for the first time in Borneo and saw an interesting comparison between the Australian SAS and the New Zealand SAS. Smudge was ordered to take his patrol and assist with a jungle training programme for the new arrivals. The Aussies' attitude was typically blunt: 'Us being trained by a bunch of pommy bastards? No way!' The Aussie SAS have their own jungles in the Northern Territories and they resented our training programme. However, in private some of their sergeants came round to Smudge and other senior British SAS NCOs and admitted, 'You Poms 'ave been here some time and we'd like to hear what you've got to say.'

The Kiwis were quite different. They were big tough men, mostly Maoris, with superb morale and they were naturals in the jungle. We got on well with them and I recall characters like Lieutenant Manuera, who later won the Military Cross in Vietnam, Trooper 'Kingie' Ihaka, and Trooper Snooks, who was built like a gorilla. He loved to carry the Bren gun and slid effortlessly through the jungle barefoot. Once I watched amazed as he and two others casually packed away forty boiled eggs between them, not for a bet like Paul Newman a year later in *Cool Hand Luke*, but just because they felt peckish!

All the same, just to bring the Kiwis back to earth, I should add that 'D' Squadron beat the Kiwi rugby team from the 1st Battalion Royal New Zealand Infantry Regiment, which astonished us as much as them and the consequent party was a night to remember.

There was a routine in camp too. The first day back, we went through a thorough debrief with the ops officer and the squadron commander and cleaned all our kit, the second day we were allowed to drink and relax, the third day we received our orders and prepared for the next patrol, and then on the fourth we went back into the jungle.

Life was simple. We were either in the jungle or billeted in a concrete 'hotel' in a seedy part of Kuching, conveniently opposite a whore house. Living on top of each other, working and drinking together month after month, all ranks in the squadron became very close-knit. Personal character traits became exaggerated and the usual behaviour patterns of the British regular army were often stretched to a limit which would have been unacceptable in any other unit. Captain Ragman was nicknamed 'Dapper' because of his dress sense. One day he was seized after a drinking session on our day off, held down and Sergeant Alfie Tasker cut off a great lock of his blond hair which always fell over his face and irritated the men. On another, we tied Jock Thompson to the fence in the yard because we were fed up listening to his stories. And Kevin Walsh, whom I had known in 1 Para when I first joined the army, had a problem with the Armalite assault rifle. Kevin was short, stocky and famously ugly, a great SAS character who sadly died not long ago. With a cigarette between his teeth, as was considered cool at the time, he swaggered into our room and gazed round at the iron bedsteads, bare boards, khaki webbing, trousers and shirts hanging everywhere on strings, towels and bars of soap left out to dry, which is always a vain hope in the tropics, and piles of spare rations which accumulated from stripping out the food packs we had to carry on patrol. Some of the men were dozing and some sitting on their beds in shorts, cleaning kit for the next patrol.

His eye lit on Jake Allsop's weapon, the American 5.56mm Armalite which had just been issued to us.

'This looks a good bit of kit, Jake,' said Kevin knowledgeably, his cigarette bobbing up and down between his teeth as he talked.

Taking his hands out of his pockets, he picked up the Armalite, admired it a moment turning it over in his hands, and before Jake could move, he cocked it, aimed it through the window and pulled the trigger.

A burst of automatic fire blew out the whole window frame and a whore across the street was shot in the arse.

'Oh my God!' said Kevin, appalled, standing in shock in a slight haze of blue smoke. 'What the fuck do I do now?'

Raising my voice slightly over the hysterical screaming from across the street, I said casually, 'Just go downstairs, Kevin, and put yourself on a charge!'

Smudge took me on a helicopter recce along the border for our next patrol, not so much because we could see anything through the canopy, but to see the flow of the endless rolling green canopy itself. The maps were so bad, with so little contour detail, that we wanted to see the lie of the land, the ridges, the re-entrants and lines of the streams under the endless acres of green trees and arching fronds.

We were escorted up to the border this time by a ten-man patrol from 2 Para out of Gunan Gajan Company base, not far from Plaman Mapu. They chose a route near the border so that we could step off their line of march, literally stepping over low undergrowth, to prevent anyone who might be tracking us from seeing the marks of our boots where we had quit the main group.

We patrolled carefully for the rest of the day over the sharp border ridge and then, in the late afternoon, dropped off the ridge to loop round on the steep slope and come back close under the ridge again for the night. Here, there was no level ground to lie on, so no one would expect anyone to sleep there, but we could sling our hammocks between the trees, and secondly, we could hear anyone blundering along the ridge above us and have plenty of time to 'bug' out if necessary, before they tracked us round on our loop in. That evening, as the sweat dried on our backs in the warm dusk after we stopped to tie our hammocks, we heard the artillery in the Paras' company position at Gunan Gajan firing off the 105mm guns onto defensive fire positions thousands of yards over the border, on paths which the

Intelligence Staff reckoned the enemy would use to approach the border. We lay in our hammocks and listened to the shells whining overhead and crashing into the greenery beyond, happy we were tucked safely under our ridge.

We moved with especial care on this patrol as this was the area where Lillico and Thompson had been wounded and the Indonesians had regular troops all along the River Sekayan which ran parallel to the border, from Jerik through Balai Karangan to Sentas further west. On our twelfth day out, we found a sign of the enemy.

I was lead scout, as usual, and peering ahead through the dripping greenery I saw the track quite clearly. It was enormous. I sank to one knee, keenly alert for enemy, and signalled with my fingers for Smudge to join me. He slipped up silently behind me. He was a good tracker, and after some time peering at the signs on the track from the shadows, he explained what he could see in a low whisper. There were several striking facts: the track, which ran parallel to the border, was very wide, maybe ten feet, which is unusual in the jungle where everyone is trying to avoid leaving signs of their presence; it had been made by a large body of men, judging by the amount of trampled mud and crushed leaves; they were all wearing army boots, the marks of which were clear; they had only recently passed, maybe the day before, or even earlier that morning, as there was no dust or detritus lying on the leaves; and they had all been going in the same direction, from west to east, from our company area to the Plaman Mapu company area. The important question was, 'where were they now and what were they doing?'

After some while waiting and listening in case anyone was using the track, we crossed swiftly, one at a time. When we were in the safety of the dark undergrowth on the other side, Smudge whispered, 'I had a good look as I crossed, and I'm sure there's a camp down the slope.'

Under his guidance, I moved forward, very slowly indeed, advancing step by step, sinking to one knee to listen every few steps, alert like a wild animal, trying to make absolutely sure we would not stumble into a sentry without seeing him first. The footprints on the track had been leaving the camp but it would be quite usual military procedure for the Indonesians to leave guards.

For nearly two hours we inched forward, straining our ears and eyes through the green foliage, for giveaway human sounds ahead, which always pitched at variance with the soft natural noises of the jungle, and for signs of straight unnatural edges among the leaves immediately in front of us, like the delicate line of a trip-wire which might be connected to a grenade. The Indonesians often laid these booby traps round a camp, as a defensive measure, as Captain Ragman had found before his ambush at Sidut. Finally, I spotted openness ahead through the trees. The enemy camp.

The place was enormous. For maybe a hundred yards across, all the undergrowth had been cleared between the tree trunks which still provided their green canopy to prevent any sign of the camp being visible from the air. Huts were dotted round with all the signs of being recently occupied by troops: muddy paths between the huts, crushed and rotting leaves, broken poles and discarded paper, boxes and hessian sacking. It was uneerily silent, though Smudge was sure he could hear 'people' sounds on the far side, out of sight down the slope.

We waited hidden in the shadows for some time, just in case the Indonesians had left a guard behind. Nothing stirred in the oppressive, damp heat except the birds and chattering insects. Smudge signalled at me to circle the camp, keeping in the jungle fringe and we moved very cautiously indeed.

It was a very strange experience moving with an open piece of ground on one side after spending all our time enclosed in green gloom. We felt terribly vulnerable, like nocturnal animals suddenly exposed to the sun.

Suddenly Derek Gorman, climbing a small bank while he glanced rapidly around, dislodged a stone which rolled down the hill sounding in our ears like an avalanche.

We froze. Long minutes passed, but nothing happened, no one came, and no one murdered us with fire, exposed as we were. Smudge later said he was sure he could smell something unnatural which made him think humans were not far but no one reacted to the noise of Derek's stone.

Had the camp been fully occupied, we would have been in real trouble. We were lucky, but plain logic dictated that, if the enemy were not in their camp, they were somewhere else in the jungle, and we all wondered what they could be doing. After Smudge was satisfied we had seen enough, we moved very carefully indeed but as fast as we dared back towards the border to make our report, first at the Paras' base in Gunan Gajan and then at our SAS base in Kuching.

The director of operations, whose authority was required to mount all Claret operations, decided we should cross the border again, this time in force with the Paras from Gunan Gajan under command of the Para company commander, and ambush the track we had found.

I was unable to go on this operation, as I flew back to Aden to assist 'B' Squadron there who had no Arabic speakers. However, a few days later, Smudge flew back to Gunan Gajan by Wessex and landed there in the afternoon of 26 April, for briefings and final preparations with the Paras.

The base was like all the others, an organised mess of rich mud, logs tied into walls, defensive trenches, sandbags, wriggly tin huts and atap roofs, the stumps of trees sticking up where the ground had been cleared and coils of barbed wire around the perimeter, all baking under the sun or drenched by rain. Beyond was the green wall of jungle on all sides.

On Tuesday 27 April, while Smudge waited in the crisp air of dawn for the Paras to go out on our ambush, there was a sudden stir round the company HQ trenches.

A Para ran out and called, 'To your positions! Stand-to!'

His patrol found an empty weapon-pit near the 105mm howitzers and regretted it at once. The gun crews ran over, jumped into the pits beside their guns, orders were shouted, shells prepared and they opened fire with a deafening salvo over Smudge's head. And followed it with another, and another, and another. The air filled with the pungent smell of cordite and a great pile of empty steaming shell cases built up behind the guns.

The guns were firing in direct support of 'B' Company at Plaman Mapu, which had been deliberately sited within the seventeen-kilometre range of the 105s. That same dawn, one hundred and fifty first-class Indonesian troops had surged out of the jungle and tried to overwhelm the few Paras left in the base. The Indonesians had obviously been watching the base. Most of the Paras were out on patrol, leaving the hasty defence to the gunners, cooks and bottle-washers who fought desperately, hand-to-hand in the weapon-pits, to drive off repeated and determined enemy attacks. During several bloody hours under the exemplary leadership of Company Sergeant Major Williams, who was later awarded the Distinguished Conduct Medal, the Paras inflicted thirty casualties to their own two dead and eight wounded, and finally drove the Indonesians back into the jungle. Though only a small battle over a company-sized position, it was vital. Indonesian success would have received huge publicity and done immense damage to the British cause.

By the time the guns next to Smudge fell silent, the pile of shiny brass empty shell cases was enormous. Gradually the story of the attack filtered back and it was plain the Indonesians on this attack had used the track we had found, and come from the camp we had seen. There is no knowing what might have happened had we found the track a week or so earlier, but we were too late. Luck is a vital ingredient in all military operations, as in life.

To counter incursions like the attack on Plaman Mapu, Claret operations became gradually more aggressive. After 'D' Squadron came home, 'A' Squadron took over under Major Peter de la Billiere and began aggressive patrolling in squadron-sized groups, sometimes with the Gurkhas, which had considerable success. In one patrol, a large Gurkha platoon killed twenty-seven Indonesians who were clearly under the impression they were attacking the usual, small, four-man SAS recce patrol. The Indonesians began to move their camps away from the border. 'B' Squadron followed 'A' with several successful full-squadron Claret operations but they were not replaced, because, in March 1966, there were definite signs that Indonesia was changing its policy and looking for peace. Sukarno had been placed under political house arrest in Jakarta due to the failed policies of his 'Konfrontasi' and the Indonesian army stayed well back on their side of the border for fear of being hit, and hurt, by Claret operations. Inside Borneo, all subversion and terrorism had been gradually reduced by the tireless work of the police and conventional troops and the danger of invasion receded.

In the jungle, Australian and New Zealand SAS patrols continued to cross the border on recces and confirmed Indonesian troops were withdrawing from the border areas, so that by the time I returned with 'D' Squadron in July 1966, there was little to be done except 'hearts and minds' patrols to maintain British influence among the remote jungle tribes.

Finally, on 11 August 1966, peace was declared because, quite simply, Indonesia's attempt to overwhelm Borneo had totally failed. British tri-service co-operation, relentless, meticulous and aggressive patrolling, police-work against the communists in urban areas, and the pursuit of the hearts and minds of the population had triumphed. Victory parades were held in Kuching, but, now the fighting was over, politics ruled the day. No British units were allowed to take part, or even be in Kuching. We were back to the old form, so familiar to British regulars and which Kipling expressed so well: 'It's Tommy this, an' Tommy that, an' "Chuck 'im out, the brute!" but it's "Saviour of 'is country" when the guns begin to shoot.'

The Malayans wanted to trumpet the success as theirs – with a little help from the British. The Royal Malay Regiment marched in triumph through the streets and no one seemed to recall that the only other time they had been in the headlines was in 1963, after being soundly defeated at Kalabakan by Indonesian troops (who were then almost wiped out by a quick-reaction force of Gurkhas).

So, we had our own victory celebrations. I had been in trouble again, and 'Punchy' Williams banished Jock Allison and me to Santubong Island, not far from Kuching. His orders sounded serious: 'Go away and fix up some boat skills training,' but this was really an excuse to stop us fighting in the bars in Kuching at such a delicate political time. Sitting on a sun-baked, sandy island with nothing about except coconut palms quickly concentrates the mind on the comforts of life, and, following Punchy's orders to the letter, we arranged a clandestine boat patrol in our rigid raider, in the dead of night, cruising noiselessly into Kuching docks for a secret rendezvous with Tony Woodhouse. His boat was filled to the gunwales with Merrydown Cider which we lovingly cross-decked to our craft and took back to Santubong Island. I don't think any of us 'deportees' to Santubong were too surprised one morning to see a flotilla of assorted craft chug round the headland with the remainder of the squadron, sent, so Punchy claimed, for 'more boat training'. I have no idea what he understands by 'beach recce parties', but we had some great barbecues with fresh meat rations, Merrydown Cider and a number of fit, though not very beautiful, young whores covertly boated out from Kuching, who enthusiastically dragged various members of the Squadron into the sea for underwater sex and a dose of the clap.

I regret not having contacted the enemy in Borneo, but very few people did. Thinking of the hours we all spent in the jungle, all patrols were hard work, most were uneventful but they formed the basis of my soldiering. Smudge, and the other sergeants I worked with on different occasions, like Alec Spence, 'Tanky' Smith, Mo Copeland and Geordie Lillico, were meticulous and what I learned from their example made the hard discipline of jungle operations seem worthwhile. Close bonds were formed between us in our four-man patrol and, though it was frustrating because I never saw the enemy, these were intensely satisfying times.

My last impressions of Borneo are of the Bungo Mountains, a remote border area southwest of Kuching where the true value of our work was clear as day. Captains Willy Firrel and Keith Farnes, Staff Sergeant Bob Crichton, Corporal Roger Tatersall and I came up river by boat and then walked into the steep hills beyond. We patrolled as carefully as before. The politicians might have been talking of ceasefire and victory, but in the jungle all men are equal, except those who cut corners. A few incursions of die-hard communists still occurred from time to time and we had no intention of being caught out. We saw no enemy, but we were royally entertained by the tribes-people.

These small brown-skinned Indians with their blue tattoos were the real essence of Borneo. Their kindness repaid several times over the efforts of our medic with his sutures, crepe and drugs. They honoured us in their long-houses with their food, music and dance, their betel-stained teeth yellow in the flickering light of their fires, and we felt good to have helped protect their way of life. This was their land. A dramatic green jungle land of steep mountain ridges joined by fantastic swaying bridges of rattan and bamboo over raging torrents of water far below, an exotic land of birds, animals, trees, flowers, and spirits which inhabit all things visible and invisible. Communism is not their way.

3

Retirement

War makes rattling good history; but peace is poor reading.

THOMAS HARDY

Camp life with no prospect of operations is always difficult for soldiers. By 1967, Aden and Borneo were over and nothing else loomed. This is an age-old problem for army commanders, and for special forces in particular. How do you occupy young men constantly at a peak of training and fitness when there are no operations?

I found it hard.

The regiment did its best to keep us busy but exercises were basic compared to today. We thought a regimental escape and evasion or a two-week NATO exercise in Germany was impressive. We were content as long as we had plenty of para-cord and masking tape, while nowadays SAS soldiers demand a vast array of weapons, air and naval assets and high-tech equipment, of which exotica like SATCOM, LTDs, and MAGELLAN are but small examples.

We were sent off on skills training. In September that year, Tony Ball and I went to the French Parachute School at Pau in southwest France on their free-fall course. The French are full of the reputation of the Foreign Legion and 'les Paras' and they have a robust attitude to parachuting. They make sure that Paras and aircrew keep up to date with their jumps and consequently their parachute jump instructors (PJIs) are so well practised you could set a metronome by the way they despatch men from their big Transaal transport planes. They fill the aircraft to capacity for every drop and empty the whole lot on one run-in over the DZ, in simultaneous 'sticks' out of both doors, left, right, left, like clockwork. In Britain, the RAF keeps adding restrictions little by little to the point where big 'sim-stick' drops are now rare and proficiency must be in question.

Tony and I enjoyed the free-fall, so when Arnhem Day came on

17 September, we repaired to a café in Pau to celebrate. After a while, four French Paras drinking in the same bar kept saying Arnhem was a disaster. True or not, we couldn't take this from the French, so we beat them all up. Horrified by this mêlée of brawling soldiers, the café owner phoned the police, and we legged it into the night across a stinking cabbage field with the wailing siren of a French police car and headlights swinging wildly through the darkness on the roads behind us. The gendarmes called in reinforcements and we were cornered by a group of furious French military police who held us at gunpoint with their MAT machine guns. This was too much. Inflamed with the spirit of Arnhem and several litres of French ale, I grabbed a MAT off one MP and proceeded to batter him with it till all the others leaped on us and we were both jailed. French-English relations were patched up and we were sent home. Tony and I were marched in to see the commanding officer who listened to our story, gave me a 'Final warning!' but nothing worse. I suppose beating up cocky French Paras is a permitted SAS pastime.

During the sixties and seventies, the regiment was inundated with requests for training teams abroad. Foreign leaders, often in the Commonwealth, had seen the successes of Malaya and Borneo and wanted their own special troops and bodyguards trained too. It was not just a question of prestige. These 'praetorian guards' were set up to keep them in power. This rush of jobs quite suited the regiment at a time when it had little else to occupy itself and it kept us out of trouble. 'Team jobs', as they were called, were not operations, but they were better than hanging about in camp and getting into trouble in Hereford. Plus, they offered the chance of lucrative local overseas allowances and lovely claims to supplement the miserable pay in those days, long before SAS Special Pay.

In October, shortly after returning from France, I was picked by Lawrence Smith to join his training team in Guyana. He was an excellent soldier who had been awarded a Military Cross in Borneo while still a sergeant major and was then commissioned. Our job was to train the Guyanese Defence Force and I found myself thoroughly absorbed. We were in the jungle again and we worked hard. There were some light moments in our rest house, or 'pub', which we found in the middle of the jungle, and we coped with the inevitable dramas, such as having to casevac Brummy Stokes with a repulsive infestation of huge maggots in his back; quite a different problem from those he faced climbing to the summit of Everest. We spent six weeks there and achieved a great deal with the GDF soldiers. I enjoyed the challenge, lifting the GDF standards from nothing to a quite reasonable level, and the experience of training local black troops came in very useful later in Africa.

However, back in Hereford I found my reputation set me up as a target again. One night after we had all had too much to drink, Danny Oldham, a big man in 'A' Squadron, took me on in the 'Grapes' pub, a famous SAS haunt. We repaired to a piece of rough ground behind the Welsh Club, badly lit by distant street lights, and set to. He was a very powerful man with immense hands and I went down straight away under a haymaker. He stood on my head and kicked me for a count of seventeen, but I refused to give up. I managed to grab his foot, hit him and turn the tables. I am afraid Major Bill Dodds, my squadron commander who had taken over from Punchy Williams, did not see this incident in the epic David and Goliath light I have described. I was locked up at once, marched in front of the Commanding Officer, Lieutenant-Colonel Viscount John Slim, and banished from the regiment back to the Paras.

Once again, I offer no excuses. I grew up in a place where it was common to carry knives and use them. We weren't so 'advanced' as some hooligans now who fix two blades separated by a penny into a Stanley carpet knife so the double cut is very hard to suture, but we were rough enough and I suppose my character attracted those who wanted to fight me. That's how I was before I took a long look at myself and settled down somewhat, later. However, it takes two to fight and the army 'system' made little effort to find out the other side of the story. None of the officers realised that I was often picked on by men who wanted to make a name for themselves, like the first time I was in trouble in America, and the other fellow got away scot free.

Of course there is another aspect that I can see more clearly now, which I do not think the junior ranks saw then and which many people reading this now might find hard to believe. The SAS was trying to make sure it was not disbanded, as it had been after the Second World War. After Malaya, Aden and Borneo provided new opportunities and the SAS did well, but their reputation was not established enough for complete impregnability at Army Board level, and many senior servicemen could not see a role for the SAS in peacetime. The anti-terrorist role, which rightly guarantees the SAS a job now, was not developed then, and nor was the conventional special forces role now so widely accepted after the wars in the Falklands and the Gulf. So, while SAS officers beavered away trying to influence army politics to the regiment's lasting advantage, the last thing they wanted was adverse publicity.

However, don't think I was the only one who enjoyed fighting. I had a higher profile, if you like, than some of the others, but fighting was very much a 'work ethic' of the SAS in Hereford at that time. A lot of us came from tough backgrounds and we used Hereford as a big playground, the women we knew enjoyed the excitement and the police were marvellously long-suffering in the days before drink-driving became a serious issue. The rivalry between us was stirred up in the pubs where we all drank and then usually settled with a fight. None of it meant very much to us, because we knew that a good scrap never made any difference to our work. Only some of the officers took a dim view.

There was one thing that always rankled. One or two officers told me I was a useless soldier. They said, 'Since you patently can't keep yourself under control in camp, you would be useless on operations, in action.' What can I say? They were probably right to come down hard on the fighting in Hereford, and I was high profile, as I say, but those officers were in no position to judge. They were never on operations with me. I don't think I have ever let down anyone on operations, I don't think anyone ever criticised my performance in action, and I do not recall ever failing to perform my duty in camp because of drink.

Anyway, I was back to 1 Para again, in Aldershot. Fortunately, the banishment was deemed sufficient punishment and I stayed a corporal. However, I was marched in 'on orders' to see the battalion second-in-command, whom I had never met before, and to my disgust he took the same view as the officers in Hereford. I stood to attention in front of him in his office and his actual words were, 'Corporal McAleese, you won't make a fucking biscuit storeman in this battalion.'

Annoyed, I replied at once, 'If that's the way you think, sir, I'd like to revert to private.'

'Request denied.'

I was puzzled by this, but I replied at once, 'Then I would like to go on the next Brecon course, please sir!'

I meant the British Army's Senior NCOs Tactics Course in Brecon, under the Beacons where I had done selection for the SAS. This course provides the core of the British Army's sergeants, the best NCOs in the world.

The second-in-command snorted at that. He said, 'Don't be a cunt, Corporal McAleese. They want highly skilled men at Brecon and you certainly won't fit. However, I'll send you on the course and if you pass, I'll eat my fucking hat.'

He probably just wanted to get me out of the way, but British Army logic is legendary and he later promoted me to sergeant to go there!

I was delighted. Brecon is not far from Hereford and I had married a local Hereford girl, Marlene Good, in 1966. She refused to leave Hereford when I was posted back to Aldershot, so, in Brecon, I was close to Hereford and we continued to try to make our rocky marriage work. She was a small, attractive, dark auburn-haired girl and I suppose she did her best. She was six years older than me and wanted to be married to a fit young SAS soldier, settle down and have children. However, I must admit, my way of life did not give us much hope. I was only twenty-five years old and wild. I alternated violently between an obsessive commitment to my work and an equally intense commitment to play. It was not that I drank any more than anyone else, just that I could not resist a scrap. Marlene enjoyed nights out too, but never understood the aggression. Her aspirations were different to mine and I don't blame her for the subsequent failure of our marriage.

Contrary to the presumptions of these afore-mentioned officers, I did well at Brecon. I was given a 'B' grade, but, when Brigadier Findlater who was in command of the Tactics School read my report, he said the results deserved better than the grade given and put it up to 'A'. I don't know what sort of results soldiers get now at Brecon, but in those days, the course was a very important part of infantry soldiering and heavily emphasised by the Parachute Regiment in particular. 'A' grades were rare and I was pleased with mine.

What was more important, I learned a great deal about good solid infantry tactics and soldiering. The course taught us everything, starting with the fundamentals; the 'Principles of War'. The age-old cynicism of the British 'Other Ranks', often useful in the hardship of war, had provided me with four short, unofficial principles so far:

1. Slaughter of the fighting men
2. Search for the scapegoats
3. Punishment of the innocent
4. Decoration of the non-participants

Now, I learned the official Ministry of Defence 'Principles' and I will repeat them here, as I have found them invaluable since. There are nine, as follows:

1. Maintenance of morale
2. Offensive action
3. Surprise
4. Security

5. Concentration of force
6. Economy of effort
7. Flexibility
8. Co-operation
9. Administration

Above these is the master principle:

The selection and maintenance of the aim

All these struck a chord in me, though I suppose I still had to learn about co-operation. In the army co-operation means knowing who is in support and knowing when to give a little for the common good, but I have always been someone who prefers to get stuck in and do the job myself, rather than waste time asking other people to do it.

These principles struck a parallel to my own life. I liked accepting a challenge and being determined to win. I have learned since that they are fundamental to success at any level, and must be instinctive in any situation. I think I applied them before, but certainly tried to do so from then on.

Unfortunately when I left Brecon after this course and went back to Aldershot, I was unable to present the second-in-command with a hat for eating as he had been posted elsewhere. Pity, too, because I was flattered and pleased when the staff at Brecon invited me to return there as an instructor. At least someone thought I had something to offer. Also, I was promoted to staff sergeant instructor. Not bad after eight years in the army, plus a bit of up and down in the process.

So began a very enjoyable period of my soldiering. Actually, it was my last job in the British Army. I was immensely helped by the officers running the course, Major Hopton and Captain Harrington-Spear. Harrington-Spear was an officer in the Royal Anglian Regiment and, after watching me grappling intensely with the techniques of instruction, giving lectures, and taking practical periods on the course, he called me over one day and said, 'Staff McAleese, ever thought of taking up a hobby?'

'What d'you mean, sir?' I replied, more puzzled than astonished. The army was my life. There was no time nor place for anything else.

'Er, a hobby,' said Harrington-Spear vaguely. He looked at me standing to attention in front of him, my hair cut down to the wood, my uniform immaculately pressed, my DMS boots gleaming, and he could think of nothing at all with which to take my mind off the military. Instead, he said lamely, 'There are other things than the army, you know.'

'Yes, sir?'

'Forget it,' he said after a moment.

But I liked him. Only later did his words make any impression, but I still don't have a hobby.

Major Hopton, a typical Royal Green Jacket officer, tall, dark-haired and fit, was also a help. He watched me giving a lecture once, on first aid, which I had spent hours preparing in my room, laboriously rehearsing it over and over in front of a mirror. My delivery was strictly by the book and when I had finished, he said, 'That was fine, but a bit stilted.'

'Sir?'

'You are an extreme man, Staff Sergeant McAleese. Take a look at yourself in the mirror. Your obsessions are your strong points, your qualities and your character. Stop trying to suppress them inside the manual of the School of Infantry. You have experience, you have drive. Use it.'

I took his advice and allowed my enthusiasm for the subjects to determine the method of instruction, rather than the other way around and I think it worked. I think the students thought so too. Even when they were soaking wet and cold, marching up and down the Welsh hills or digging filthy dirty trenches and filling them in again, I was always there with them, encouraging them and trying to pass on my own enthusiasm for soldiering.

I felt that these infantry officers gave the Brecon school depth and balanced the sometimes selfish obsessions of the airborne, the Parachute Regiment and the Special Air Service. In fact, I grew to respect the line infantry regiments, particularly the Argylls, though maybe my old grandfather's ghost affected my judgement. Overall, I saw that although Mr Average Top Student was a Para, so was Mr Average Bottom Student, while most line infantry NCOs produced steady 'C' grades. They were good men with experience to offer and I enjoyed working with them.

My nine years were up. I enjoyed working in Brecon very much, but officers in the Parachute Regiment had told me that I had reached my ceiling in the British Army, that my record stood against me and I could expect no further promotion. This was a bitter pill to swallow at twenty-six years old. I knew nothing else and I wasn't interested in anything else.

So, on 1 March 1969, I retired from the British Army.

I owe my early training and experience to the Parachute Regiment and to 22 SAS, but, as it turned out, I did far more soldiering elsewhere.

4

Catharsis

> Be ye transformed by the renewing of your mind, that ye may prove what is that good, and acceptable and perfect will of God.
>
> Romans 12: 2

As a Catholic, but not a very good one, I might say that the next few years were my time in the wilderness. Sister Loyola and Father Brett would rise up at the sacrilege, but the analogy ends there, abruptly. I did not go to a high place, to observe the world. I saw the world from a very different place altogether, among the low-life. I was tempted and gave in.

This was a grim part of my life and for a time I debated whether to include it in this book at all. I'm not proud of what happened, but then I thought I should present the whole picture. If I did not mention it, some smart-arse would bring it up and accuse me of trying to hide it. I don't want that. I have said I'm not making excuses for myself. My life has been about soldiering, I'm proud of my achievements as a soldier, I've served in three different regular armies and I won't allow myself to act like so many Walter Mitty 'mercenaries' who prefer not to talk about their past. Besides, I learned a lot in these next miserable years.

·I did not make a very good civvy. In fact, the first thing I did was to try and join the United States Army, to go to Vietnam. A well-known SAS officer, nicknamed the Rat, who left the army as a colonel, took a considerable risk for me by pulling strings with friends of his in RAF Air Movement and fixed a flight for me from RAF Lyneham to La Guardia Airport in New York. I equipped myself with a passport and visa and arrived in the USA with no money to find bureaucracy was alive and well. The US Army recruiting officer was perfectly happy to sign me on, but first he wanted me to obtain a US work permit. When I went to the Labor Office, they were quite happy to give me a work permit, once I was in the US Army.

Depressed and penniless, I was walking down Broadway and bumped into Tim Holt, who had won the Military Medal in the SAS in Malaya. He was broke too. We both went to a hospital and gave blood for a few dollars. Finally, I succeeded in phoning my contact in RAF Air Movements and he wangled my flight home. On reflection, I think it was probably a good thing I was prevented from joining the US Army. I don't think I would have survived Vietnam.

I got a job laying gas pipelines. This was the golden period of British North Sea Gas development and I worked up and down the country on sites in Fife, and at Braintree and Hereford. However, I was still married to Marlene and when I came back to Hereford between jobs I saw all my old mates who were still in the army. I found this hard to bear. I was on the outside, looking in where I wanted to be, my marriage was in tatters and I was having to come to terms with civilian life at a time when the student revolution, peace marches, long hair, beads and bells were in full swing. It sounds odd now, but I used to go to work on the gas pipeline in Hereford dressed in my Parachute Regiment smock. I changed into work clothes on site, and at the end of a day's work, I put the smock on again. I resented being a civilian and I was disgusted by the 'you-owe-us-a-living' attitude in people at that time. I wanted to show I felt differently. I suppose I took it out on Marlene, we argued constantly and it made no difference when, in 1969, she produced my first child, a son we called Jason.

The Hilton Assignment was a brief light in the darkness. In June 1970, I received a telegram from Lawrence Smith who had finished his time with the army, saying there was a lucrative prospect of earning £5,000 for one night's work. I was immediately interested, especially as I felt confident in the nature or ethics of the job if it came via someone like Lawrence Smith. I was even more encouraged when the follow-up contact was made by John Ragman, who had been in Borneo with me and had been awarded the Military Cross. If there had been any lingering doubts they were dispelled when he took me to a black and white block of flats in Kensington in London where the offices of Watchguard were located and where I met David Stirling, founder of the SAS in the Second World War in 1941. With him were a room full of people. Of the twenty plus men there, I knew more than half, as they were all ex-SAS soldiers. Stirling and Ragman did not give us all the details, to preserve secrecy on a 'need to know' basis, but they gave us a sketchy outline in which they explained that we were being asked to commit ourselves to an operation in Libya and must be on stand-by till called forward. Given the people running this job, and that we knew the revolutionary new leader Muammar Gaddafi had seized power from the Libyan King Idris in Tripoli only the previous September, none of us had any qualms about agreeing to join in. We were each given an envelope containing £200 and left to await 'call-up'.

Nothing happened. Eventually, I was amazed to read about the whole operation in the national newspapers. I found out that we had been planning to raid the prison in Tripoli, ironically called the Hilton, and release all the anti-Gaddafi political prisoners before withdrawing via the beach nearby. The British Government found out what was intended, decided it was all too embarrassing and aggressive and the operation was blown by British MI6.

This was a real let-down, and, about the same time, Irene, a girl I had met in Hereford that winter, reported me to the police for kicking in her door and back-handing her. She was a slim girl with brown hair and long legs perfectly shaped for the mini-skirt which was all the rage then. Our relationship rocked violently from extreme excitement to violent brooding rows. She became a dangerous obsession for me. Our affair finally shattered my tottering marriage with Marlene who divorced me in February 1970 and was the cause of my spending nearly two years in Gloucester Jail.

To start with, in June 1970, I was given three months for kicking in Irene's door and three months for smacking her, both suspended sentences. When I did it all over again in November the Justice of the Peace implemented both previous sentences, added some more and sent me away for nine months.

HMP Gloucester was old-fashioned: slopping out, army-style food, full of low-life and it never bothered me at all. Remember Lethamhill Road. I spent as much time as I could in the gym working the weights, a number of my friends in the SAS visited me regularly, and I got on well with the prison officers who were mostly ex-army or police. I was put in charge of the detail in the mailbag sewing shop, which may sound grand but in prison is the bottom of the pile, and immediately ran into trouble with the prison's sub-culture.

Sewing mailbags may sound a straightforward job to you, but since a few pence was given for each finished bag, rules had been invented by the prisoners to benefit the old lags. The understanding was that new men had to do a week's 'training' at the end of which they received only a nominal sum, which might just cover them for a bit of tobacco, irrespective of the number of bags they had sewed. The old lags took the rest, booking in all the new men's bags as their own. I decided this was unjust. Everyone should get paid for the number of bags they sewed. That day, a thin-faced man who had spent years in and out of prison, an old lag though he had never done a real lagging (i.e. served a sentence longer than three years), took a finished bag off one of the new younger men, gave it to me and said, 'Book this in for me, mate.'

'That's not yours,' I said. As the prisoner in charge of the shop, I recorded the number of bags each man had sewn.

He sneered unpleasantly. 'You better book it as mine, mate; I've got ways of fixing guys like you.'

To which I replied, 'And I've got ways of fixing guys like you.' And I hit him.

He staggered back, and suddenly ducked out of the bag shop to find the nearest prison officer who was on duty outside the door.

Standing right beside the screw, he screamed at me, 'Come on, you bastard. Take me if you can!' He waved his hands at me, encouraging me to attack him again. He knew perfectly well that, whereas he did not care how long he was in prison, I risked an extra sentence for fighting.

I glanced at the prison officer and, to my delight, he tactfully turned away. So, I hit the guy again, as hard as I could. Needless to say, the prison officer saw nothing and I had no further trouble.

On 28 May 1971, I tore off another sheet from the missionary calendar hanging on my cell wall and read, 'Be ye transformed by the renewing of your mind'. An hour later, I walked through the gates into Gloucester city to the bus station, free again. I have never forgotten the text, though the timing wasn't quite right. Irene was waiting for me in Hereford and we swung back into another violent roller-coaster chapter of our relationship which ended predictably with me standing before the Bench again. I was back inside Gloucester nick by 16 August for a second six-month stint of weight training.

I read a good deal and had plenty of time to think about my life. The prison was not rich in reading material, and it was common to find that prisoners had deliberately torn out the last page, but the *Reader's Digest* was allowed and I found much to read there which mirrored my reflective mood. Maybe that's why they allow the *Reader's Digest*. The majority of the prisoners were thieves and conmen who spent their whole lives in and out of jail and I don't think many of them bothered too much with articles like 'Unless You Deny Yourself' by A.J. Cronin, or 'The Joy of Doing Good on the

Sly' by the Reverend Gordon Powell, which I found in the *Reader's Digest* and still have, or Patience Strong's 'Quiet Corner' in the *Sunday Mail*.

Believe it or not, I began learning calligraphy during my weeks inside. As you might imagine, I had plenty of time and got rather good, laboriously copying out Patience Strong or 'Quotable Quotes' like, 'Only a life lived for others is a life worthwhile' (Albert Einstein). Of course, the other prisoners watched me doing this and I ended up writing letters home for them, to wives and girlfriends. One man who could hardly write his own name dictated to me as follows, 'My dearest darling beautiful wife, I miss you very much, my dearest darling beautiful wife, and I am looking forward to seeing you again, my dearest darling beautiful . . .'

A crowd of others round us nodded appreciatively.

'For fuck's sake,' I interrupted, pen poised over the inkwell. 'She's got the message! What d'you want to say?'

He looked hurt at that, paused and continued, 'My dearest darling beautiful wife, you will notice my handwriting is different. This is because I'm taking calligraphy lessons here . . .'

There is no shame in prison.

Out again, I worked with Bob Varey over the winter of '71–72, but by June I was in trouble with Irene once more. She just got to me, drawing me in like a bee to a honeypot. We got wildly involved with each other, and then as always ended up arguing like cat and dog. One night I went from the pub to her house to find she was out, but the rest of her family were waiting for me. Her mother and brothers began a screaming argument, a fight ensued and the beak sent me back to Gloucester, this time for another six months.

This time, the weight training, calligraphy (which was quite good by now), and a good deal of reading sorted me out. I never felt that I was a villain, a thief or a criminal. I was in prison over a woman, for drinking and fighting, which seem to me clean enough reasons but this time I had resolved the whole thing in my mind. I had done my time and that was that. I had reached the bottom, seen the low-life there and wanted no part of it. It was time for a change.

The doors of Gloucester Prison closed for the last time behind me in December 1972 and I went back to Hereford. Irene found me near the old stone bridge over the River Wye and began her usual game. She strutted along the pavement ahead of me, tantalising in her mini-skirt like some houri in a Hollywood movie. This time I stopped, turned around and walked away.

— 5 —

Interesting Work Abroad

Oddly enough, a virtue that brings its possessor pleasure and profit is held suspect in our intricate ethical system. Why should this be so?

HERMAN HESSE, from *If the War goes on . . .*

In 1975, I was thirty-two years old, working on the oil rigs, like so many ex-soldiers, and bored. So when Bob Varey said he had seen an ad in the *Daily Mirror* offering 'interesting work abroad' I thought, why not? This turned out to be the 'Rhodesian Contract' and it was very bizarre indeed.

On Saturday 27 May, three of us, Bob Varey, Norman Duggan and I, went up to the Centre Court Hotel in London from Hereford. We sat about in a large conference room, curtains drawn, facing a stage, and around 7 p.m. the drama began, just like something from a movie. All the lights gradually dimmed, leaving us in darkness till suddenly spots lit the stage curtains which began to slide open. A small man with a long face appeared neatly dressed in a suit and he began to give us an extraordinary briefing. This was my first sight of John Banks, who had been dishonourably discharged from 2 Para in 1969 for driving a car without insurance. Behind him, a big sheet hung on the wall on which someone had drawn a free-hand map of Africa, with 'Kariba Dam' written on it free-hand in huge letters right in the middle. Banks had taken trouble with the stage effects. He dropped his voice and began to speak softly and penetratingly using maximum amplification on the public address system.

'All those who have scruples about fighting for the black man against the whites should leave the room now,' he boomed.

Only a few got up and left the room. I reckoned there was plenty of time to leave later if necessary and we were all too intrigued to

60

walk out at once. However, there was a lot of muttering and John Banks, sensitive to this, wisely announced there would be a tea break. I took the opportunity to talk to some of the others and quickly realised that the place was full of dreamers, Walter Mitties and space-cadets with no military experience whatsoever. One very young-looking eighteen-year-old wearing a natty combination of suit and baseball boots, tried to convince me he had been fighting with Frelimo against the Portuguese. Another, called Les Aspin, certainly came from Norfolk, East Anglia, in the UK, but insisted he was from Norfolk, Virginia, in the USA and swore blind he had been working for the CIA. He later claimed in a book to have single-handedly killed four Palestinians who burst into his hotel bedroom to assassinate him, and even said he threw one out of the window to his death on the pavement below.

The briefing continued. Banks told us there was a big op coming off in Rhodesia. He had been asked to find two squadrons of mercenaries to fight out of bases in Zambia against the Rhodesians and we were to use medium machine guns. He meant the Vickers water-cooled MMG which is good value in defence but massively cumbersome and particularly unsuitable for mobile operations (we never used it in the Rhodesian SAS). The three of us from Hereford listened intently, but Banks's briefing matched the whole atmosphere and was entirely phoney.

Once he found we had been in the SAS, he was at pains to impress us and revealed that he had some secret backers for this operation. All ears, we listened fascinated as he told us he had been to a covert meeting with Paddy Mayne in a caravan on Hankley Common. Colonel Paddy Mayne was one of the first great SAS names, who was awarded three DSOs for bravery in the Western Desert and commanded 1 SAS. He left the army after the war and went back to Northern Ireland. Banks's claim was certainly impressive as Paddy Mayne had died in a motor accident two decades before in 1955. I later found out that the story had more to do with deceiving his wife as Banks was screwing a bird in this caravan on Hankley Common at the time, the dull bit of sandy ground near Aldershot which the Paras use for balloon jumps.

Banks had to come up with something about 'backers' because he had to explain how he was paying for the hire of the conference room, how he paid for expenses and how he managed to afford handouts. He gave £200 to Bob, Norman and me, probably because he wanted ex-SAS soldiers to balance the young dreamers we had met during the tea break. Banks had been a Para and if he stopped to think, he was able to tell the difference between a complete bluffer and some-one who had a little soldiering experience. Later, as Banks's own delusions developed and the cash rolled in, he didn't bother to try.

However, most journalists who follow mercenary stories cannot tell the difference. Or, more likely, they prefer not to. Most opted for Banks's story, leaked by him to the press, that he had gone to another secret rendezvous with a 'tall aristocratic officer' in a 'large country house near Hereford'. The implication was clear. Colonel David Stirling, who had certainly been behind the Hilton Assignment, was the backer, 'the Paymaster', with other decorated SAS officers in the shadows. The press also implied these men enjoyed the tacit approval of the British Government. This scenario was supported at long distance by the fact that Britain was far from cosy with Ian Smith of Rhodesia. Such speculation made more suggestive and exciting copy than the sordid truth and suited the arrogant imaginations of Banks and journalists alike.

The Rhodesian operation was plainly fantasy and we went back to Hereford where I was living with my sister Molly. I thought no more about it till Banks phoned and asked me to help him with security at another weekend meeting, this time in the Post House Hotel in Heathrow. On Saturday morning, I arrived in a suit and tie to find a group of nineteen people who looked even stranger than the first lot, in jeans and loud coloured T-shirts, swinging heavily tattooed arms like muscled gorillas, and, needless to say, they spent most of their time sitting at the bar telling each other war stories.

'I was in the Foreign Legion,' said one. 'I flew a glider into Dien Bien Phu in '58.' Apart from the fact that he would have been four years too late, the Legionaires parachuted in, and this fellow didn't look old enough to have been a pilot then, sixteen years before.

'I was a marine,' replied his co-drinker. 'A commando.'

'Yeah? I work for Mossad,' said a man with a mass of fair curly hair.

'We came across your guys when I was in the CIA ...' said a fourth.

'I was a navy diver for seven years,' said another, enormously fat man on a bar stool. 'I was with the Special Boat Service then. A medic. Of course, that was after my radar technician's course which I did to supplement my sonar skills.' He twisted with difficulty on the stool to bring me into the circle at the bar and said, 'So you were in the SAS as well?'

How could a man do so much in so short a time? Amazed, I nodded, actually catching myself considering his question seriously, when I knew perfectly well I had never seen nor heard of him in Hereford before in my life.

He smirked knowledgeably and shouted, 'Barman! Another round of beers!'

All the drink went on expenses which Banks paid for and I began to wonder what the point of it all was until a reporter for the *Daily Mirror* turned up, on Banks's tip-off. The meeting was supposed to be a continuation of the Rhodesian operation but that was all nonsense. Fantasies are no good without publicity, which the journalists willingly gave him.

After the press left, I decided to find the man with the mass of curly hair. He had been behaving very strangely, peering at me from behind pillars and ducking out of sight round corners. I decided it was time to have a talk. In his room, he backed away from me, saying, 'John Banks told us if we did anything wrong, you'd kill us!'

I was speechless. The man was completely bald and on the dressing table stood a hairdresser's polystyrene head supporting a fine, curly blond wig.

More bemused than angry, I went downstairs to find Banks who airily said, 'Oh that? I told them you were the adjutant of the SAS and that you would not hesitate to kill them if they misbehaved.'

Such was the 'mercenary' world of John Banks, but the casual attitude to 'killing' had a more sinister impact the following year.

By the Sunday, Banks decided the farce had gone far enough and told me to dismiss the men. Of course, as soon as they heard the jamboree was over, the hotel telephone lines were jammed with orders for bottles of gin and whisky on room service and some could hardly lift their suitcases as they staggered out of the hotel. The final bill must have been vast. The price of fantasy, and, do not forget, publicity. Banks drove me to his house where he thanked me when I left and said cryptically, 'Peter, there could be pressure on. You'd better take this.' And he pressed a loaded .32 calibre pistol into my hand. Puzzled, I returned to Hereford and handed it straightaway to one of the officers in camp.

Of course, Banks phoned again. A few days later, he offered me £60 a week to act as his security advisor, which was reasonable money at the time, so I agreed. He wanted to sell commercial security, and needed my enthusiasm and experience to make presentations to clients, to persuade them we could train their bodyguards and security officers. This was a genuinely good idea. At this time the so-called 'security industry' was only just starting and there was money to be made by new firms in the market. If Banks had not allowed his penchant for intrigue and fantasy to ruin the plan, we might have made it work. Management for the Churchill chain of hotels came to us and Banks spoiled a good presentation of mine by calling himself Patterson. Of course, the hotel's security boys immediately recognised him as Banks. His face had been all over the newspapers as the central figure of the mercenary stories only weeks before. Once again, it was clear nothing would come of these plans and I went back to Hereford.

This, then, is the shady world of mercenaries and security men, where it is difficult to separate fact from fiction, where most of what you hear is lies, but, beyond that grey twilight zone of nonsense, there was (and still is) a hard core of reality.

Ironically, it was directly because of the publicity generated in these first ludicrous fantasies that John Banks was contacted to supply men for an actual contract. On Saturday 17 January 1976, I was sitting in Molly's house in Hereford when the phone rang and a voice said, 'Is there a Major Nick Hall there?'

I had never met a 'Major Nick Hall' but the line went dead before I could ask for an explanation.

This happened again so the third time I was surprised when the caller announced, 'This is Major Nick Hall speaking.' He explained that he was a colleague of John Banks and there was a job abroad, with pay and expenses. 'If you're interested, come to the Tower Hotel tomorrow and we'll tell you what it's all about.'

The following morning, I packed some overnight things, dressed in a suit and took the train to London. I was under no illusions about John Banks and the rest but the chance of excitement abroad made scaffolding in Hereford look pretty dull.

We sat about in one of the bedrooms and I recognised a number of the same faces I had seen before in the Post House Hotel. The door opened and a tall upright man of medium build with a pasty face came in and introduced himself as Major Nick Hall. He said he was an officer of the FNLA (the National Front for the Liberation of Angola). He seemed about twenty-five years old and I don't think any of us were convinced by his rank. I did not at that time know that he had been a private in 1 Para where he had been court-martialled for selling weapons to the Ulster Volunteer Force and sent to prison for two years with a dishonourable discharge from the army. With him were John Banks and Les Aspin, the man who had single-handedly taken on the PLO in a hotel room, and they briefed us about the war in Angola.

On 10 November 1975, the Portuguese had announced that they

were leaving Angola after five centuries of colonialist rule. On the same day, two liberation movements fought a battle twenty-five miles outside the capital Luanda. Holden Roberto, the leader of the FNLA, was defeated by the Marxist troops of the MPLA (the People's Movement for the Liberation of Angola), so it was the communist-backed MPLA who celebrated Independence Day in Luanda while Holden Roberto retired to Ambrizete, a hundred miles up the coast. In the south was another group, UNITA (the National Union for the Total Independence of Angola), led by the bearded Jonas Savimbi who was supported by South Africa.

The USSR then stepped in to bolster the MPLA. First, 'advisors' arrived in Luanda, then Fidel Castro willingly supplied thousands of his black Cuban soldiers (who were a nuisance to him in Cuba at that time). Most important, Russia supplied plenty of arms; the ubiquitous AK assault rifle, T34 and T54 tanks, and artillery in the form of mobile 122mm Katyushka rockets, known in the Second World War as 'Stalin's Organs' because of the horrendous noise they made when fired. This massive effort shocked the United States which tried to solve the problem with money. President Ford agreed to allocate $32 million to prevent Angola becoming communist. The fund was managed by a handful of CIA agents but the reaction was too late and produced too little on the ground where it mattered, facing the reality of the MPLA.

African armies usually fight each other with the minimum martial contact, moving from town to town terrifying the opposition with propaganda. When the attack comes, resistance is slight because most of the enemy have run away. Those foolish enough to stay can expect little mercy. The hallmark of African wars is slaughter. I have heard it said that 90 per cent of casualties are the result of massacres and atrocities, mostly after the fighting is over, and after my time in Africa I can believe it. This was certainly true in Angola.

However, the MPLA was a serious proposition. Stiffened by Cubans, Soviet arms and the Soviet doctrine of concentrating the maximum forces in the attack, the MPLA had a distinct military advantage over its rival FNLA. Like a juggernaut, the MPLA advanced along the long thin roads through the bush taking town after town, and by the time we all met in the Tower Hotel, Holden Roberto's FNLA was confined to the north of the country.

Nick Hall did his best to paint the FNLA in the best light, but those were the facts. He finished off with, 'We need tough guys. Men who aren't afraid of fighting tanks and overwhelming odds.'

I can't say what the others thought about that, but there were about twenty-four people in the room and they all accepted a first payment of £200 each and a Sabena airline ticket to Kinshasa. Flight 614 left Heathrow that evening for an overnight stop in Brussels before carrying on to Kinshasa. Passports were no problem. Banks and Hall had foreseen that most if not all would come without their passports and spent hours on the telephone and visiting the Belgian Embassy. Presumably, the British made no connection between John Banks of recent mercenary fame and the new manager of a group called the Manchester Sporting Club, nor thought it odd that such a club should carry identity cards in the name of the SAS! (Banks called his company Security Advisory Services). Anyway, they had no objections to letting us out of the UK, the Belgians were happy to clear us through Brussels, and plainly we would have no difficulty flying into Kinshasa. Holden Roberto was related by marriage to President Mobutu of Zaire who allowed him a base in Kinshasa.

Banks and Hall had been given very little time to supply men for the FNLA and kept up the momentum. Without delay, we drove to Heathrow. I went with Hall in a car, while the rest piled into a coach. By the time they reached the airport, the total number had shrunk to twenty. Four or five had gone absent with their cash, stepping out of the coach at traffic lights on the way, preferring to spend their money at the bar rather than face 'tanks and overwhelming odds'.

I left Britain as a trooper in the new mercenary army and I was one of the few who did not get paralytically drunk that night in the hotel in Brussels. I enjoy my drink but not when I am working and, however Mickey Mouse this adventure seemed to be, I stayed off the booze. Perhaps 'Major' Nick Hall was impressed with this, as, by the time our Sabena DC-10 landed at Ndele Airport in Kinshasa, he had promoted me to captain.

We waited on the plane for all the other passengers to leave and then emerged into the hot, sweet-smelling, oppressive African night to find Holden Roberto standing by a car on the tarmac. He was a tall stocky black man dressed in a grey light-weight suit wearing dark sunglasses which he was never without. He appeared tired, like a man with his back against the wall, but he shook us all by the hand as we filed past and we all replied as instructed by Nick Hall, saying, 'How d'you do, Mr President.'

Feeling dirty and exhausted after our long flight, we walked across the tarmac to a gate beside the terminal buildings. The whole place was in a terrible state of repair, with paint peeling, concrete walls chipped or broken and windows smashed. Outside the perimeter fence, we boarded an old American-style bus and followed Holden Roberto's car at speed over bumpy potholed streets littered with garbage to a restaurant where he gave us all dinner. He was surrounded by a crowd of black bodyguards wearing slacks and bright calypso shirts bulging with under-arm pistols. With them was a white man, called 'Canada' Newby. After dinner, 'Major' Nick Hall, Holden Roberto and Newby climbed into the big limousine and led us on another mad drive through the sprawling city to the other side of Kinshasa. Holden Roberto lived in a large white villa called Kirkuzi which was set in spacious grounds on a rise overlooking the city and was guarded by patrols of well-armed black men.

It was late, we were exhausted, but we were immediately issued with Belgian-style army uniforms, belt webbing and pouches, boots, .30ins-calibre M2 carbines with several 30-round clips and one magazine. Four of us picked FNs, the Belgian equivalent of the British .762mm SLR. Contrary to what has been said, these M2 carbines were in good order, though there was some grousing because some of the men with British Army experience were more familiar with the SLR. Admittedly, the SLR is easier to clean and has more hitting power than the .30ins-cal but it is strange how perceptions change. Nowadays, everyone wants the M16 (Armalite), a smaller calibre still at .556mm, but everyone recognises that the ammo is lighter and you can carry much more of it. Important, that, in a firefight.

Perhaps because we now looked more like soldiers, 'Major' Hall announced we were to drive to Angola that same night. He told me to inform the rest and we set off again in the old Yank bus. No more than fifteen minutes later, still inside Kinshasa, we were stopped by a Zairean Army road-block. In the manner of black African troops, all the Zairean soldiers pointed their rifles at us and expressed ignorance of our 'mission'. To my horror, everyone in the bus started leaping to their feet, cocking their carbines and there were shouts of 'Let's shoot our way out!' I saw our expedition ending in a bloodbath before we even reached Angola and took command. I calmed them down, made them all unload their carbines till we reached Angola and put an armed man in each corner of the bus. Outside, an interpreter sorted out the road-block and we set out again. Others have written up this incident as taking place inside Angola, where it doubtless looks better on their combat CV, being in the war zone.

The bus rumbled on towards Angola, 200 miles away. We spent a very uncomfortable night lying across the seats trying to sleep as the bus jolted along through the darkness. The roads were so bad that we occasionally had to detour into the bush to avoid potholes and everywhere I saw the remains of cars and trucks which had simply broken down or crashed and been left for want of spare parts.

At dawn, we reached Luvo, a largish place on the Zaire-Angolan border, and crossed into Angola for the final leg of our journey to Sao Salvador, another fifty miles southeast where Holden Roberto had his headquarters. This town was no different from any of the others we had passed through, with peeling whitewashed flat-roofed houses, a few with Cape Dutch fronts, very colonial and very Portuguese, with loose-limbed black Africans wandering about in desultory groups in streets filled with rubbish, or just sitting, waiting, with small black children playing in the dust, and the warm air was rich with the rank smell of decay. Our bus passed the police station which was patriotically flying the red, yellow and white FNLA flag from a pole on the roof and then turned off the main street through big wrought-iron gates into the grounds of a large colonial-style palace. This was the FNLA HQ and it looked very run-down indeed.

Stiff from our journey, we stumped out of the coach and stood about. I was wondering at a number of black soldiers slouching about under trees wearing only their underpants when a tall English officer appeared suddenly at the top of the steps of the house. He was neatly dressed in uniform, in the rank of captain, with a moustache and a military bearing. He surveyed us from the steps, waved his hand at us, his face a picture of disgust, and demanded succinctly, 'Who the fuck are these fuckers?'

This was Mick Wainhouse. He stood there like an officer on parade and cursed everyone for having long hair, being dirty, unshaven and overweight. I must admit I felt rather guilty as I was not as trim as I had been, but I was reasonably fit and saw no point in lambasting men who had been travelling solidly for thirty-six hours. I sent the others off to find billets upstairs in the palace and had a quiet talk to Wainhouse on my own and cooled him down.

Once again, we were not to know that 'Captain Mick' as he was called had been a private in the Parachute Regiment and, like Hall, Callan, Copeland and others, had been dishonourably discharged from the army. Maybe his court martial proceedings had given him an extra opportunity for studying officers' behaviour, because he aped their mannerisms rather well.

Callan appeared and I must say he made me apprehensive. He was of medium height, tanned, well muscled and looked very fit. It takes a lot to make me frightened, but I could see he was a complete maniac by the arrogant way he strutted and threatened. All round us, everyone was running about standing to attention in front of everyone else, stamping feet, saluting, shouting orders and generally carrying discipline to extremes which would have been ludicrous in any regular army. There was something dangerous about this man which warned me to act very carefully with him. I was on his ground and vulnerable. Remember, all these people had been brought together at short notice, with no allegiance to each other. A pecking order had to be established out of nothing, with no army system, traditions, ethics nor any body of law to help, in other words by force of personality alone. Callan, Wainhouse, Charley Christodoulou and Nick Hall were the first in, and Callan had taken charge. It was as simple as that. These were the men hired to help Holden Roberto and his FNLA and the whole lot of us were being funded by the CIA, just as the Cubans fighting with the MPLA were the vicarious agents of the Russians. While the enemy were about seventy miles down the road at Damba, this was the absurd situation at the head-quarters in Sao Salvador. It was the mercenary jungle at its worst.

Callan asked me for my background, which I told him. He did not volunteer his own. His real name was Costas Georgiou, born in Cyprus in 1951, and had been a moderately successful Para until he foolishly decided to rob a post office in Belfast, with Wainhouse. The postmaster observed them driving up and down the road and telephoned the nearest army base.

'I'm going to be robbed!' he said to the Para officer on duty.

'How d'you know?'

'Take it from me,' replied the man. He had been robbed numerous times before by the IRA and recognised the signs.

'All right. Can you give me a description of the men?'

'To be sure, I can,' said the postmaster drily. 'They're in uniforms of the British Army, wearing Para berets and driving one of your Land Rovers!'

This ill-conceived frontal assault was typical of Callan, as was his threat to kill the officer prosecuting him at his court martial. He was given five years and dishonourably discharged.

While I was talking to him, a black soldier came up to us. Callan snapped at him, 'What is it?'

'Sir, we've got no food or ammunition.'

'Fuck off!' Colonel Callan shouted in the man's face and drove him off with a few broken words of Portuguese. Then he turned to me and said indignantly, 'Can't you see the trouble I have with these people?'

We went in his Land Rover for a drive round the town. The streets seemed filled with more black soldiers carrying rifles and wearing nothing more than their underpants. I remarked on this and Callan said absently, 'I requisitioned their uniforms.'

He pointed out the salient features of Sao Salvador as we bumped along the potholed streets. The place was dominated by the palace and the police station. Outside the town on the edge of the bush, he showed me the airstrip and I saw how Sao Salvador was built on an escarpment overlooking a lovely valley full of green trees and grazing land.

Back in the HQ, everyone was trying to get their hands on weapons of their choice, mainly AKs, which they simply grabbed off passing black soldiers. Typically, no one was satisfied with what there was available. Callan told me there was a shortage of weapons, but I made my own tour of inspection and found a large shed behind the palace full of weapons and ammunition. There were no FNs but there were plenty of Soviet AK assault rifles, boxes of brand new M2 carbines complete with magazine pouches and rifle cleaning kits, a couple of American 106mm M40A1 recoilless rifles, a couple of Soviet anti-tank RPG rockets, American 66mm light anti-tank weapons, the free-flight disposable missile launchers called LAWs, and plenty of ammunition. In brief, it is complete nonsense for anyone to say we had a shortage.

There was an atmosphere of chaos in Sao Salvador and especially round Callan which had nothing to do with the proximity of the MPLA. He was totally unpredictable, manic and brutal. He called over a black man who was wearing a new camo' hat he wanted to give to one of the new arrivals. When the black FNLA soldier didn't spring to attention quickly enough, Callan screamed at Sammy Copeland and another mercenary to take the black away and beat him up, which they did. For an hour we could hear the man screaming inside the palace before they flung him out into the dusty yard covered in blood. It was common to see, or hear, black soldiers being beaten up and it added to the atmosphere of anarchy. I don't know what Holden Roberto thought of this, or even if he knew, but hitting people who can't hit back, black or white, has never been my style. Unfortunately beatings were only just the beginning.

By evening, the new arrivals were in some shape. At least, the pecking order was established, with a trail of broken sunglasses, the budding mercenary's indispensable accessory, trampled underfoot to prove who had lost out in various petty little arguments, and we went to bed. Callan gave me a room on my own and I slept deeply until a terrified mercenary burst into my room in the middle of the night shouting, 'We're being shelled! We're under attack!'

I rolled out of bed and ran to the window. Great flashes of light lit the brooding African night, with cracks of distant thunder, but this was an electrical storm, not the MPLA gunners. Some of the men had never been out of England and they were very inexperienced.

A couple of days later, I was pleased when Callan let me pick six of the men for a separate detachment. I took Brummy Barker, Mike Johnson, Doug Saunders, Stuart McPherson, Mick Rennie and John Tilsey. We drove to the airstrip and flew to San Antonio di Zaire, about 150 miles from Sao Salvador, in a Fokker Friendship piloted by a Portuguese and paid for by the CIA.

This was my first real look at the battleground and the first time I appreciated the sheer size and emptiness of Africa. Dry grassy hills rolled out in all directions beneath us, covered in scrub bushes, spreading baobabs and low thorny trees, and I could see the importance of the roads which linked each lonely town in the bush. San Antonio di Zaire was in the northwest corner of Angola, rather out on a limb, but it was an important coastal town on the south bank of the Congo River estuary. Zaire lay several kilometres away across the water, on the north bank.

From the air, I could see that San Antonio was ideally placed to defend. The town was built on the side of a flattish triangular peninsula sticking out into the mouth of the river. The road to the town from the south passed a crossroads at Corpus Christi which I indentified as a crucial defensive position. However, it was clear that the only escape once the attackers blocked the land approaches would be by boat from the quayside where the local fishing boats were tied up.

Holden Roberto met me in the town and explained he believed it was vital to hold out against the MPLA who had already taken Ambrizete, the next important town south about 100 miles down the coast. If the MPLA took San Antonio, he said, there would be nothing left to the FNLA except an enclave in the north, pressed against the border with Zaire.

I installed my small group in a villa in the town and drove out to Corpus Christi where some nuns lived in a convent. It was perfectly obvious that an immense effort was required to organise any sort of defence. The whole town was in a state of virtual anarchy. FNLA soldiers ambled round without any sort of discipline, the black civilians had given up, complaining that the FNLA stole food and anything else they wanted. There was talk of rape, and the two hospitals we went to, one civilian and one military, were utterly disgusting, fly-blown, stinking of gangrenous rot, with dirty bandages lying about and no drugs.

Angry more than depressed by all this, I asked Holden Roberto to gather the people together on a worn basketball pitch in the centre of the town. We looked out on the sea of black faces, Holden Roberto adjusted his black sunglasses and shouted, 'This man is the new commander of San Antonio di Zaire.' He turned elegantly from side to side, looking over their heads, trying to muster enthusiasm, a spare, somewhat menacing figure. 'You will come to him if there is anything you need. He is in charge of everything!'

No one seemed very impressed, but then, the place stank, they were starving and I don't think anyone cared who ruled them: the FNLA, the MPLA or UNITA. Come to that, for me, the state of the place rather took away the pleasure of being called the supremo of a whole town for the first (and only) time in my life.

There seemed little point defending somewhere as close to total anarchy as San Antonio was when we arrived. There was no sign of law and order, even African-style, among the civilians, while even the rudiments of military discipline were lacking among the soldiers. I decided the place needed ripping into shape at once. I detailed my small group to make various assessments, of the weapons available, of the numbers and state of the FNLA troops, of the rations and ammunition, and went myself on a closer look round the town. On the outskirts, near the river, I discovered a large warehouse belonging to Petrango, Angola's petrol company. Amazingly, while the country starved for lack of organisation amid the ravages of civil war, it was full of food.

'All this,' I told the black man in charge, waving my arm at the boxes of rations stacked inside, 'is requisitioned.'

He was terrified, not by me, but for his stores, and reminded me of a certain type of British quartermaster sergeant who likes his stores neatly arranged on the shelves out of use, and, therefore, out of harm's way.

I tore off a sheet from my notebook and wrote him out a receipt for the entire shed, signed simply, 'Peter.' He was happy with that, and I have often wondered if he got into trouble, if he survived. Back in our villa HQ, I ordered the food to be issued to the 800 black FNLA soldiers so they had no excuse to steal from the civilians.

These soldiers were useless. They had been trained by the Chinese at Kinkusu in Zaire and spent their time learning stupid communist slogans rather than training with their weapons which they had hardly fired, even on the range. Their commander was a large black man called Commandante Lima who had been a policeman in the United

States. He passed his time working on a boat down on the river, presumably preparing for his escape. I can't say whether it was his American police experience or the way of life in Africa, but when two smugglers were brought in with boxes of cigarettes they had tried to smuggle into Angola, Commandante Lima generously waived the usual death penalty, took charge of the cigarettes for his own profit and let the smugglers go.

On the second day, I got Commandante Lima to gather all the townspeople on the basketball pitch again. I don't know what they all thought of a stocky white man getting all fired up on their behalf, as none of their own leaders seemed to have bothered, but they really perked up when I announced that the riverside fish market was out of bounds to all soldiers. I even saw a few smiles when I explained the soldiers now had their own food and would not be allowed to loot any more. I told the people that if there were any infringements, complaints must be made direct to me in our little villa in the middle of town. I finished by saying I had found a vast quantity of flour, in Petrango's warehouse, and I wanted bakers to bake bread. There was no shortage of volunteers. For the time being, we had solved the food and discipline problems. There was enough food and flour to feed both civilians and soldiers. Thanks are overdue to Petrango.

We got several generators going and restored electricity to the main buildings, including the two hospitals which we cleaned up. I used the FNLA military police for this job, huge men in dirty white helmets with MP painted on the front and armbands. For some reason I could not explain, one particularly massive MP sported a single sinister black glove. Certainly, human rights were not top of the agenda in San Antonio di Zaire, or anywhere else in Angola. Out on a limb in San Antonio, none of us knew just how true this was in Maquela where the self-styled 'RSM' Sammy Copeland had moved to conduct operations. In between mad dashes at the advancing enemy, these two were conducting their own grown-up version of *The Lord of the Flies*, torturing and murdering blacks without compunction.

I was worried at the lack of intelligence in my sector, from Holden Roberto, who had not returned to see me, from Commandante Lima or anyone else. So, when I heard a light plane overhead, I drove out to the airstrip outside the town in one of the Land Rovers I had commandeered from another Petrango shed. I found a Portuguese pilot standing by a Cessna. He said he worked 'for the Americans' without elaborating on that and agreed to take me on an air recce. I needed to find out how close the enemy had come. Rumour said the enemy might be approaching through the bush to our south. We took off and flew towards Ambrizete, following the coastal road which I could see was in an appalling state of repair. We saw nothing, so we turned east towards Tomboco, along the road. Again, there was no sign of enemy forces, nor did there seem to be many locals about.

On my return to San Antonio, I sat down in our small house and wrote a Military Appreciation, depending heavily on the training I had received at the Brecon Tactics School, for I had never had to do an appreciation like this in the SAS. I looked at all the factors I thought were important, such as the available intelligence, our own forces (seven of us whites and 800 black FNLA), the enemy forces we could expect to attack us, and detailed weapons, ammunition, food and the tactical possibilities. Then I finished off with my principal conclusion, which was that there were various local skirmishes going on in the Maquela and Sao Salvador districts, but there was no overall control or staff work of any kind to coordinate the anti-communist FNLA effort. My conclusion was that trained staff and logistical support was needed at once. I gave the report to the Portuguese pilot who promised to give it to the 'Americans' he worked for.

One morning some days later, the precarious rule of law and order I had instituted fell apart. A group of black civilians appeared at our house all jabbering at once. The FNLA soldiers were busy looting from the fish market in direct contravention of my orders. 'Let's go!' I said to my group of six and, with the huge black MPs, we grabbed some rubber batons we thought might come in handy, piled into Land Rovers and drove down to the river to the fish market where we set about the looting FNLA soldiers. The locals were amazed and delighted and shouted their encouragement. 'Viva O Peter!' they cheered. 'Viva O Comandante!'

Feeling rather pleased with this Robin Hood style action, we put the men we had arrested in the Land Rovers, dumped them at the town jail and went back to our house for a brew.

This may sound rather rough justice, but you should understand that at the same time, acting on Callan's order, two mercenaries murdered a black FNLA officer called Zeferino for stealing tins of pilchards. By the end of January, Callan and the other lunatics with him had probably murdered more than 200 blacks, excluding those they claimed to have killed in action. They were murdered on 'suspicion' of being spies, for infringements of discipline, for fun and to see what certain weapons did to the human body. Callan decided to test Charley's shotgun for himself. He called over a FNLA soldier, stuck the barrel in the terrified black man's mouth and blew off the top of his head, leaving nothing but his jaw-bone. Many were shot behind a mud hut in Maquela by Callan and others, while Sammy Copeland preferred to take the blacks to Quiende bridge where he shot them, pushed them over the parapet and watched them fall in the river.

We knew nothing of this, having left Callan in Sao Salvador, and our problems were mild by comparison. Two days after the episode in the fish market, the MPs came to say that the jail was full. I went down and found the place looked like the Black Hole of Calcutta! With all the men we had arrested, the prisoners were standing shoulder to shoulder, hardly able to move and suffocating in the intense heat. I ordered, 'Let them out!' meaning release only the soldiers we had arrested at the fish market, who had suffered enough after a beating and a couple of days in the overcrowded jail. However, the MPs, always men to overdo an order, promptly opened the doors of the jail and the whole lot streamed away to freedom, including all the long-term prisoners and a murderer who promptly vanished into the bush.

Meanwhile we had been organising the defences. I saw that there was a terrible mix of weapons among the FNLA troops. Some had Russian Kalashnikovs, firing Soviet 7.62mm by 39mm medium rounds, some had FNs, firing standard NATO 7.62mm by 51mm, and others sported Spanish CETMEs, also firing 7.62mm NATO rounds but using different magazines which would not fit in the FNs. This would be a nightmare for ammunition resupply in combat. I told Commandante Lima we would divide the FNLA into four groups and redistribute all the weapons. There was considerable resistance to this, because some liked their AKs, or FNs, but I insisted, and we ended up with four companies which at least carried the same weapons: one with all the AKs, a second with all the FNs, a third with the Spanish CETMEs and a fourth carrying an impossible mix of carbines, Sten guns, shotguns and all sorts which I kept in reserve in the middle of town.

I placed my few men with the FNLA companies and we started training. I had seen little enemy activity from my air recce, but the word was that they were loafing about in Ambrizete only an hour or so down the road and there was not much time to knock our soldiers into shape. The six men with me were excellent, no matter what they were accused of later, and worked hard and enthusiastically, encouraging the black soldiers. I made out a simple training programme, starting with the basics; weapon handling, some range work, section battle drills and fire control. While this was going on, I selected defensive positions round the town and in between training periods we set the FNLA soldiers to digging trenches and filling sandbags.

A day or two after giving my report to the Portuguese pilot, he flew back in with two Americans, John, who was very fat, and Stuart. They wore civilian shirts and slacks and offered no explanation of who they were. Stuart said he had been a US Marine and I assumed they were CIA. They said, 'Who wrote this Situation Report?'

I owned up and John said, 'Can you take Ambrizete?'

'Yes,' I replied. 'But I'll need trucks to get there, ammunition to take the place and resupply to hold it.' I was beginning to see the frustrations of staff work. The lack of communications was probably the most acute problem. I had no idea Callan and the others had moved down to Maquela more than a week before, that Jamie McCandless, an enormous ex-SAS soldier, had been the first white mercenary to be killed in an ambush, or that John Banks, now elevated to the rank of 'Major' in the FNLA, had flown into Kinshasa with another draft of new mercenaries on 29 January.

I said, 'I need radios.'

The Americans promptly flew in radios, American style PRCs common in the US Army in Vietnam. With this new source of supplies came the suggestion that we should begin to prepare for a breakout south towards Ambrizete. They also said they would give me some rigid raiders. These were steel boats with outboard motors which took a section of ten men, like those I had used on the rivers in Borneo, and which I could use to loop south along the coast during the advance on Ambrizete.

I managed to raise the FNLA Headquarters base station in the palace in Sao Salvador where I heard 'Fuzz' Hussey's voice. He was an ex-SAS soldier and he was manning the radio shack. He told me, 'Some boys have come out, but I'm on my own and I can't say any more.' I knew his voice and he sounded very odd. I felt something was badly wrong.

I used the Cessna again to make another air recce. This time I landed on the rough airstrip at Tomboco where I spoke to a Portuguese mercenary called Colonel Bento. He said his men were starving for lack of food and he was delighted when I told him about the Petrango food stores. By this time, I had found another store in San Antonio, an even bigger aircraft hangar full of food which I 'liberated' with a second promisory note that full payment would be made after the war: I arranged with Colonel Bento for the FNLA

Fokker Friendship to fly in rations to the Portuguese at Tomboco, and also to our people at Sao Salvador.

However, all our efforts in San Antonio di Zaire, and come to that, the FNLA effort everywhere was destroyed by what happened next. There is no doubt in my mind that the Americans I had met were keen to help. They had the finances and were already supplying me, but it all fell apart.

On the morning of Thursday 5 February, I was making another appreciation of the town's defences with Brummy Barker, whom I had known in Support Company in 1 Para when I joined up. He was in the anti-tank platoon and his advice was crucial in defending the town against the MPLA tanks. He agreed that the key to defending San Antonio was at Corpus Christi, just outside the town, where there was a small river and marshy ground which was impassable to tanks. My plan was to move a company of FNLA out to the area and we were talking about this as we drove back to town when we saw the Fokker Friendship coming in to land. Holden Roberto and his bodyguards turned up at our villa HQ in town with an attractive blonde American reporter called Robin Wright. Holden Roberto looked worn out. I asked one of the others to show Robin around, just to get her out of the way, and we sat down to talk.

Speaking in broken English, he said, 'Terrible things have been going on with the others. At Maquela.'

'What?'

'Killings,' he said with an air of defeat.

Sensing disaster, I grimly wondered if he meant blacks or whites, but he added, 'Many men, also white men. Colonel Callan gone for three days. I want you to take over. Please? You go now, with me, to Maquela, to sort it out?'

Even through his bad English, the picture was not encouraging, and it struck me as typical of my luck that all of a sudden I was expected to be the saviour of this mess. I must say the idea did not appeal. Roberto had heard these stories by word of mouth and he had no more idea than me what we were likely to find on landing in Maquela. Other mercenaries, who had 'deserted' from Maquela by jumping into the Fokker during an admin run to Maquela the day before, said they expected Callan to return any moment with a large number of mercenaries. I knew very well that Callan completely controlled his henchmen who would do, and seemingly had done, anything he ordered. There was no news of Callan's other two associates, Sam Copeland and Shotgun Charley. All in all, it did not sound as if Callan and the rest would take much notice of me or

Holden Roberto's new decision to put me in charge.

However, we took off in the Fokker for Maquela, Holden Roberto, his bodyguards and I with Mick Rennie as my support. I left Brummy Barker in charge of San Antonio in my absence and refused to allow Robin Wright to come with us. God knows what Callan would have done with a woman as pretty as her when he found out she was a journalist. Few soldiers get on with reporters, especially not British Army soldiers with experience of media reporting in Northern Ireland.

We left San Antonio under a brilliant blue sky but as we approached Maquela we faced a great tower of black cloud. Visibility was limited, the rain lashed across the windows and the pilot refused to land. Instead we flew to Kinshasa, only about thirty minutes' flying time north.

In Kinshasa we drove from the airport to Holden Roberto's secretariat in the big villa on the hill above the city, and I tried to piece together the threads. I found one man called Dave Tomkins in Mama Yemo Hospital (a very grisly, dirty place in a similar condition to the hospitals we had found at San Antonio). One of his grenade booby traps had exploded and wounded him in the arse, but he knew very little of the massacres except hearsay. Others added their evidence but it was sketchy. 'Major' Nick Hall had spent most of the time in Kinshasa, sleeping all day and living it up all night in the Kinshasa night clubs, such as the Intercontinental Hotel, where he terrorised black girls and swaggered about for the benefit of reporters like the BBC's John Simpson. I discovered we had collected another self-styled captain, an American called Tom Oates who was an ex-Los Angeles policeman. He wore a ridiculous, bright scarlet beret, squeaky-clean camouflage fatigues and polished boots, and he had hardly crossed the border into Angola. Barry Freeman, a mercenary who had allegedly been involved in the killing, understandably played down his involvement, but the story which emerged was truly appalling.

Briefly, on Sunday 1 February, only a day after arriving, a number of the new intake of mercenaries had been ordered to set a night ambush on the south side of Maquela facing the expected approach of the enemy. In the dark, they had seen a vehicle approaching, not recognised it as one of theirs, and fired a rocket at it. In fact, the Land Rover contained Dempster, Freeman, Boddy and a new man called Max who were severely shaken but, amazingly, unharmed. Believing themselves to be under attack by a large force of enemy, the ambush party then piled into trucks and drove pell-mell for the border where they were turned back by an ex-SAS soldier called Terry Wilson. Then they drove to Sao Salvador but met Callan on the road. After some confusion, Callan brought everyone back to Maquela, found the town had not been taken by the enemy and called a parade in the square, lining up the new intake, unarmed, and surrounding them with his henchmen and a number of Portuguese mercenaries. When the Land Rover party explained how they had been 'treacherously' attacked, Callan lost his temper and ranted about the 'cowards' who had tried to 'murder' his men. He screamed at the accused men to strip to their underpants, which older hands recognised as his usual prelude to a killing, demanded to know who had fired the rocket and, when a young man called Phil Davies owned up, Callan shot him on the spot, firing three bullets into his head. Then, casually, he ordered several of the Portuguese to throw the body over a low wall, and told Sammy Copeland, 'Take them away, Sergeant Major. You know what to do with them.'

Copeland, it seems, was delighted. Perhaps he was bored of killing blacks. He took Barry Freeman, Tony Boddy, Chris Dempster, Paul Aves, Andy McKenzie and a Portuguese called Uzio, they shoved the eleven condemned men into the back of a Dodge troop carrier, drove them outside the town and gunned them all down.

I was badly shocked, more so when I heard that my cousin, Tom McAleese was reported to be among the dead. Thankfully, the report later turned out to be false.

The images of this disaster would not go away and I never stopped moving that day. I thought of the shame it brought on British soldiers, of my cousin, and the senseless criminality. As the story of the massacre leaked out, an atmosphere of doom settled on Holden Roberto's camp in Kinshasa. It deepened on hearing that Tomboco had fallen. I met the Portuguese Colonel Bento who said he had blown a bridge on the Ambrizete-Tomboco road but the enemy tanks had found a way round. In spite of my suggestion, he had no intention of going back. To add to our troubles, it seemed the enemy had ended their rest and refit and they were on the move.

The military situation was grave. My initial assessment of the dangers of not having any staff support, command or control was confirmed. The Americans had poured in millions of dollars to support the FNLA. A good deal was creamed off en route, but there was plenty left to buy the tools of war. Contrary to what anyone may say, there were enough radios, arms, ammunition and all the necessary supplies. The problem was that no one was coordinating any of it. All this equipment was hidden in sheds and lock-ups all over Kinshasa, but no one was in command to pull it all together. Holden Roberto was not strong enough to control his undisciplined murdering mercenaries, he spoke little English, and this was Africa, where chaos and corruption was endemic in peace and rampant in war.

The massacre at Maquela had to be pursued. Holden Roberto had realised that when he had flown to see me at San Antonio. The political consequences were nothing short of disastrous for him. When the news burst on the world, his support would vanish. In mitigation, the very least he could do was show he was doing something to clear up the mess. He asked me, 'Will you go to Maquela? To arrest Callan and the others?'

I felt inadequate for the task. This was an adjutant's job, a policeman's job. I don't think like a policeman, I was not trained as a policeman but I knew I had to go. Besides, no one else wanted the responsibility.

That night, I spent some time working out exactly what I was going to do once the Fokker landed in Maquela. It was easy for Holden Roberto to say, 'Arrest them!' but I could not see these maniacs coming quietly.

I was up very early the following morning, 7 February, and dressed with a bullet-proof vest hidden under my combat shirt. A small group gathered at the villa. Holden Roberto was wearing his dark glasses as usual, but the sharp edge of his control had gone which gave away how worried he was. With him from the night clubs came 'Major' Nick Hall, wearing uniform for a change, and Mick Wainhouse, who may have been intrigued to see what his old colleague Callan had been up to. Tom Oates, complete with pressed fatigues and scarlet beret, made up the group. We drove to the airport and the Fokker took off at 6 a.m.

There was little talk during the flight. As we approached Maquela I looked down and saw a Land Rover with a mounted Soviet Degtyarev 12.7mm machine gun driving onto the airstrip. I frankly admit I was worried. Callan plus his cronies and firepower like that would be hard to beat on my own.

But I was committed. The Fokker lost height, landed and taxied to a halt. All the others immediately hopped out and doubled away from the aircraft to the sides of the airstrip pretending to take up defensive positions, ready to see who came out on top, I suppose. A blasphemous thought flashed through my mind. At that moment, I understood what Jesus had felt like in the Garden of Gethsemane, abandoned by everyone and facing the Roman soldiers.

The Land Rover drew closer and I saw just Copeland and Shotgun Charley aboard.

'How're things, lads?' I asked cheerfully. According to my plan, I produced a map, spread it out on the ground, and asked them to give me a brief.

Copeland knelt down in the dust, putting his AK beside him on the ground and began to talk. I watched him carefully as Shotgun Charley wandered over to look at the map. As he came within reach, I kicked Copeland's AK out of the way with my foot and began setting about Charley with the but of my M2 carbine.

He dropped his shotgun and screamed, 'I wasn't even fucking there!' He knew perfectly well why we had come.

I stepped back, covered them with my carbine and told them I would kill them at once if they moved a muscle. Copeland just stared.

Of course, the rest came running over as soon as they saw it was safe, and we all drove into Maquela with Hall and Oates shouting for blood.

Maquela was a shambles. The usual whitewashed colonial flat-roofed houses were wrecked, garbage littered the deserted streets and there was a terrible smell of death.

We found the rest of the mercenaries sitting dejectedly in a burned-out building in a state of shock. They were utterly drained with the constant fear of being shot too. I galvanized them out of the house and lined them up in three ranks. Once they saw we had arrested Copeland and Charley, the accusations flooded out and we learned that nothing had been heard of Callan since he had disappeared into the bush on a vehicle patrol with a handful of other 'mercs' to recce the Cuban positions.

Hall set up a 'court martial' which was nothing more than a kangaroo court. Holden Roberto, the Commander of the FNLA in Angola, was present and provided some semblance of authority. He certainly knew exactly what was happening even though he spoke little English, but the fast pace was dictated by 'Major' Hall. Naturally, there was no shortage of witnesses. They queued up. They had all seen Callan murder Phil Davies on parade, an extraordinary and quite inexcusably callous act, though no one present had actually seen the other mercenaries killed outside the town. Sammy Copeland was found guilty of 'mass murder' but Charley 'Shotgun' Christodoulou was acquitted.

Copeland was sentenced to death by firing squad without further ado.

Once the sentence was declared, numerous people began jostling to take part in the firing squad.

'I'll do the bloody thing myself,' shouted an enthusiastic young man who was in 21 SAS, a Territorial Army SAS regiment which recruits in the south of England.

The firing squad was selected and took its place, still arguing. Copeland stood a little way off. Holden Roberto made a last-ditch attempt to salvage something of justice. He spoke up and suggested that Copeland should be handed over to the British authorities in Kinshasa, and that the matter should be dealt with by the British police.

Nick Hall shouted him down, bellowing, 'This man must be executed!'

Suddenly, taking advantage of the momentary confusion, Copeland made a break for it. He jinxed left and right through the bush and nearly escaped, but the firing squad was so keen to shoot him that all they had to do was lift their carbines and a fusillade brought him down wounded. Casually, one of the mercenaries walked over, drew his pistol and shot him dead.

In retrospect, I blame myself for what happened. I weakened and let matters get out of hand, allowing men like Hall to force their will against my better judgement. We were all working for Holden Roberto and those two were his so-called 'officers', but I should have taken control. Killing like that is not my scene, though Copeland was certainly guilty and none of us felt any sympathy for him. Further, I want to clear up an accusation made against me, typically by people who have never taken the trouble to speak to me about it, and make it absolutely clear that while I was unhappy with what was going on, I made no suggestion whatsoever to exchange Copeland for Christodoulou. There were some terrible things done by various people under Callan but it is certain that Copeland was guilty. He had led the execution party which had cold-bloodedly murdered eleven British citizens. He rightly suffered a rough justice.

In fact, I will never forget the scene of the killings. Some of the men thought they knew where to look and we drove out of town in a Land Rover. A detailed search was not needed. We drove up a hill and I could smell the place at once. I stopped the Land Rover. I got out slowly, unbelieving, feeling a great sense of emptiness as I stared out over the gentle slope of the valley which dropped away from the road. Copeland had told them to try to escape and the eleven corpses lay scattered in ones and twos among the dry green grass and thorny bushes, tapering away to the last victim who lay some 100 metres away. The bodies were bloated, fly-blown and rotting horribly but I could see they had been grotesquely murdered, shot to bits, limbs torn off with bursts of automatic fire. For fun. One body was kneeling, his head hanging over a bush, the twigs covered with his brains which had been blown out of the front of his face.

I whispered to myself, 'God in heaven! How can men do this to their own?' I have never seen anything like it. I felt ashamed to be a British soldier.

But the war went on. The enemy were closing in on the FNLA Sao Salvador-Maquela pocket in a classic Soviet pincer strike on the two roads through the bush from the west through Tomboco and from the south through Damba. Advance elements were only a few kilometres from Maquela.

Morale among the guys was understandably low. I gathered the shattered group of mercenaries together and I told them the situation as far as I knew it. There was no disguising the facts. The communist MPLA and Cubans had the upper hand, looked like seizing the whole of Angola and I bluntly finished with, 'Those who want to go, leave now. The rest will carry on.'

Armchair critics had their opinions of this war, but always with the benefit of hindsight. You should know that when I asked that question, all the 'big men' from the Foreign Legion, the TA SAS, and the Paras, in that order, fucked off. Oh yes, they all had various plausible excuses, which were all bullshit. The men who volunteered to stay were old hands, many from the Second World War, and young men with no previous military experience, who were bloody impressive.

As a result of the depletion of our numbers, we were in no position to hold Maquela and I gave the order for the men who stayed to fall back on Sao Salvador. While in Maquela, I had also found that our supplies were very low, particularly diesel fuel. There was nothing left except what was in the vehicles already, probably a lot less than sixty gallons. Since I was now cast in the role of 'Commander', whether I liked it or not, and since there was no one else ready or capable of doing it, I flew the half hour back to Kinshasa to find the Americans again and ask for more of their support.

When I got there I found more bad news. San Antonio di Zaire had fallen. On Saturday 8 February, Brummy Barker had chosen to go hunting rather than move the 106mm M40 recoilless anti-tank rifle and a company of FNLA into the position we had agreed at Corpus Christi. When he got back he found the tanks rolling up the road without means of stopping them and in minutes the port was in communist hands. The FNLA soldiers had evaporated into the bush and the rest of the men, with Robin Wright, were chased through the town to the river where they only just made good their escape in a boat. I expect they were pleased that I had had the foresight to put it there. They reached Americans in Zaire on the northern bank of the Congo who arranged for them to fly to Kinshasa. Barker quite literally missed the boat and was taken prisoner.

At the same time, the news of the massacres at Maquela leaked out to the world's press.

'Mercenaries in Big Killing!' screamed the headlines, and Murray Davies of the London *Daily Mirror* reported later, 'I saw the horror of Massacre Valley!'

When I met the two Americans, John the fat one and Stuart the ex-Marine, they were glum. They agreed to supply fuel but they said, 'These killings have really screwed us. The State Department has ordered us to hold off completely, and if we get caught helping you, we're in the goddamn shit.'

The communist enemy were making the most of the massacre, using the propaganda coup to show the capitalist system 'at its worst'. Costas Giorgiou, the 'Colonel Callan' for whom, astonishingly, various journalists had a 'sneaking admiration', did more damage by his criminal killings of blacks and his massacre of white mercenaries than the enemy were doing with their army. After the news broke, the United States dissociated itself as fast as possible from Holden Roberto's mercenaries and the FNLA. At that point, if not much earlier, Angola was lost to communism, and there was nothing the few mercenaries left could do about it.

However, we all tried for the next week or more, while the FNLA soldiers deserted over the Sao Salvador palace wall in large numbers every night.

In Sao Salvador, those who remained went out on patrols to identify enemy positions and intentions and prepare the Quiende bridge for demolition.

In Kinshasa, the two Americans had reluctantly agreed to give me five vital airlifts of diesel fuel we needed to move our vehicles, and also radios for the lads, under cover of supplying the Zairean army. Nick Hall was supposed to have coordinated the delivery so that it came to us (after all, he was Holden Roberto's 'senior staff officer'). I arrived at Kinshasa's Ndele airport at 5 a.m. and the Fokker landed two hours later with only three drums of diesel. Someone had ripped us off. I was furious. At eleven o'clock, Nick Hall, in civvies, finally arrived at the airport with Holden Roberto and I lost my temper with them both. Hall had done nothing, having spent all night drinking and chasing women in the Kinshasa Casino, while Roberto put on his 'shy and timid' act. It didn't wash. By that time I knew that during wars in Africa, especially in Angola, a lot of innocent people die off the battlefield. Holden Roberto's FNLA was as bloody as all the rest, and he knew it.

The corruption in Kinshasa was getting me nowhere. I decided I must get back to Sao Salvador, but the Fokker was grounded for repair (in retrospect, perhaps deliberately so, because the Americans had been funding this plane all along). I looked round for something else with Dave Bufkin, a recently arrived American pilot, and found the Cessna parked up near a hangar. It was guarded, but a few weeks in Africa had added a worldy-wise cynicism to the refreshingly clean violence of my youth. I bribed the black guard for the keys and stole the Cessna. Dave Bufkin, who had been a crop-duster in the States, flew us both the half hour south to Angola using a Shell road map.

As we approached Sao Salvador, I was suspicious at once. Whereas normally there were crowds of people milling about in the town, this time the place was deserted. I told Dave to land anyway, but none of our men in the town could explain why the locals had vanished. They said there were a couple of Land Rover patrols out along the roads southwest, towards Quiende and Tomboco, looking for the enemy, but since there were no radios there was no intelligence reported back from them. I told Dave to turn round and we took off again for a look round.

Dave flew towards Maquela and after about fifteen minutes I saw them. What a sight! It was the biggest armoured column I have ever seen, stretching for a mile or more back along the dusty road through the bush. Bufkin had an awful lot of guts. He flew us low right along the column so I could see everything. The Russian BRDMs and T54 tanks were easy to spot in their typical harsh green Russian paint, though they had made a good effort to conceal some vehicles from the air by removing the canvas canopies and tying bushes to the metal frames. This neatly broke up the shape of the vehicles and made them impossible to see among the scrub trees of the African bush till we actually flew right over them. At the back of the column were endless trucks filled with Cuban and Angolan soldiers and plenty of massive forty-ton articulated supply vehicles filled with combat resupplies. I counted about seventy fighting vehicles and estimated some 2,000 troops. It was a hell of a sight.

'We've seen enough! Let's go back,' I said drily to Dave, and we returned to Sao Salvador where I got all the guys together by the steps in front of the palace.

'Who feels like fighting?' I asked sarcastically and when several put up their hands I told them flatly, 'Well, you're going to have all the fighting you ever wanted.' And I told them what we had seen from the air.

While I was talking to the men, two small Chinese tanks appeared in the road and turned into the palace grounds. Horrified, we watched one smash through the wrought-iron gates and lumber towards us. It flattened the flag pole and headed straight for the steps of the palace where we were standing. We scattered. Engine roaring and tracks grinding, it lurched halfway up the steps and halted. A big black tank commander emerged from the turret.

'Great!' I shouted as I watched him extricate himself from his tank. 'We've got tanks!' They were certainly not the last word in tank design but better than nothing against the armoured vehicles I had seen from the air.

I had no sooner spoken than this gallant black tank commander jumped down from his tank and legged it, disappearing through the broken gates into the town.

Dave Tomkins appeared in the second tank. Though not fully recovered from his wounds, he had discharged himself from Mama Yemo Hospital in Kinshasa and volunteered to lead these small Chinese tanks and a vehicle with anti-tank missiles down to Angola. He was obviously in pain and I advised him to go back to Kinshasa. I found a Portuguese bulldozer driver who could drive the tank instead.

We made preparations to defend the town but I don't think anyone expected to be able to repel the Cuban/Angolan armoured columns. There was some excuse for wondering why we were bothering at all. The town was deserted, people had gone to ground in their houses or disappeared into the bush to await developments, all but one hundred of Holden Roberto's FNLA soldiers had also deserted Sao Salvador, we could expect no resupplies from the Americans after Callan's behaviour and our leader, Holden Roberto, was in Kinshasa with his FNLA 'senior officer' Nick Hall.

The air of doom worsened when one of the black soldiers with me fired off his rifle by mistake. At once they all started shooting wildly and several more took the opportunity to desert. A group jumped on the anti-tank truck mounted with our 106mm M40 to drive it off. I lost my temper and leaped aboard after them, physically throwing them off it again.

Aged eight, at Number 15 Lethamhill Road, Glasgow.

My grandfather, 'Old Miles', in the uniform of the Argyll and Sutherland Highlanders, aged twenty-six in 1914.

Lethamhill Road as it is today. The site of Number 15 is on the left of the picture. Barlinnie Prison is visible on the right (my father's cell was on the top right).

In Bahrain with 1 Para in December 1962.

On operations with the SAS in the Jebel Barash area, Aden 1966.

The fort at Ataq in Aden.

With 16 Troop of the SAS in Aden, against the background of the Jebel Barash.

As a fresh-faced SAS Trooper in Borneo, 1965.

During the attack on the ZANLA camp at Muroro, with the Rhodesian SAS.

Flying back from the Muroro camp attack with George McLagen.

Preparing to attack 'DK', a ZIPRA camp in Zambia, with the Rhodesian SAS. The informer who led us to the camp is sitting on the ground.

'DK' camp burning after the attack.

Wearing typical Rhodesian Special Branch garb, including 'nutcracker' shorts (note drum magazine on AK47).

With Jim Addison and SEPs (Surrendered Enemy Personnel) I had trained for the Rhodesian Special Branch at the end of an operation in the Keep Three area.

With Jane and Pete Donnelly at Bindura registry office, 24 January 1980.

Mick Rennie came back from his recce along the Sao Salvador-Tomboco road and reported the enemy in that direction too. Again I felt suspicious. We were out on a limb in Sao Salvador, we only had a small corner of Angola left in our control, two enemy columns were closing in like the horns of a bull on the only two 'main' roads and a glance at the map showed me that our retreat would soon be blocked off when the armoured column I had seen from the air reached the Lucosso-Cuimbata crossroads.

Again I saw no realistic option but to withdraw. The decision to retreat is easy to talk about, bloody hard to take on the ground. Also I knew there were several mercenaries (including Callan) still unaccounted for on patrols of which nothing had been heard for some days. However, there was nothing our little group of thirty mercenaries could have done at that time to alter the course of the Angolan war. The march of world politics had strode past us and we were now a lost cause. I gave the order to pull out of Sao Salvador.

Not far outside the town, one of the little tanks threw a track. We left it and drove on towards the Lucosso-Cuimbata crossroads passing great crowds of black refugees. Among them we saw deserting FNLA soldiers carrying all the loot they had stolen. Everyone was trying to reach Zaire.

We dug defensive trenches at the crossroads just in case we were surprised there by an advance party and I sent Dan Aitken with some others to blow the river bridge just beyond, on the Maquela road. They returned two hours later and confirmed my gut feeling that we had been sitting in a trap in Sao Salvador. The Cubans had been only one kilometre away when they had blown the charges and dropped the bridge.

If I had not pulled the men out of Sao Salvador when I did, the Cubans would have taken the crossroads, cut us off and many more mercenaries would have been captured. At that stage, the outcome of the war was not in question.

While we were at the crossroads, I got a message to drive to the border where I found the two Americans again. They confirmed it was hopeless. For the last time, I returned to the lads at the crossroads and gave the order for complete withdrawal to Kinshasa. The last mercenaries left Angola to the communists on 17 February.

Holden Roberto and Nick Hall were furious.

'Why have you deserted your positions?' shouted Nick Hall, back in uniform again. 'You should be court-martialled!'

Bluntly, I told them the situation. Angola was lost. Had been for a long time. As I spoke, I wondered if these two could have done more than just spend their time lurking in Kinshasa, but I kept this to myself. My position was weak. I was in uniform as a white mercenary working for a defeated black Angolan leader in someone else's country.

The Americans had also heard that two patrols were missing and let me take the Cessna (which they had recovered from Sao Salvador) out the following day to see if I could find them. I took a radio in the hope of raising someone on the ground. There was nothing. Only one young boy, from Barry Island in Wales, emerged from the bush in Kinshasa a week later after a two-week escape and evasion from deep inside Angola. He had been with Mick Rennie's patrol driving towards Tomboco when they had been ambushed and split up. Without any training he had instinctively done all the right things to avoid capture, not stayed in huts, hidden at night under bushes, stolen food and crossed the border to safety. It was an impressive performance.

Thirteen mercenaries were missing (some for days) before being captured. Later, after a show trial in Luanda, four were executed: Callan and Andy McKenzie, Brummy Barker (who always complained of his bad luck) and Daniel Gearheart who was executed for being an American. The rest were imprisoned. They are all out now. The others who did appalling things while pretending to be soldiers got away scot free. The British police investigated the massacre, but not any of the other killings of blacks. When Freeman and Dempster returned to England, they were arrested and questioned about their part in the massacre of the British mercenaries at Maquela, but a decision to let the whole matter drop was taken by Prime Minister Harold Wilson at Cabinet level.

I hung on in Kinshasa till the end of March, staying in a shed at the back of Holden Roberto's villa. I went to see the two Americans who were slumming it in the Hotel Intercontinental and we discussed their plans to mount a guerrilla campaign. Of course, after the terrible publicity of the mercenary killings, this was nothing more than a CIA pipe-dream.

The British Embassy was very stuffy and formal but I helped them put together a list of as many names as I could, so they could inform relatives in Britain. An aggregate list is given in Appendix A, from my original list and other later sources. There was still doubt about exactly who had been murdered at Maquela and killed in action as no one had kept a record of the latest arrivals or could remember their names.

Holden Roberto withdrew into his villa and refused to speak to any of us. Finally, when only Dan Aitken and I were left, I persuaded the two Americans to talk to Roberto. We had no money at all and they told him to pay for plane tickets for us to return home. On 23 March, after two months in Africa, I flew back from Kinshasa on Alitalia flight AZ827 to Rome and then by AZ282 to Heathrow, London, with very little money in my pocket.

6

Trigger Time

You must remember, this is Africa. They think nothing of doing filthy, beastly things to each other.

LORD SOAMES, British Governor in Salisbury

'What are you going to do next?'

'I'm going to join the French Foreign Legion,' I replied morosely, staring into space over a pint in a pub in London. After another intense but disastrous affair with a girl in Hereford, I was bored and depressed and had taken the train to London with just enough money to reach Paris.

Murray Davies was a reporter I had met in Kinshasa when he was covering the end of the Angolan war for the *Daily Mirror*.

He laughed and said, 'Forget it. If you like fighting, why don't you go to Rhodesia? They've got a hell of a fight on their hands.'

I nodded. An ex-SAS friend in Hereford, Chuck Hinde, had told me the Rhodesians were really going for it, on their own, and surrounded on all sides by hostile black 'Front Line States'. Chuck was then in the Central Intelligence Organisation (CIO), on leave in England, so he said, but I found out later he was doing 'passport work'. This meant leaving Rhodesia by scheduled air flights, travelling to another country, usually in Europe, from which he could innocently enter one of the black Front Line States as just another tourist on a scheduled flight. Once inside the target country, he could carry out a covert attack or assassination. ZANLA's Operations Chief, Herbert Chitepo, was blown up in his Volkswagen car by Rhodesians on 'passport work'.

I said, 'Sounds great, Murray, but all good ideas need finance and I've hardly got enough to cross the Channel, let alone reach Rhodesia.'

'I'll give you the money.'

What a stroke of luck! He generously gave me £200, which was a lot in those days, and I flew to Rhodesia on New Year's Eve of 1976.

In Salisbury, the luck ran out.

I went straight to the Army Recruiting Office and while my papers were processed, I stayed in the Ambassador Hotel and kept out of trouble. By contrast, several other new arrivals, including a man about my build and appearance, spent their time drinking and whoring on the town.

Some days later, to my horror, the Recruiting Office told me I was unsuitable and refused to sign me on. I was really at a loss and deep depression loomed, but fortunately I ran into Chuck Hinde again. He listened sympathetically and set up a meeting for me with Jack Berry who was in Rhodesian Intelligence.

'I see you like the dusky maidens,' said Berry cryptically in his office.

'What're you talking about?' I replied, puzzled.

'Don't give me that shit,' he said bluntly. 'We check out all foreigners who come here to join up, and you didn't pass the test.' He told me a covert surveillance team had followed 'a short stocky man with a moustache and intense blue eyes' who spent all his time out on the town screwing black women. They had mistaken me for the other man in the hotel who looked like me! I confirmed this with my room number.

On 4 January 1977, once satisfied my intentions were good, I was allowed to sign on in the Rhodesian Army as Number 728200. I immediately volunteered for the Rhodesian SAS, went to Cranbourne Barracks in Salisbury, and began one of the most serious periods of my soldiering career.

I had joined the army of a country which was locked in a fight to the death. Mr Ian Smith, the Rhodesian Premier, headed a government which refused to countenance a change to the system where 240,000 whites held total political and economic power over 6 million blacks. He had steered the country through the Unilateral Declaration of Independence from Great Britain and by 1976 Rhodesia had no international friends. Even South Africa was under tremendous pressure from Dr Henry Kissinger, the American Secretary of State, to stop supporting Rhodesia with arms and oil. It is not surprising that the atmosphere amongst all Rhodesians, not just those in the army, was tense.

A glance at the map shows that the country was surrounded by antagonistic communist black states. My experience in Angola the previous year came in useful, because the Portuguese withdrawal from Angola on one side and Mozambique on the other, both countries which succumbed to post-colonial communist regimes, placed great pressure on Rhodesia. Both communist governments, along with Zambia and Botswana, gave safe haven for the black communist organisations outlawed in Rhodesia. The two principal groups were Joshua Nkomo's ZIPRA and Robert Mugabe's ZANLA. Communist bloc countries, headed by Russia and China, were applying a sort of domino theory to Southern Africa, as countries became communist one after the other, with the object of making the whole of Southern Africa communist.

The Rhodesian communists were Joshua Nkomo's ZIPRA (the Zimbabwe People's Revolutionary Army) and its political wing ZAPU (the Zimbabwe African People's Union) which recruited from the Matabele tribal lands. The fighters lived in camps in Zambia and infiltrated Rhodesia from the north and west, from Zambia looping south through Botswana to cross Rhodesia's long western border with Botswana.

The second and largest communist group was Robert Mugabe's and the Reverend Ndabiningi Sithole's ZANLA (the Zimbabwe African Nationalist Liberation Army) and its political wing ZANU (Zimbabwe African National Union) which recruited from the other side of Rhodesia, from Mashonaland where the Shona tribe was the country's biggest population group. They had built some very large training camps in Mozambique, which was seriously Marxist and gave ZANLA great support, and they infiltrated Rhodesia through the thick bush along her 1,300-kilometre eastern border.

In fact, only 220 kilometres of Rhodesia's 3,000 kilometres of border was with a friendly nation; South Africa was friendly, but international pressure was increasing to stop the South Africans assisting the white regime in Rhodesia. Quite simply, the Rhodesians had their backs against the wall, and there was no time for frivolity. Even the drinking and womanising was pursued with intensity.

By the time I arrived, both Robert Mugabe's ZANLA and Nkomo's ZIPRA had carried out countless attacks on the local population and the blacks suffered more than the whites. The newspapers were filled with a constant stream of accounts of brutalities from all over the country. One of the most grotesque incidents occurred just before I arrived, in December 1976, when ZANLA terrorists attacked the African families on a British tea estate in the Eastern Highlands because the blacks refused to stop working for the owners. The ZANLA 'fighters' lined up and machine-gunned twenty-seven of the men, then kidnapped the women and children by walking them back to their training camps in Mozambique. By

Christmas that year, 716 civilians had been murdered by terrorists but only 61 were white.

Training for the Rhodesian SAS matched the mood of the country. I buckled down to it, enjoying the feeling of being back in a regular army with a clear purpose, but I found the first phase frustrating. Recruit training is fine when you are seventeen years old and fresh to uniform, but I was thirty-four and for me the first six weeks were absurd. There was the usual regular army obsession with imposed discipline, endless drilling, digging holes, filling them in again, and making up 'bed blocks' in the billet, which meant folding the bedding to an exact measurement which we checked with carefully measured lengths of string before the inspection. In fact, it was easier to make up the bed block, leave it on the bed and sleep on the floor. Colour Sergeants Kruger and Paul Fisher were insanely keen on a vast number of star jumps for every infringement. I have always thought that punishment should be relevant to the training. Leaping up and down like frogs in drill uniform certainly improved our fitness, but it did nothing to better our drill.

I discovered Rhodesians just love wearing shorts. Sometimes we just wore PT vests and at other times we wore camouflage shirts with a full complement of webbing pouches on our belts, but we always seemed to wear shorts. One awed American said, 'The Rhodesians are the only goddamn soldiers who have ever been to war in their underwear!'

Most of the men with me were little more than half my age, called up for their National Service, straight from civilian life. The SAS had to select men like this because the only alternative source, the Rhodesian Light Infantry (RLI), was fed up with having its best men poached by the SAS. In fact, the Rhodesian SAS found the system worked reasonably well, as they were able to teach men to think in SAS terms from the start rather than have to reteach them. Of course Rhodesia was at war, so they had the great advantage of testing everyone very quickly on active service as soon as they finished selection and training. Furthermore, by direct contrast with most recent British Army campaigns, soldiers in Rhodesia expected to see and fight the enemy every time they went out on patrol.

This was probably why the weapon training and live firing exercises were realistic and good. For another six weeks, we lived in the Gwaii River Mine area, north of Wankie National Park, and worked through an intensive programme. I loved it. There is no better feeling than being really fit and totally involved in training when you know it will lead to action. Every morning, we started with PT before a busy schedule of speed marches in full equipment and live firing with a wide variety of Western and Soviet weapons.

The Rhodesian Army depended on captured equipment so, apart from the usual FNs and GPMGs, it was essential to train with Soviet arms, AKs, RPDs, the DSchK 12.7mm HMG, the anti-aircraft KPV 14.5mm super-heavy MG, the US 106mm M40 recoilless rifles and so on, many of which I had seen and used before. In addition we did plenty of realistic mortar shoots and imaginative battle drill exercises in the bush, always firing live ammunition of which there never seemed to be any shortage.

We became very brown, lean and hard and we were ready for the SAS selection course. Mere walking over the hills meant nothing to us any more, so the instructors deliberately set about trying to wear us down. This was called the 'Rev' and it was twenty-four hours of continuous PT. We were made to do anything the instructors could think of as long as it was really tiring and pointless. Anyone not totally mentally committed to passing would give up. In the UK, we had something similar during British SAS selection and called it 'sickener' but it did not last twenty-four hours solid and we were allowed to eat normally in the cookhouse. In Rhodesia, we were given only water, glucose and salt tablets.

They gave each of us a brick. We had to carry the bloody thing everywhere.

'These bricks are your loved ones!' shouted the instructors. 'You know what women are like. They hate being left alone. At *any* time.'

All the bricks had girls' names. Mine was called Elsie. One man had a brick called Arthur because he was an ex-Royal Marine. For hours they made us climb in and out of an empty swimming pool, stark naked, time after time sliding down the water-less slide till our arses were raw, and finally, around 4 a.m., I dropped Elsie on the concrete pool floor, breaking her in two.

'Stop everyone!' screamed the instructors, horrified. 'McAleese has dropped his loved one!' In the dark, naked, we formed up in three ranks and gave Elsie a solemn funeral with full military honours. Then she was unceremoniously dumped in a dustbin. I was given another brick which, to underline my promiscuity, was called Elsie too.

The actual selection course was short after all this and took place in the Matapos mountain area, where Cecil Rhodes is buried. We turned out in complete patrol gear, with full ammunition scales, our FN rifle, loaded of course, and an 80-lb rucksack. And they gave us a log. One huge telegraph pole between twelve of us.

'This log likes travel!' they shouted. 'Take this log to Bambata Caves!'

Rhodesian SAS selection is much more emotional and more group orientated than British SAS selection. In the UK, if you don't want to carry on, no one cares. You're just invited to 'have a brew and jump in the truck'. In Rhodesia, it was a bit more like the Parachute Regiment 'A' Company in Aldershot.

'Keep a tight arse and you'll pass!' we shouted together as we sweated to carry our log for fifteen kilometres up and down hills which looked like Ayres Rock in Australia, were just as hot and quite as horrendous. We never reached Bambata Caves with our log. No one does. They don't even give you the right map. The point is the effort of trying.

We finished off with a week of walking about thirty kilometres a day in full kit and rucksack. At night we slept on the ground rather than waste time returning to barracks and the medics injected our blistered feet with yellow proflavin to harden the skin. Out of the hundred who started, I was one of about twenty-five who finally passed.

During this selection period, on leave in Salisbury, I met Jane Crist. She was, and still is, a tall gentle person, with soft dark hair and big brown eyes, a beautiful person, but with a certain inner calm which I think comes from her quiet conviction in her beliefs as a Roman Catholic. She was born in America of an Irish American father who achieved fame as the role model for J.P. Donleavy's drunken fictional character Sebastian Dangerfield in his book *The Ginger Man*. She had been living in Salisbury for two years, where she was training to be a nurse at the Andrew Fleming Hospital, and we met at Sharon Hinde's apartment some while after Chuck Hinde had been killed on operations. Jane was there with her little four-year-old daughter Emelda and as soon as I saw her, I knew I wanted her.

Determined not to let her go, I played the 'sweetie trick' on Emelda. While Jane was talking to Sharon Hinde, I chatted up Emelda, gave her a couple of sweets and casually asked her where she lived with her mummy.

'Alderbury Court,' the little girl replied, her eyes fixed on the sweets in my hand.

When I had a couple of days' leave, I just happened to be walking through Alderbury Court and rang the bell.

You will probably wonder what on earth such a person could find in one of the 'brutal and licentious' such as me, and I can't really say, but we fell in love. I admit that I may not have put it quite like that to her, but that's how I felt. I always get hopelessly absorbed with the women in my life, but I can honestly say this was true of no one more than Jane. Almost, perhaps, my feelings amounted to obsession. Maybe she loved me for that, as we were happy then in Salisbury, in spite of the risks to life and limb in Rhodesia at that time.

My continuation training finished with more Soviet weaponry, laying and lifting mines, parachute jumps from Dakotas, and Klepper canoe training on Lake MacIlwain. Then I joined 'A' Troop, in Kenyemba in northern Rhodesia on the Mozambique border, and we went on operations.

My first operation with the Rhodesians was against FRELIMO, the Mozambique black national army. This was not the first time the Rhodesian SAS had fought FRELIMO inside Mozambique. In 1973 and '74 the Rhodesian SAS had been obliged to cross the border and conduct specific operations against FRELIMO from a place called Macombe, as the conscript Portuguese troops spent their time sitting about in their bases afraid to go out. Portuguese troops were never very good at controlling FRELIMO guerrillas but at least they had kept the lid on the problem. So, Portugal's withdrawal from Mozambique in 1976 was a strategic disaster. It fuelled black African communism and nationalism and exposed Rhodesia's whole eastern flank. Rhodesia was left with no support at all along the 1,300-kilometre border. By the time I arrived, FRELIMO was in power, supplied with shiploads of arms by the Chinese and giving full support to Robert Mugabe's ZANLA, allowing them to open more routes of infiltration into Rhodesia through the excellent cover of the low scrubby trees which covered the broken hilly country of Mashonaland. These routes were also used to bring new black recruits out of Rhodesia to the huge ZANLA training camps in Mozambique where Cuban, Russian, Chinese and East German 'advisors' came to train and indoctrinate them. Once trained, the guerrillas, or 'terrs' as we called them, slid back through the bush into Rhodesia to cause mayhem and death.

Our job was to ambush one of these routes. Dave Berry, who had been in the SAS in Macombe and who ultimately received the Bronze Cross of Rhodesia for bravery, was our patrol commander and set the four of us in position among one of the typical outcrops of rock in the bush, hidden in the scrub grass and low thorny trees over-looking the track which passed in front of us in a slight dip in the ground. For three days no one came along and we sat silently in the heat, concealed among the low bushes and rocks, taking it in turns to sleep, basking in the soft warmth of the day and grateful for the slight cool of the night. Then, Dave received radio permission to pull out. (We used Morse as it is less subject to static and interference over long distances than voice.) We began to creep away from the track between the boulders, trying to minimise the crunching noise of the dried fern-like grass which covered the ground when suddenly the last man out turned round to check his back and spotted four enemy in distinctive green FRELIMO uniforms moving along the track. Swiftly and noiselessly we slid back unseen into our ambush positions and opened fire. We killed all four. I remember that Baz Joliffe was most effective with his RPD, the Soviet light section machine gun. We searched them for documents and left the bodies for other guerrillas using the infiltration route to find.

Operations with the troop continued relentlessly. In contrast to my experience in Aden and Borneo, when contacts with the enemy were rare, we expected to meet them every time we went on patrol. And win. Our morale was high, though the pace of operations never seemed to let up and reflected the continuously worsening political situation.

We ambushed another track and this time the guerrilla was riding a bicycle. They often used bikes; they could move faster along the winding trails through the trees, give nothing away from footprints and no one would normally be suspicious of bike tracks. I often wondered if the idea came through the Chinese from the Vietcong's use of bikes in Vietnam. We also did vehicle operations, on one of which Corporal Ian Suttil, an ex-British Royal Marine, was blown off his truck by a landmine. He sailed past me and broke his arm on landing. Ian never had any luck. He was wounded four times, once passing an apparently dead terrorist who then leaped up and shot him, and was finally killed on a cross-border raid into Mozambique with the SADF. On another, led by Lieutenant 'Dangerous' Darrel Watt, we did a vehicle sweep looking for terrorists in an area where the thorn bushes were so bad we carried three spare tyres per vehicle. We spent the day stopping to change burst tyres and all night sitting up repairing the tubes in our overnight laager position. We had a tremendous mix of weapons on that patrol which was typical of the campaign, as there was so much Communist bloc weaponry supplied to the ZANLA and ZIPRA guerrillas. We even had a Russian 12.7mm and a Browning .50 cal on the same truck.

After six weeks of operations, we came back to our camp in Salisbury for ten days to clean up, refit and prepare for the next six weeks. During these ten days, we were allowed leave. The Americans in Vietnam went for R and R, or Rest and Recuperation, but the

Rhodesians, with an endless routine of non-stop ops for six weeks with ten days off before the next six weeks, headed for the bars and the women with the same passion with which they pursued the enemy and rechristened their leave 'I and I', or Intoxication and Intercourse.

I went to see Jane and we found her daily shifts at the hospital were really awkward. She worked from 7 to 12 a.m., and from 5 to 11 p.m. and the Matron was very strict indeed with the student nurses. I used to wait impatiently for her in her apartment and listen out for her coming back along the avenue outside which was lined with lovely big jacaranda trees. The purple blossoms fell all over the place and I could hear them crackle under her feet as she walked back up the road to see me. Sometimes, if she knew exactly when I had my week off, she would work a seven-day stretch of night duty which entitled her to nearly four days off and we would spend the whole time together.

Back on operations, our enemy was ZIPRA. We were to attack Namumba Farm, just inside Zambia on the northern bank of the Zambezi River. Special Branch sources and recce patrols confirmed that ZIPRA guerrillas used the old farm as a staging point when crossing in and out of Rhodesia. ZIPRA were trained by the Russians along more conventional military lines than ZANLA, as Nkomo's eventual plan was to invade Rhodesia in full strength. They usually crossed into Rhodesia in uniform, looking like soldiers, but their terrorism was as brutal as anything ZANLA could offer.

'Missionaries are the enemy of the People,' said ZIPRA leader Albert Ncube, trotting out the awful tired phrases which the communist guerrillas used to excuse their killings, and he fearlessly murdered the Right Reverend Adolf Schmitt, the former Roman Catholic Bishop of Bulawayo, another priest and a nun. The Bishop's successor, the Right Reverend Henry Karlen, sent a message to Joshua Nkomo and Robert Mugabe saying, 'Is this the reward for our work for the Africans?'

Captain Bob McKenzie, who was awarded the Silver Cross of Rhodesia for his continued leadership and bravery, gave us a very thorough briefing on the Namumba Farm attack. Then we piled into a big 3-ton Mercedes and Rodev 'Unimogs', which had been sold to the Rhodesians by the departing Portuguese, and drove north from Salisbury through Makuti, then on to the edge of the Kariba basin. Everything seems big in Africa but the view from the escarpment overlooking the Kariba valley is truly impressive, across the trees and grasslands of the huge valley floor with the immense Kariba lake lying in heat haze far off in the distance. We zigzagged down the steep escarpment onto the floor of the valley and set up our forward base. After a further recce, McKenzie, whose preparation and planning were always excellent, gave his detailed attack orders. After final rehearsals, we assembled the canoes and carried them through the grass and trees to the Zambezi, arriving at about 2 a.m. The Klepper was the only collapsible canoe rugged enough for special forces infiltration (and is still used by the British SAS) but it is designed to carry only two men. The river was about 100 metres across at this point and McKenzie decided we would carry a third man: one paddling at the back and two lying over the front. On command, we all slipped down the muddy bank into the slow-moving dark brown water and paddled silently to the black line of the opposite shore. As Mo Taylor was on his way back to the Rhodesian bank by himself, a great shape suddenly burst through the glistening surface under his canoe and dumped him in the water. A vast hippo opened its mouth angrily, wallowed and disappeared. Mo Taylor was gone, and there was no time to look for him in the dark.

The river bank was green and lush, like England, but as soon as we moved off, we were back in typical African bush; thorn trees, boulders and long tough grass. As planned, we divided into two groups, the assault group and cut-off group, and, as the first streaks lightened the eastern sky above the spreading baobab trees, we attacked the farm.

I, and every second man, carried an RPD to give the maximum firepower and we opened up with everything. I was close to McKenzie in the assault party, next to Imre Baka, an American serving with the Rhodesians, and we cut down two ZIPRA who ran across our front, clearly disorientated by the firepower, noise and suddenness of the attack. The enemy dropped two or three 60mm mortar rounds on us without effect and we swept through the farm, driving most of them out towards the cut-off groups beyond. One enemy held us up for a couple of minutes firing from thick bushes which all three of us peppered till he stopped. As we went past, I thought of Ian Suttil and looked back, saw the enemy soldier lying down and noticed he was still very much alive, holding his AK ready to use. I fired a burst into his chest. The black terrorists often feigned dead like this. Overall, Namumba Farm was a success. We killed seventeen enemy, most as they tried to escape through the cut-off groups by the river, and Mo Taylor turned up next day, half-drowned but in one piece. Unfortunately Mo was killed later on another operation.

These operations were high in effort and low in results. Killing four or even seventeen terrorists may sound rather horrid but it simply was not enough. The number of ZIPRA and ZANLA guerrillas operating inside Rhodesia was increasing year by year, from 400 in 1974, to 700 in 1976 and to 2,500 by the time we did that patrol in early 1977. They were losing some, captured and killed, but seemed to have no trouble recruiting, even forcing young blacks from their villages to join the big guerrilla training camps in Zambia and Mozambique. There, safely beyond the reach of the Rhodesians, morale was high, numbers swelled and if a few were killed when they went back to fight for their cause inside Rhodesia, the number of successful terrorist attacks continued to increase. ZANLA were hard to detect. They went back to their villages, mingled with the people and struck out in civilian disguise, though some were assigned to different areas so they could 'lean on' the locals if necessary. On 7 February, another seven white missionaries were massacred at St Paul's Catholic Mission, near Mrewa, only thirty-seven miles from Salisbury. Rhodesia was losing the war and many officers wanted to hit back.

We got the chance at Chimoio.

Before I describe the battle, I must explain the background, because this operation was no ordinary one-troop cross-border op. The decision to go ahead was taken by Prime Minister Ian Smith himself, advised by his Combined Operations HQ. It is amazing, in retrospect, that the Rhodesians only formed a ComOps HQ in March 1977. Before that, the war had been regarded as a police operation with military support, rather like the British experience in Malaya, Aden and lately Northern Ireland. The new structure put the emphasis the other way around (see Appendix B). It brought together under one political-military control all the essential elements needed to win the battle against the terrorists. But it was too late.

On Monday 21 November, we were ordered to drive all the way back to Salisbury from an operation in Mabalauta, right down in the southeast. When we arrived back, tired and dirty, we were told to prepare our personal equipment for a para jump. OPSEC (operations secrecy, or the need-to-know principle) was very good. We thought we might be attacking a FRELIMO/ZANLA base at Malvernia, a small town on the border in Mozambique on the end of the Maputo-Malvernia railway near the border with South Africa. We were way off the mark. We arrived at Salisbury military airfield at midday and were told to wait outside a hangar. A PJI (Parachute Jump Instructor) came out with a look of amazement on his face. He had caught a glimpse of the briefing map inside and said, 'You want to see what you're going to fucking attack this time!'

When we were called in, I saw at once what he meant. We were on for Chimoio, the biggest ZANLA training area in Mozambique. It was massive. We sat down with the RLI on bleacher benches which had been specially set up in the hangar and listened to the intelligence briefing from the SAS I.O., Captain Scotty McCormack.

For more than a year, intelligence had been collated from the Rhodesian Special Branch and the Selous Scouts who had sent two-man patrols ninety kilometres deep into Mozambique to reconnoitre the whole target. The Chimoio camps occupied an area of twenty-eight square kilometres near the town of Chimoio, formerly known as Jilla Peria, on the railway line which led from Beira on the Mozambique coast to the Rhodesian border in the southeast. No less than thirteen separate ZANLA training camps had been identified in this area, containing between 9,000 and 11,000 guerrillas. Air photograph interpreters had counted 700 on one rifle range alone. They were being trained by Cuban, Chinese and East German advisors and supplied with all the weapons and equipment they needed on the railway straight from the docks at Beira. The Rhodesians wanted to attack with only ninety-seven SAS and eighty-eight RLI troops.

SAS Commander, Major Brian Robinson, gave the finest ops brief I have ever heard. He was a small, wiry terrier of a man who was the driving force behind the success of the Rhodesian SAS and he really wound us up for the fight that day. He, McCormack, and the airforce commander, Group Captain Norman Walsh, had pushed ComOps for over a year for this operation, arguing against staff reluctance to commit so many valuable resources of men and planes to a project in which the odds were so heavily stacked against us. Failure would be a serious blow to morale, deeply embarrassing, and any lost assets would be impossible to replace. Senior officers were also constrained by the limit to cross-border operations which had always been till then only forty-five kilometres. However, by November 1977, the government realised they had to do something dramatic about the guerrilla camps, to hit back at ZANLA, and they gave the go-ahead.

Major Robinson used a superb model made up on the hangar floor, with aerial photographs stuck together to give a realistic impression of the whole target area. He explained we could only attack five of the thirteen camps, because the place was too vast an area and we lacked numbers and assets. We were to parachute onto the five parts of Chimoio in groups around the target area to form a tight Airborne Envelopment 'Box' to hem in the enemy and prevent him escaping, like lines of guns at a shoot. Then Vampire and Hunter ground-aircraft, Canberra bombers, and Alouette helicopter gunships flying out of temporary admin bases were going to bomb and strafe the camps for several hours. Finally we were to fight through to the centre of the camps, attack the secretariat and cause as much devastation as possible before withdrawing by chopper to Rhodesia. If successful, it would shake ZANLA to the core.

'We've totally stripped everything from everywhere for this op,' said General Walls in his introduction. Walls had been in 'C' Squadron SAS with the British in Malaya and was now the Supreme Commander of the Rhodesian Armed Services. Major Robinson listed our attached resources: aged Vampires, Hunters, six Dakotas, thirty-two Alouette III choppers, a DC-8, Canberra bombers and a mountain of logistical support, most critically AVGAS to refuel the short-range choppers. The logistical problems were immense but had all been solved. We hoped. The Daks could reach out from Salisbury to Chimoio and back, but the Alouettes could not, so the Rhodesians had invented the Forward Admin Base concept, setting up a self-protected base inside enemy territory which the Alouettes could use to refuel quickly and not leave their station over the fighting area for too long.

Using the model, Robinson explained how the Vampire and Hunter ground-attack planes would be used. Six Dakotas would drop the ninety-seven SAS and forty-eight of the RLI, twenty-four per aircraft, and some of the Alouettes would put down the other forty RLI troops, four per chopper, who would be flown from Grand Reef airbase via Lake Alexander nearer the border, where the command and control chopper with Group Captain Walsh would orbit high over the camp to direct operations. The Alouette 'K-car' gunships mounted with twin .30 cal machine guns would circle giving fire support. As he talked, he pointed out different coloured circles and points suspended above the big model which indicated the flying patterns of each aircraft, cleverly building up a clear picture of what was going to happen all around us as we fought through on the ground. As we listened, I began to feel the tension of the impending operation building up inside me, thinking of the para jump onto a hot DZ, the distance inside enemy territory, the sheer excitement.

At the end of the briefing Major Robinson said to the RLI, 'Good luck!' Then he turned to his own SAS and added, 'Professionals don't need it!' Which really pissed off the RLI but it was done with the dry, hard humour typical of soldiers before action. We all knew Chimoio was going to be dangerous work.

That evening we were billeted in an isolation compound on the airfield, to preserve OPSEC, and we spent the time preparing our kit. I remember a tremendous atmosphere of commitment, everyone mucking in helping each other. That evening, they gave us free soft drinks and beers which really told us how seriously they were taking it, but no one drank more than a couple before lying down on the floor to catch some sleep.

On Wednesday 23 November, we were up at 3 a.m. We drew and fitted our parachutes in the hangar. There was an atmosphere of intense concentration and common purpose, everyone helping each other in pairs to pull up the straps and adjust the webbing. I was paired with Steve Kluzniak, a tall fair-haired rather studious-looking man who was an excellent soldier. I tucked my Russian RPK behind my shoulder straps and Steve checked my harness. We heard the Daks' engines roaring outside and walked out to the aircraft. Six Daks did not make a second Arnhem but it was a stirring sight and I don't think any man among us could deny the thrilling rush of adrenalin and excitement when we took off and headed into the brightening southeastern sky, one aircraft droning purposefully after another. Shortly after seven o'clock, we reached Lake Alexander near the border in clear morning light. Perfect weather for parachuting. We circled round over the placid waters of the lake before our final run to target and I shall never forget the sight, all the Dakotas circling round, the dozens of Alouette choppers stacked up waiting to go and further out the fast-moving jet Vampires and Hunters holding off like eagles before their ground-attack run-ins.

Meanwhile, out over the enemy camp, a lone civilian DC-8 piloted by Jack Malloch flew low over the muster parade taking place and thousands of ZANLA dived for cover thinking they were under attack. The DC-8 passed and minutes later, when nothing further happened, all the guerrillas emerged from their foxholes and formed up to continue their parade in the belief they were safe after all. The deception plan had worked.

Sixty miles away over Lake Alexander, Group Captain Walsh and Major Robinson in their command chopper gave the order to attack. The Dak pilots streamed out for the run-in.

Inside our Dak, everyone appeared to be asleep. All round me were men festooned with para harnesses, weapons and ammunition, leaning against each other, their heads lolling. These Paras were apparently so cool they could sleep as we roared through the sky on our way to the drop zone. However, adrenalin was racing inside them all. Their eyes were closed but no one could actually sleep. Somehow they all sensed the despatchers moving decisively to the door, and when they heard their orders in their headphones every man snapped fully alert.

'Prepare for action!' yelled our despatchers over the noise of the plane. We all stood up, and automatically started our parachute drills, mentally running through the sing-song mnemonic, 'Top hook and pin! Bottom hook and pin! Static line cleared to left-hand side! Stowage of the static line and centre pack tie!'

'Tell off for equipment check!' yelled the despatchers. We shouted our response, one after the other, and shuffled towards the open door, a long line of helmeted grim-faced men strapped with gear and weapons. I was near enough to the door to see the tops of the yellow-green trees flash beneath us, the big baobabs and scattered African huts only 400 feet below. Operational jump height. We were close now. A Vampire jet roared past rocketing a cluster of farm buildings on the target area and I could see an Alouette K-car swinging round with its .30 cannon blazing at the ground. I checked my watch. It was thirteen minutes to eight, exactly as Major Robinson had ordered.

'Red on!'

I felt wild, aching to get out, to get started.

'Green on, GO!' I shuffled and stamped towards the open door and leaped into the rushing air.

My 'chute had hardly opened before I was nearing the ground and I plunged straight into a tree, my parachute hopelessly tangled in the branches. All around there was the racket of the K-car choppers firing, the explosion of the jets' rockets but, more personally, I could hear bullets cracking past my head. I looked round desperately for the bastard firing at me. I couldn't see him and there was no time to climb out of my harness completely so I yanked the capewell attachment clips at my shoulders to release myself from the 'chute, fell out of the tree onto the side of an anthill, still in the harness, and struggled to release my RPK from under the straps. I fired off a couple of shots at where I thought the guerrilla was hiding but then Big Steve Kluzniak shouted he could see the man behind a tree. Steve had landed more easily and was out of his harness. He fired at the terrorist, despite the fact that the butt of his RPK had broken on landing, while I scrambled out of my harness completely.

Staying in cover behind my anthill, I watched Steve to see where he was aiming and located the man's fire position not far away. I opened up on him too. Suddenly, I heard quite distinctly the tell-tale click of the hammer on an empty chamber which told me he had run out of bullets. To my amazement the bastard tried to surrender, having seconds before been happily trying to kill me as I hung from my 'chute. What a fucking neck! I shot him, and Steve and I moved to join the others.

Bob McKenzie formed us into a stop line, hiding spread out in the dry grass and scrubby trees, waiting for ZANLA troops running away from the K-cars which were wheeling and circling overhead. From time to time, terrorists in ones and twos would break cover, trying to get through our line, and we shot them as they came.

At midday, we began to move forward, careful to keep our line straight so we would not shoot each other by mistake and we began to flush them out, one group after the other. Really, it was a slaughter. We took a lot of fire but it was mostly inaccurate. They had been poorly trained by the North Koreans and Chinese who had fired them up with political slogans, taught them lots of dialectical non-sense about the masses, but very little about individual fire and movement and battle skills. They simply had no chance against trained, disciplined troops. A lot tried to change out of their uniforms into civvies or just run away naked, but we looked for the tell-tale piles of coloured clothes and found them all the same, hiding in bushes, under tree trunks and in holes in the banks of a dried river bed we swept through. Some fought, some pretended to be dead, and some who I thought were feigning death were actually dead, the victims of the tiny steel flechettes from the anti-personnel bombs dropped by the jets that morning. You couldn't always see the tiny rips caused by the flechettes in their rumpled uniforms but I always fired a couple of rounds at the chest, just to make sure.

By three o'clock, we halted the line on the edge of the centre of the camp, where we could see the communist secretariat and admin huts; large wooden huts with corrugated steel roofs, African grass huts and white army bell tents scattered among the trees. Our tracer set fire to some of the grass thatched roofs and fires blazed all round us creating a scene of utter mayhem, with the smell of burning, the constant noise of gunfire and the explosions of rockets and bombs further away. One hut turned out to be an ammunition store and suddenly exploded, sending a fireworks' display of RPG rockets zooming off in all directions across the camp.

We reached our objective, the communist party secretariat, and found mountains of documents and ledgers stacked inside big trunks, called trummels in Rhodesia. It was a gold mine of information for the Special Branch. I had never realised what detail the communists keep about every single party member. They even had information on who was sleeping with whom.

So far, we had only had two wounded in 'A' Squadron, but I heard on the radio that Frans Nel, a young fair-haired Rhodesian in 'B' Squadron, had been shot dead by a woman terrorist. Let no one tell you the women were innocent bystanders. They trained and fought just like the men, sometimes better.

A group of us in 'A' Squadron found a little white Peugeot truck near the secretariat which had been stolen from North Side Service Station in Salisbury and had a service sticker inside showing it had been in Salisbury only three weeks before. With Steve Kluzniak, Rob Rodell, Chunky Chesterman, Dick Borman, and I, Bob McKenzie used it to drive round the camp picking up the enemy's 14.5mm anti-aircraft guns and other equipment we wanted to take back to Rhodesia. He said, 'We felt like Kelly's Heroes all tooled up and perched on the bonnet and roof of this pickup.'

Shooting and explosions went on all day all round us as other SAS and the RLI worked through other target areas further away. I spent the rest of the day blowing up large enemy trucks and other vehicles, doing the maximum amount of damage we could. I can honestly say it was a lot of fun.

The attack had been a complete surprise and success so far. Our commanders assessed that the enemy were disorganised and incapable of counter-attack so they decided to leave us on the ground overnight. When darkness fell, we hid among the trees in an ambush position of all-round defence and waited lying on the dusty baked earth under the trees, keeping all our gear on, I took it in turns with Steve Kluzniak, who was near by, to sleep or doze, our weapons cradled ready to use. The shooting died away at dusk and in the silence ZANLA must have thought we had pulled out, because they began to emerge in small groups out of the darkness, calling out, 'Comrade! Comrade?' We imitated them, calling back, 'Comrade! Yes!' When they came on towards us, we shot them. All through the night there were bursts of fire from all round.

All this may sound very hard-nosed, but these were people who were being trained to go back to Rhodesia and kill. They weren't innocent civilians, like the people who they killed in buses and schools, like the eight men and women and four children of the Elim Pentecostal Church Mission they killed at Vumba in the Eastern Highlands. These victims were raped and bayoneted to death by twenty of Robert Mugabe's ZANLA. The ZANLA guerrillas were not, in the words of ZANLA commander Josiah Tongogara to US Ambassador Andrew Young, 'Moving round villages conducting political seminars and singing songs.'

They killed their own as well. The following morning we went back to the farm building which had been attacked by the Vampire as we parachuted in and found four prisoners who had been murdered by ZANLA just as our para drop started. Their hands were tied behind their backs and they had been shot in the head.

An odd thing happened near here, where we found a store of rations with Portuguese markings. One of our guys called Andy Johnson found a can of milk, drank it and immediately went into shock. He collapsed on the ground kicking and spluttering and shouting in panic. He was casevaced at once in an Alouette and recovered, and I later discovered that our own very dear and lovely Special Branch had somehow got access to these rations during Portugal's withdrawal from Africa and poisoned them. What swine! you may say, but the fact is that the gloves are off in guerrilla warfare and enemy soldiers are fair game. On both sides. For example, in Malaya during the Emergency, the British Special Branch poisoned enemy food caches or put ground glass in rice rather than lift or destroy the food. A wounded or sick enemy is better than a dead one: he is an embarrassment for them to look after and is not likely to give the others much confidence. A dead guerrilla is a martyr who can be buried with stirring songs and forgotten. Come to think of it, that's rather the same for soldiers anywhere.

The Chimoio plan had been well thought through. We spent some time that morning burying homing beacons in the ground so that, after we had gone when the camp was reoccupied and bulging with guerrillas again, our bombers could home in and bomb them to bits.

We made a second sweep of the camp, working through the area where we had found so many of their trucks and Land Rovers. The sheer size of Chimoio, an area of twenty-eight square kilometres, meant there were masses of places to hide. We had landed in the middle, scattering the guerrillas in panic, and we wanted to find as many as we could before we had to leave. Forty were hiding in a ravine and a brief firefight flared up till their resistance collapsed under the discipline of our fire orders, good individual fire-and-movement and accurate shooting. They broke and ran and we killed them all. As you may imagine, the overall 'body count' was huge. This antiseptic American phrase is the newest label for an ages-old military obsession to quantify the outcome of a battle. At Chimoio the count was enormous, well into the hundreds, and duly trumpeted by soldiers and press alike. I accounted for thirteen, excluding those 'shared' when one enemy is hit by several people at once. As may be imagined, the impact of this attack on ZANLA was immense.

Before we left later that afternoon, we set fire to everything. I lit a gas cooker and ran along the thatch roofs of the party huts, lighting the dried straw which caught immediately. In minutes, the fires spread rapidly through the trees and great clouds of black smoke billowed into the sky. To add to the chaos, bullets they had hidden in the thatch cooked off in the heat, exploding everywhere.

Finally, that afternoon of the second day, Alouettes lifted us out back to Rhodesia, to Lake Alexander and then to Grand Reef airbase at Umtali. We flew back to Salisbury feeling dirty, hot and tired but pretty pleased with ourselves and we were all looking forward to a good session in the bar to tell our war stories. Instead, as soon as we landed, we were put straight back in isolation on the airfield again. ComOps were so delighted with Chimoio, they wanted us to attack another big ZANLA training camp without delay.

This was Tembue. It was estimated there were 6,000 guerrillas there, so it was not as large as Chimoio, but it was more than twice as far away, right the other side of the Cabora Bassa dam lake, northeast of Salisbury, 200 kilometres inside Mozambique near the Zambian border. If things went wrong there, there was no easy way out. However, ComOps reckoned that we could use the same trick twice in quick succession, on the basis that the enemy were still in utter disarray at Chimoio and would have no time to learn the lessons, let alone pass them along to Tembue. That, at any rate, was staff theory.

We caught up with a bit of sleep on Friday, but only after we had reorganised and prepared our equipment, and received another set of excellent orders from Major Robinson. The plan was exactly the same, but the Forward Air Fields (FAFs) were even more important because of the greater distance from the Mozambique border to Tembue. ComOps set up two Admin Points inside Rhodesia, at Mount Darwin and near the northern border at Chizweti, one big one inside Mozambique called the Train because it was so busy feeding helicopters in and out, and one very close to Tembue, some 200 kilometres inside enemy territory.

Next morning, early on Saturday 26 November, we jumped in on Tembue at precisely the same time as at Chimoio. ZANLA never knew what had hit them. All day, we fought through the bush in our sweep line, with endless small contacts and firefights, walking slowly and methodically through the bushes and low trees as we flushed them out. At a river bank, Steve Kluzniak and I were working together, one covering the other, when we suddenly came under fire from thick bush, near a series of trenches protecting a sloping approach to the Tembue river. We sprayed the bushes but we couldn't see our man and both ended up diving for cover into the same trench, a long narrow slit in the hard red earth.

'You seen him?' I asked furiously as we sat at the bottom of our trench.

Steve shook his head. But our man knew where we were. We watched his bullets smacking into the red earth at the top of our trench.

After a few minutes, sitting helpless, afraid to move, I lost my temper. I dived out of the trench and zigzagged fast to another one. Bullets cracked past. As I ran, I tried to see where the bastard was hiding, looking for smoke or flash from his muzzle, or giveaway movement in the bushes. Nothing. I dived for cover into another trench and still he kept sniping at us. I shouted at Kluzniak. He had seen nothing.

I tried again, determined to find the bastard. I rolled out of my trench and doubled forward again, leaving Kluzniak behind to cover me in the dense smoke billowing from burning huts not far away. No sign. Still the ZANLA soldier stayed hidden, and, as our sweep line moved slowly on, we had to leave him. His accuracy was nothing to shout about, but he was one man who certainly knew his field craft.

We moved from action to action, once flushing out nearly fifty ZANLA from a ravine in a tremendous rattle of automatic firing. On all sides, unseen actions took place, punctuated by the bigger .20 cannon of the K-cars which we could call in with our ground-to-air A76 radios. We heard on the radios that the others in the SAS and the RLI were having as much success as us. The ZANLA command were totally disorientated and their fighters desperate to run away or hide. That night, we lay up in ambush just as we had at Chimoio, and several of the guys near me fired at terrorists trying to come through us in the night. We got little sleep but though we were 200 kilometres inside Mozambique, we felt very confident. We had taken no casualties and inflicted terrible losses on the enemy. I never realised how many till the tally was made the following day, a Sunday. They stopped counting at 1,200 dead but the total at Chimoio and Tembue was well over 2,000. In two days ZANLA had taken a terrible beating.

As we pulled out ready for the choppers to fly us back to Rhodesia, I heard that another troop had rescued a black Selous Scout who had been held captive in a deep pit. The Selous Scouts were excellent troops, a combination of white and black Rhodesians, who moved in groups of ten, to ape the communist section strength, or just in twos, so they could move swiftly and unnoticed. They had courageously recce'd both the Chimoio and Tembue camps, to confirm Special Branch information, and supplied us with the detail we needed to make the attack. This man, a black NCO, was lucky we turned up. The black guerrillas always treated black Rhodesian soldiers far worse than they treated whites, torturing them mercilessly before they were allowed to die.

These were remarkable operations. I wonder how many countries anywhere in the world would have had the political guts to mount these attacks, let alone be able to muster the necessary military skills. Political and military commitment was required from the very top, from Ian Smith and General Walls, to the very bottom, from the likes of me and Steve Kluzniak. In the middle, officers like Robinson and Walsh faced immense staff coordination and logistic problems, posed by distance, refuelling of the short-range Alouettes, ammunition resupply, and the bringing out of captured enemy documents and equipment. All this meant working out new solutions never before tried and putting them into effect for the first time on high-risk operations which, had they gone wrong, would have caused unthinkable losses to men and aircraft and dealt a terrible blow to Rhodesian morale. Impressive, no matter what you thought about the Rhodesian regime. They committed a mere 185 troops against fantastic odds.

Jane was well aware of the dangers but she never tried to stop my work in the SAS. As a nurse, she was constantly faced with the realities of the war when the wounded were brought in to the hospital. She never said anything, but she must have been very worried before the Chimoio and Tembue raids. Later, she told me the hospital had been cleared for action to receive the expected high casualties. Whole wards had been emptied waiting for us to fill the beds. None of the hospital staff knew what the operation was to be, but it was going to be big, and Jane knew very well that I would be on it.

The pressure did not let up but it varied. On one cross-border operation in trucks, we had to come back through the Rhodesian Cordon Sanitaire minefield, the CORSAN. This was an extraordinary feat of military engineering, a barrier of mines 830 miles long to prevent guerrilla infiltration across the Mozambique border. This was the second biggest minefield in the world after the US minefields across the DMZ between North and South Vietnam and I believe it was a total waste of time and money. It ignored the fundamental military principle that an obstacle is not an obstacle unless covered by fire; i.e. unless observed by soldiers, which the CORSAN wasn't. The enemy just ignored it or removed it. Quite often, rains washed away the fragile African soil and revealed the mines standing out of the ground.

On this occasion, we waited on the Mozambique side and watched as Rhodesian Army Engineers cleared a breach for our trucks. They had just finished when I saw a major walk forward. His foot hardly brushed the ground at the side of the breach but the earth erupted and his leg disappeared in a cloud of red spray. He was casevaced to Jane's hospital in Salisbury where the poor man's daughter was a nurse. Everyone was involved in the war in Rhodesia and maybe this serious atmosphere of commitment intensified our affair.

The whole country was embattled. Everyone in the country knew someone in the services which fielded year by year an average of 25,000, equivalent to more or less a tenth of the white population, and everyone suffered from United Nations sanctions. There was no chocolate or real Scotch whisky, for example, though the Rhodesians proudly made a whisky substitute which was truly revolting. The attitude among the whites was that Rhodesia had an answer for everything the international community could do to her. However, all this pressure was too much for some people who quit, on what was called 'the chicken run' or 'taking the gap', rather than hang on to witness inevitable defeat. They took what little they could, but no financial stocks or funds were allowed to be transferred out of the country so their apartments stayed empty and unsold. With the market at rock bottom, Jane and I moved to an excellent place in Beveridge Court in Avondale district.

There was no end of work for the SAS. The commitment to killing the enemy, which we did with practised efficiency on more or less every patrol, was intense and life in the Rhodesian SAS was rather humourless, in contrast to my experience in the British Army. Maybe this was due to the fact that Rhodesia was certainly under great pressure, maybe it was a difference in national characteristics, or maybe it was because the Rhodesians in the Rhodesian SAS were under pressure from foreigners like me. There were men from Britain, America, France, South Africa, Canada, Zambia, Spain, Germany, New Zealand, Denmark and elsewhere. Some called us the Rhodesian Foreign Legion. In 'A' Squadron, twenty-eight of the thirty-three were foreigners, excluding numbers of the Rhodesian Territorial SAS who unquestioningly served their six months a year call-up, excluding other times when they were called on for various big operations. The Rhodesians called us foreigners 'Nanny knockers' (those who slept with black nannies in white households because they could not break into the clique of local white women) and argued we were just visiting for the 'fun', whereas they lived there and were fighting for their livelihoods and future. This may have been the crux of it, for the future was bleak and, in retrospect, defeat inevitable, but whatever the reasons, the Rhodesians in the SAS certainly retained a distinct consciousness of themselves. From the outside, anyway, they grouped together in a subtle, but none the less real, self-protective clique.

Of course, Rhodesian officers and senior NCOs knew each other very well, often having been to the same schools, such as Plumtree, Peterhouse and Churchill, of which they were very proud. Indeed, I remember one officer who always wore his Plumtree School socks in uniform, and, when he was unfortunately blown to pieces on a mine, the joke among us foreign swine was that the only way they had identified him was by finding one of his legs stuck in the branches of a tree still encased in his Plumtree School colours.

The 'Russian Front' as we called the southeast, was hard work. The terrain was difficult, flat and sandy so it was nearly impossible to cover our tracks, the local Africans were very antagonistic everywhere and Mozambique's FRELIMO troops actively searched for us in this area more than any other. Knowing we were usually about twenty strong, they gave themselves the advantages of working in groups of fifty or more and used 82mm mortars and HMGs. Our target was often the single road and rail link from Maputo to the coast and, as soon as the locals spotted a Dakota overhead, they reported it and FRELIMO would sweep the area. They moved along beside the railway line, checking the sand for our spoor behind the clumps of sandalwood typical of the area which provided the only cover to hide in. Then they would attack with everything they had, confident the Rhodesians did not normally use air cover inside Mozambique.

So, the Rhodesians adapted their tactics. Eighteen of us in 'A' Squadron jumped into Mozambique and deliberately left tracks which we hoped would be seen by the locals to draw the FRELIMO troops onto us. The idea was to use airstrikes to give them a bloody nose which might dissuade them from tangling with us in the future. We were moderately successful. We dug in in slit trenches, walked to a nearby road and fired some rounds to attract attention. While waiting for a reaction, we placed a parachute in a tree but to our dismay had no response. I never saw any enemy, but Captain Colin Willis in 'B' Squadron called in an airstrike on a column of seventeen trucks and destroyed them.

On another occasion, near a small town called Maxalia, we walked in covertly, to avoid the locals spotting a para entry. On all external ops we wore plain green uniforms, and no dog tags, so that if any members were killed they could be written off by the authorities. All callsign members were assigned book numbers so they could be identified over the radio if killed or wounded, and all had their blood group written on the chest of their plain green shirts in felt-tip pen. Callsign members were also 'blacked-up' so they could be mistaken for FRELIMO at close quarters, and camouflage cream – sometimes mixed with mosquito repellant – was constantly reapplied at each halt, which for us was normally ten minutes in every hour. On this occasion we were even 'disguised' in ZANLA uniforms, but we took casualties. As we moved through the bush, we surprised a group of ZANLA who reacted fiercely, firing RPG7 rockets through the scrub trees and opening up with heavy small-arms fire. The man next to me, called Tony Nesbitt, went down under a fearsome burst of AK, shot in the leg. The enemy drove off and I gave him first aid. To reassure him I joked about his wound. 'It's a really beautiful neat hole, Tony. No exit wound, but the entry hole is really lovely!' He groaned with laughter till the pain got to him.

On the same op, on 6 December 1977, Dick Borman was not so lucky. If people are honest, they would admit Dick was not much liked, maybe because he was always harping on about his religion or maybe because he had no sense of humour. One day, Steve Kluzniak, Frank Tunney and I were sitting in cover in the scrub having a brew when we heard shooting some way off. Some of our lads had gone that way and, between sips of tea, I remarked with deliberate black humour, 'With a bit of luck Dick Borman's got it.' Everyone laughed, but when they brought a body back, it was Borman. What's worse, the poor man died in a clash between two of our SAS patrols, and, to cap it all, there were no choppers available to bring out his body. We had to wedge him in the branches of a tree where he stayed for two days to prevent animals, rats and so on, eating him.

I must admit, the incident made us wonder if the choppers would have come for us if there had been a wounded man waiting for casevac. The modern soldier assumes he can depend on 'hot extraction' with choppers, but the fact is that there are sometimes shortages and other priorities. I think here they rightly decided a Selous Scouts live operation was more important than a dead SAS soldier.

There were numerous camp attacks after Chimoio and Tembue but never quite so big. Muroro, a ZANLA camp, was one which sticks in my memory for what happened to me there. We jumped at a quarter to eight in the morning as usual, and found that the camp was deserted. The Selous Scouts had reported 1,800 there but we swept through the scrub and the body count tallied only twenty-five. This was an unremarkable score for the Rhodesian SAS, which was called 'a bad day's jousting', but Muroro was a turning point for me. As we stalked through the trees and long dry grass, sweeping the area, a black guerrilla suddenly leaped up right in front of me, no more than a couple of paces away, like a rabbit flushed from the long grass. Stupidly, he turned to run. Instinctively, I lifted my FN to my shoulder and straightaway shot him in the back of the head. To my horror, his skull literally exploded. His brains blew all over my face and chest webbing. His body collapsed on the hard ground. What shook me was the unthinking speed with which I had reacted to shoot another person, so efficiently and without compunction. The lesson stayed with me all day. There was no time to clean up. I had to stay in our sweep line carrying that man's brains all day, stuck to my webbing, stinking and fly-blown.

Maybe it was justice, but I nearly got left behind at Muroro, deep inside Mozambique. Four of us were tidying up the parachutes we had hidden on jumping in. This was a nerve-wracking job, as the terrorists would sometimes try to find the cache to ambush us when we came back, or booby-trap the parachutes. We were absorbed checking the sandy ground for signs that the enemy had been around and the last Alouette took off without us. I looked up, somehow warned that something was wrong, and ran in front of it waving my arms to flag it down. Thankfully the pilot saw me. All the way back to Salisbury, I could not shake off the memory of killing that man at Muroro. The images of his exploding head would not go away. They never have. I was thirty-five years old and his death marked the moment in my life when I began to see myself as others saw me.

My old ladies in Salisbury would have certainly declared this a sign of weakness. They were a group of charming old women who 'adopted' the foreign soldiers serving in Rhodesia. They took this duty very seriously, in loco parentis as it were, and they were more committed to the fight than the soldiers. They always showed a keen interest in our successes and regularly sent me and the other foreigners nice letters, knitted socks or balaclavas which the Rhodesian Army faithfully brought out to us on helicopter resupplies while we were in the bush on operations. During our leave, these old ladies insisted we visit them, and, because they were all part of the white war effort, the Army Staff made precise appointments for us.

Suitably scrubbed and wearing a clean shirt, tie and slacks, I often went to tea in their apartments in a smart district of Salisbury. God knows what they thought of me, a short, stocky Glaswegian with staring blue eyes, a bent nose and hair cropped to my scalp, but for an hour or more, I would perch on a chintz armchair, delicately sip tea from a cup, and face a circle of white-haired Rhodesian ladies who pressed me for stories of the fighting. While they fed me with an endless supply of dainty cakes and toasted comestibles, they genteelly plugged me for the most gruesome details. The war was our only topic of conversation. For all their apparent frailty and charm, they delighted in hearing about raids like Chimoio and Tembue. When I said goodbye at the door and thanked them for their kindness, one old lady would always whisper, 'Remember now, Peter. You'll get one for me, won't you?'

The Kavalamanja camp attack began in the bar. At least, it was late Friday afternoon when the SAS were put on stand-by and not many were left in camp. Captain Bob McKenzie ordered me to round up the men, so I hopped in a Land Rover and toured the old haunts of Salisbury, dragging them out of places like the Coq d'Or, the Golden Dragon, the Sahara Bar and the Monomatapa Hotel where they were drinking beer and talking shop. They came willingly, as camp attacks were popular. There is no more thrilling way of going into a fight than by parachute. We were all psyched up with the jump before we even touched the ground, we were confident of winning the firefight and there was always the chance of a bit of loot. Russian weapons were popular souvenirs, like the Tokarev automatic pistol or the new AKM assault rifle.

Kavalamanja was one of Joshua Nkomo's ZIPRA camps, just inside Zambia and not far from the Mozambique border, where the Mkariva River joined the Zambezi River. The Zambezi was enormous at this point, flowing in a great slow bend eight hundred yards wide between a mountain on the Rhodesian side and low, marshy ground by Kavalamanja on the Zambian side. Two Selous Scouts, Captain Chris Schollenberg (one of only two holders of Rhodesia's highest bravery award, the Grand Cross of Valour) and Sergeant Chibanda (later awarded the Silver Cross of Rhodesia) had watched the ZIPRA camp from high ground inside Zambia, cut off from help by the river. They lay hidden on high ground for days to produce a report of enemy activity and estimated there were some 175 terrorists armed with AKs, anti-aircraft 14.5mms, 12.7mm HMGs and they identified numerous items of East German equipment. Heavy summer rains delayed the operation, but they stayed in their hide with a box-office view to watch us jump in.

On Sunday 6 March, our usual 08.00 hours P-Hour was put back due to bad weather and our Para-Dakota skimmed 100 feet over Nyamvuru Mountain at ten o'clock on the run-in. We jumped with a company of the Rhodesian African Rifles (RAR). The RAR began their sweep through the camp while we formed stop groups on the northeast side. Our task was to contain the terrorists and hold off the regular Zambian Army if it turned up on the dirt track from Feira (now Luangua), not far away. It didn't. In fact, Rhodesian radio intercepts picked up frantic calls from the Zambian Army at Feira to the capital Lusaka asking for reinforcements in case Feira itself was next on our list!

In the camp, the weather and dense jessie bush slowed progress badly and most of the enemy escaped under cover of darkness that night across unguarded flooded ground on the banks of the Zambezi. The final score was forty dead ZIPRA. I had little fighting to do but we found a large quantity of Russian CE compact plastic explosives and I had a great time setting the demolitions to blow a large cache of Russian weapons we could not bring back. The explosion was deafening and blew the leaves off the trees for hundreds of yards round.

ZIPRA were conventionally trained by the Russians and better troops than ZANLA who were nothing more than terrorists in civvy clothes. We noticed the difference when we attacked 'DK-1', a ZIPRA camp near Lake Kariba.

We drove in Unimogs from Salisbury to Binga for briefings and final rehearsals, and at last light Alouette choppers flew us low level to a drop-off point sixteen kilometres from the camp. Our march in was certainly covert. The weather was foul, it poured with rain all night and we could hardly see the man in front, so no one else could possibly have seen us. We carried rucksacks with spare ammo, a day's food, sleeping bags and ponchos (before the era of Goretex!). The packs weren't heavy, but we were sodden, muddy and tired when we reached the forming up point for the camp attack just before first light. As the soaking trees emerged from darkness in the miserable grey dawn, we crawled forward through the mud in the cover of bushes and long grass to the start line.

As soon as we stood up to begin the attack, they opened fire and a furious battle started, ripping leaves from the trees all round. We put down a heavy weight of fire and moved forward step by step, bound by bound, in controlled fire and movement through the bushes and long wet grass. We pushed them back onto a slight rise, but they were as fired up as we were, shouting, 'White bastards! Come on, white bastards!'

Almost the whole squadron cornered a group of ten in some bushes, where we taught them the important difference between 'cover from view' and 'cover from fire' by blasting the patch of bushes and killing the lot. Driven by us and the .30 cannon from an Alouette K-car above, the rest withdrew towards a river bed where they ran up against one of our stop groups. Boxed in, they fell back from the stop group towards us again and we gradually crushed them, once again moving our patrols together in 'bounds', firing from the kneeling position to see over the low scrub and grass, and moving short distances in a low crouching dash to fire again. The fighting pressed them into the river bank where we finished them off with A8 grenades. These were South African grenades, crude but effective: a wodge of PE inside a column of metal washers. The final score was seventy-eight dead ZIPRA and two wounded SAS, but they fought hard. ZIPRA were well armed with brand-new Kalashnikovs and trained as conventional soldiers by their Russian advisors, so they stayed and fought. ZANLA were terrorists who mostly seemed to work on the principle of, 'If you kill and run away, you live to kill another day.'

The Rhodesians were keen on mines. The CORSAN must have absorbed a lot of staff work, time and money, and the Rhodesian SAS used mines extensively too, for similiar reasons, to dissuade the guerrillas from using infiltration routes.

The Rhodesian SAS did a lot of mine operations on the north side of Lake Kariba, in Zambia. One dark night, a Kiwi captain who had been in 3 Para, Chunky Chesterman, Rob Rodell and I were taken over the lake in a civilian motor boat to a point some two hundred metres off the Zambian shoreline. We lowered two Klepper canoes over the side and carefully stowed our heavy kit. Two more men were going to paddle us in and bring the canoes back to the mother craft, so two of us lay over each canoe and they paddled us to the dark shoreline. We waded off with our gear and the canoes slipped away into the darkness. Ashore, we hoisted our rucksacks, which were heavy with one 12-lb anti-tank mine each, and set off into the thick scrub. Our target was a road along the lake which was used all the time by the Zambian army supplying the ZIPRA camps to the southwest. This MSR (Main Supply Route) was about thirty kilometres from the lake but the high savannah bush was dense, like dry jungle, and allowed us to walk during the day without fear of being found. We stopped at about eleven o'clock when the sun was too hot and lay up till three before going on again. We reached the road just before dusk of the second night, watched it carefully for a couple of hours and then moved in to lay our mines.

The road was not surfaced and our plan was to lay one mine every kilometre or so. The South African anti-tank mines we carried were nicknamed 'Chocolate Cakes' because they were round and painted a chocolate colour. They contained a charge of about 13 lbs of Amatol and detonated under a pressure of only 11.8 kgs or 26 lbs. We also carried a special mining kit which consisted of digging tools, poncho, para-cord, a brush, and carpet over-boots to avoid leaving the spoor of the soles of our combat boots. Having selected where on the road the mine was to go, I laid out the poncho on the ground beside it, scraped back all the topsoil and put it carefully on one side of the poncho. At that time a lot of people made the mistake of digging the six or eight-inch hole straight down, but most of us always dug holes with sloping sides, because if it had straight sides sometimes the vehicle would catch just the corner of the mine (which was approx ten inches in diameter), press it out and not set it off, or the wheel would jump across the straight sides and not touch the mine at all. Champfered sides caught the wheel no matter what.

While a couple of the others kept watch up and down the road, I put the mine at the bottom of the hole. The most dangerous part of the process was arming the mine. The Rhodesian SAS lost eleven men killed laying mines, so I always took care. Before back-filling with soil, I very gently tied a length of para-cord to the mouth of the pin holding the MV-5 pressure-release switch. This fitted into the 75 MD-2 detonating cartridge which stuck out of the side of the mine. Then, after back-filling, I warned the others and retired to safety at the side of the road. Wrapping the string round my fingers, I gently pulled out the pin with my para-cord. Nothing happened. After a short wait in case of a delayed fuse, I went back to tidy up the topsoil and very gently brushed it over to conceal the handmarks in the dust.

Once all our mines had been laid, we marched back through the savannah to the lake where we took a bearing on Binga from the water's edge. The lights of Binga could always be seen from the Zambian side and once we had radioed the bearing to base, they knew where to send the boat to pick us up under cover of darkness. However, we took care to retire into the savannah till it was time for our rendezvous with the Kleppers, just in case the Zambians patrolled the lake edge and found us. A friend of mine was killed like that, because he was too ill with malaria to walk back inland and wait in safe cover.

I was never convinced by the use of mines in Zambia. After that patrol across the lake, I recall sitting at Binga and listening to the controlled explosions of the Zambian regular army engineers blowing the mines we had just laid. The noise carried quite clearly across the surface of the lake. It is rumoured that on one occasion a brave and foolhardy black Zambian engineer spent twelve hours defusing a mine fitted with anti-lift, anti-prod and anti-light devices.

By contrast, the mines we laid on the important enemy roads in Mozambique in the southeastern area, which we called the Russian Front, seemed worthwhile. The road and rail system there was used extensively by ZANLA moving into Rhodesia.

However, compared to our employment attacking enemy camps, I don't think the success of mines justified the loss of eleven men from the Rhodesian SAS, out of a total of forty-two who gave their lives for Rhodesia.

7

The Death of a Country

Life is really simple, but men insist on making it complicated.

CONFUCIUS

I was promoted to full corporal in the Rhodesian SAS in two con-
secutive promotion conferences, but at the start of 1979, I realised I
would go no higher. I do not think I fitted in. The bald fact is that I
was thirty-seven years old, fifteen years older than men of the same
rank, and where the younger guys held their senior ranks in awe, as
men older than them and more experienced, I did not. Of course, I
respected the senior ranks as fine professional soldiers, men like
Sergeant Major Lutz, Captain Bob McKenzie, Major Brian Robinson
and Major Graham Wilson. They did a good job, but they were not
gods. However, there is a pecking order in the relationships between
ranks and personalities in any army unit, especially one as tight-knit
and specialised as the SAS, and I attracted criticism because I was
not a standard fit in the mould.

Rumour travels fast and my reputation had followed me from
England, by damaging gossip rather than by an official report, and
coloured any name I might have had for good operational soldiering.
I was actively trying to shake off my earlier image and I only had one
fight in the Rhodesian SAS, with a Sergeant Andy Langley during
my recruit training. Langley was a big ex-US Marine with Vietnam
experience from 'B' Squadron who was not much liked. He enjoyed
terrorising the recruits and he made it clear to other instructors that
he was going to 'fix' me and see I went to jail. I suppose he singled
me out as the oldest recruit. He walked in to our billet one evening
while we were watching *Waterloo* on video, switched it off and shouted,
'I'm Langley, I don't like you. I've got the highest pain tolerance in
the goddamn world and I can't feel your pain!' His problem was that

I was by then a very keen and fit recruit and I gave him very little to criticise. Finally, he ordered me to call out the time as we marched along on the parade ground, and I shouted, 'Left right, left right, LEFT!' always finishing with a 'left!' in the British Army style.

He objected, shouting, 'You're fucking wrong, boy!' Which I did not much like. 'You have to say both 'left' *and* 'right' and finish with a 'RIGHT!'

You will probably find this rather a petty distinction, but Langley drew himself to his full height over me, worked himself into fury and screamed with triumph, 'I'm going to put you in jail for this!' Being me, I thought I might as well go to jail for something important, so I punched him and laid him out. So much for his pain tolerance. I think most people were secretly rather pleased at Langley's fate, but Major Robinson rightly gave me twenty-eight days in jail for battering one of his sergeants. I never regretted it for a moment. After all, Langley deserved it.

Or maybe I made myself unpopular for refusing to obey an order to kill a black man. I was on a four-man patrol led by a Rhodesian corporal and we were lying hidden in bushes ready to ambush a track used as an infiltration route by ZANLA terrorists. However, an elderly black civilian wandered down the track dressed in dirty shirt and worn trousers and, by sheer bad luck, he spotted the Claymore anti-personnel mine one of the other guys had put out to hit the enemy and which was poorly concealed. I watched the old man's expression change as he became aware of the small rectangular mine standing on little metal legs in the undergrowth. Horrified, he gazed into the bushes where he suddenly realised there were armed soldiers hiding, looking at him.

'Shoot him!' whispered the corporal beside me.

I refused, and whispered back, 'If you want to kill him, do it yourself!'

He insisted, 'I'm giving you an order!'

I took aim and fired deliberately wide. The black vanished, showing a surprising turn of speed for an old man.

The corporal lost his temper, blaming me for compromising the whole operation, and we had a furious argument out there in the bush. It was true we had to leave the ambush, but the shot, wherever it had been aimed, would have compromised us, let alone having to deal with the dead body, the spoor of dragging him away and the blood on the track. Besides there were a group of children close by who would have heard, and seen, what we had done.

The plain fact was that few prisoners were taken by the Rhodesian

SAS. I am keen to be the first to kill the enemy, especially in the heat of a firefight, but I have never been someone who could kill a civilian in cold blood. I will leave that to men like Callan, Copeland and other mercenaries in Angola. I was unpopular because of this incident, but in fairness I do not think this was so much for refusing the order, which would have compromised the ambush anyway, but for not fitting in with the Rhodesian system. In 1978, the Rhodesian SAS had swelled from being just 'C' Squadron and had become the 1st Rhodesian SAS Regiment. There was therefore a lot of promotion flying about but the political state of Rhodesia at the time and the inescapable fact that the war was getting out of hand made the atmosphere in the SAS (I can't speak for the other Rhodesian infantry regiments) even more embattled than ever.

The number of terrorists operating inside Rhodesia relentlessly continued to rise, from 2,350 in April 1977 when I joined the SAS, to 5,598 by November of that year, to 6,456 by March 1978 and 11,183 by January 1979 (These are the Rhodesian Government's own figures).

I can understand that the Rhodesian officers and senior ranks felt cornered, frustrated by political restraints to their military plans, and unwilling to be specially tolerant of outsiders. As you have read, there were plenty of foreigners in the Rhodesian SAS, and a goodly few are buried in the cemetery in Warren Hills by Lake McIlwaine, but we were never fully accepted. Some did better than others, like Steve Kluzniak, but we were always different, and I suppose my own profile has always been higher than most. I know that one of the regiment's later commanding officers, Major Wilson, was a fine soldier with all three of Rhodesia's highest bravery awards, the Grand Cross of Valour, the Silver Cross of Rhodesia and the Bronze Cross of Rhodesia, but he did not approve of me. I suppose my record in the field was spoiled by the various incidents I have outlined above, because he never worked with me on a patrol and he must have formed his opinion by hearsay.

Anyhow, the plain fact was that I was a 37-year-old corporal and did not fit. I tried a transfer from 'A' Squadron to 'C' Squadron in the newly formed regiment but it made no difference, so when an old friend from the British SAS and 3 Para, Sergeant Major Jock Hutton, told me about his work for the Special Branch training blacks as Auxiliaries, I applied for a transfer. Several of us foreigners applied at the same time, for similar reasons, including Steve Cleary, Ron Cook, big Jim McGuire, Frank Tunney who was an Aussie, and Paddy Gibline. We all marched in to see the Rhodesian Regimental

Commanding Officer at the time, Lieutenant-Colonel Garth Barrett, who lost his temper. 'You bastards aren't transferring,' he shouted, furious we had taken our own initiative to leave the regiment. 'I'm posting you!' With that, he tore up all our transfer applications and threw them in the bin.

What a blow to our pride! This illustrates SAS thinking, because, although we had served as well as any in the field, a 'posting' rather than a 'transfer' meant that we would no longer be entitled to the few perks enjoyed by Special Forces (which included the Special Branch): this was the $33 a month extra pay called 'SAS Gunner Pay' and 'Special Unit Allowance'. So, the CO struck a terrible blow to our pockets as well! Plus, being posted from the SAS made us available for any general duties and at the mercy of the bureaucrats in Army HQ.

We ended up standing to attention in front of a postings officer in Army HQ in King George VI Barracks in Salisbury. He had clearly been briefed by Garth Barrett. He hardly glanced at our records of service before shouting, 'You've arrived at last, eh? Well, you bastards aren't going to Special Branch! If I say you're being posted to Gwelo, you'll go to Gwelo, and if I say you'll be posted to a black battalion that's where you'll go!'

He was getting into his stride when his sergeant major walked in and I was just thinking maybe we could appeal to him as equals in the time-honoured game between NCOs and officers when Paddy Gibline gave a great sigh of despair. He had battered this sergeant major in a fight in Cally's bar not a week before!

That was a dark day. However, we extracted ourselves from the officer and sergeant major in the postings office and in desperation I contacted Jock Hutton. He arranged an interview with a Special Branch officer called Chief Superintendent Mac McGuinness. Mr Mac, as everyone called him, interviewed us and declared, 'I can use people like you!' Without delay, he sorted out the postings office, we were all transferred to his department, and we kept our pay. He was an SB Commander attached to the Selous Scouts, who thought very highly of him. He had the widest connections imaginable, he was never fazed by anything, even in these last chaotic months of Rhodesia's existence and he always appeared in a cheerful mood, singing and joking. This was indeed a change from the Rhodesian SAS. And so was the work we did.

By the beginning of 1979, the war with ZANLA and ZIPRA was at stalemate. The Rhodesians had not surrendered a single town or piece of territory to the communist terrorists, but were terribly stretched in all provinces. At a tactical level, the Rhodesians won virtually every engagement and achieved a consistent kill ratio which never fell below 6:1 and was as high as 2000:1 at Chimoio and Tembue. These huge cross-border successes eventually forced the leaders of Zambia and Mozambique to press Robert Mugabe and Joshua Nkomo to participate in peace talks offered by the British in late 1979. This was a remarkable political result arising from military action, considering the shortage of equipment and manpower always suffered by the Rhodesian Army, but on the world political front, Rhodesia's position was worse than ever. In the words of the Selous Scouts Commanding Officer, Lieutenant Colonel Reid Daly, 'There had been a time when Rhodesia had been held up as an example of fine race relations, but now we were the pariahs. Only black rule, not multi-racial rule would satisfy our enemies, or even our friends.' World opinion pushed Rhodesia relentlessly into the hands of the hard-line communists in ZANLA and ZIPRA. Obstinately, Rhodesians tried to shut out reality but, as Reid Daly said, 'The stink of political defeat, which always pre-empts a military defeat, had begun to seep like blood poisoning into the veins of the Security Forces and into the veins of Rhodesia itself.' My next year in Rhodesia more than proved he was right.

Mr Mac sent me to Bindura.

There was a definite feel of the Wild West about Bindura. It was a small town about fifty miles northeast of Salisbury in the middle of ZANLA's Mashonaland. A population of about 1,200 whites lived there with some five thousand blacks but no one knew exactly how many because no one had bothered to count them. The blacks worked mainly in the Trojan nickel mine and in the large citrus plantations all round which gave off the most wonderful scent of orange blossom along the roads in the spring.

The Special Branch base was in a 'fort' made of corrugated iron sheeting, to prevent people seeing what went on inside. There was one wide main street, sleepy and deserted, which featured the usual necessary collection of shops, banks, and stores, and behind this on either side the Rhodesians lived in spacious houses in some style. In time, Jane followed me to Bindura and we set up house in a large villa conveniently near the SB fort. There were two parts to the hospital, one for whites and one for blacks and, when she qualified, Jane worked in the black section where she was the only white nurse.

There were a collection of bars, most notably the Bindura Country Club which was in the middle of town and the Coach House Hotel at one end, where increasingly frantic parties took place as the white

Rhodesians realised they were losing the country they had made theirs.

Far from losing pay, Mr Mac had me promoted to sergeant and I went with some of the others to prepare for the reception and training of black Auxiliaries. On 30 January 1979, Rhodesian whites loyally followed the advice of Prime Minister Ian Smith and 80 per cent voted in favour of a new constitution which they knew would lead to a black-dominated parliament. Since 1977, Smith had been talking to Bishop Abel Muzorewa, who led the United African National Council (UANC), and the Reverend Ndabaningi Sithole, who controlled the ZANU Patriotic Front. Both these black nationalists had agreed to come back to Rhodesia for elections. Neither had great support and they had no connection with the Chinese-trained ZANLA terrorists of Robert Mugabe and the more conventionally Russian-trained ZIPRA troops of Joshua Nkomo, both of whom refused to participate in the elections.

On 24 April, Bishop Abel Muzorewa won fifty-one of the seventy-two black seats in the hundred-seat Parliament and was elected Rhodesia's first black Prime Minister. Now, having agreed to renounce terrorism, his UANC and Sithole's ZANU Patriotic Front had to come back to Rhodesia and join the fight against ZANLA and ZIPRA. To further complicate matters, there was another Auxiliary group formed from surrendered enemy personnel (SEPs) from ZIPRA. Frankly, it would be an understatement to say none of these groups got on with each other.

We drove trucks to Salisbury airport in the greatest secrecy to meet the first of Muzorewa's guerrillas. One hundred of UANC flew in from Libya where they had been training courtesy of Muammar Gaddafi. You can imagine how they felt flying right into the lion's den. Mr Mac had arranged for the civilian aeroplane to unload them in total seclusion at the top end of the airport and they probably thought they were going to be summarily executed. If that didn't make them sweat, then the heavy overcoats they were wearing against the Libyan winter certainly must have. February is pretty hot in Rhodesia. Their discomfort probably increased by the minute, for the SB men who were detailed to drive the trucks had been drinking bottles of whisky while waiting for the plane, and one drove his truckful of astonished guerrillas straight into the airport gate as we left, flattening it. The final insult to the Rhodesian image was that we had to keep stopping on the dangerous fifty-mile drive through bandit country to Bindura while these drunks relieved themselves up against the wheel. I was to discover that Special Branch employs the strangest people, especially it seems, in the last throes of a military campaign.

The UANC soldiers were put up in an old army barracks in the fort and we started to train them. The object was to use them to fight the ZANLA guerrillas infiltrated among the Shona villagers in our region. This had been tried before, with mixed success, and it was not entirely cynicism which made the Rhodesians nickname these black auxiliaries as 'tame terrs'. They were not always so tame. One group of black ZANU PF nearly 200 strong had been 'trained' and then run riot. Out of control, they had seized their white liaison officers and threatened to kill them if their increasing demands were not met. The liaison officers managed to talk their way out but reported the ZANU PF had dug defensive bunkers all round their camp and were in a murderous mood. The Rhodesians had no patience for that sort of behaviour. An SB liaison officer called Pete Donnelly, who was known to this group of ZANU PF, drove out to their camp and issued them all with smart red baseball hats. They were impressed and put them on. Next day, the Fire Force made a full camp-attack assault, boxed them in with stop groups and swept through the camp while Alouette K-cars floated round above blasting 20mm cannon at anyone wearing a red baseball hat. In all, 178 stroppy ZANU PF died.

Understandably, there was little mutual trust between the Rhodesians and auxiliaries, except where groups had personal supervision, and the Rhodesians often gave them AK bullets with only a couple of grains in the charge, in case they went on the rampage.

For me, all this was quite an eye-opener, to find out what had been going on in this war while I had been head down on serious operations fighting with the Rhodesian SAS, on a continuous round of camp attacks, mine laying, ambushing and other cross-border operations. The rest of Rhodesia seemed to have taken an altogether more bizarre attitude to life.

'I've lost the monkey on the operating table,' said Steve Hartful to me one evening at the bar of the Bindura Country Club where several others were sitting round on the upholstered wicker chairs enjoying bottles of Tshumba beer under the slow turning fans.

'What happened?' I asked.

Steve looked sad. He was an American training to be a doctor in Salisbury and he spent his call-up periods working for Special Branch. The monkey was a tame animal which lurked on the mown lawns round the club and persisted in masturbating on the verandah, ejaculating all over the clean red stoep paint. This gripping sight

fascinated the women and Steve had righteously decided such outrageous behaviour was not in the public interest. The solution was,
he thought, to put his medical training to the test by castrating it.

He shook his head. 'There's a shortage of anaesthetic so I used an
elephant tranquilliser and it never came to!'

God help his patients, wherever he is now.

Quite probably the nature of Rhodesian Special Branch work
reflected the desperate internal and external security situation which
the country faced at the time, and exchange or 'au pair' operations
with the South Africans were an example.

Before describing my part in one of these, I should explain a little
the serious side of Special Branch or you will think it was all about
drunks and animal experiments. In a conventional war, Military
Intelligence collects information about the enemy, sifts it and
produces useful intelligence. In a civilian war, when terrorists are
mixing with the population inside and outside the country, military
intelligence is supplemented by police intelligence, which depends
on sources of information among the civilian population and basically
comes through two branches, the Criminal Investigation Department
(CID) and the Special Branch. However, the police CID is not ideal
from a military point of view because its work is too open. Its object
is to bring criminals to justice. Everyone can see what the CID does:
scene of crime work, arresting, interviewing and giving evidence in
court. In counter-terrorist operations, so much of police effort must
be covert, for all the same reasons Military Intelligence is covert,
which is where Special Branch fits in. Naturally, when terrorists
operate from safe havens over the border in neighbouring countries,
SB interests follow them, what they called 'going external'.

There are good historical examples of successful co-operation
between Special Branch and the army, notably during the Malayan
Emergency (1948–60). There is also an interesting parallel between
the British Special Branch working with the SAS and specialised
surveillance units in urban Northern Ireland, and the Rhodesian
Special Branch working with the SAS and the Selous Scouts
reconnaissance patrols who were brilliant in rural Africa. I imagine
the principles of operation in both cases are very similar.

In its search of the enemy, Rhodesian SB came into contact with
the South African Police (SAP). They had the same enemies. South
Africa was supposed to be taking a low profile in its support of the
Rhodesian regime, after the United States had put the pressure on,
but the communist enemies of Rhodesia were the enemies of South
Africa, or allies of their enemies, so the two countries came to a

secret arrangement. South African security forces would operate secretly in southern Rhodesia and Rhodesians would do various secret jobs for the South Africans.

The Rhodesian Army was desperately stretched, so the South African Defence Force (their army) had a base just over the border inside South Africa and came over to fight in Rhodesia in some strength, as a complete Fire Force unit. Their targets were ZANLA or ZIPRA terrorist groups located by the Selous Scouts, or groups of the (then) illegal communist African National Congress (ANC) hiding from the South Africans just inside southern Rhodesia.

Of course the whole thing had to be politically deniable. Naturally, the world would have been shocked to learn the truth of the collusion between Rhodesia and South Africa. So the SADF Fire Force, its Paras, helicopters and all, was completely equipped and dressed as Rhodesian, and 'sterilised' of anything which might give away their real origin. In return, the Rhodesians carried out secret attacks on targets for the South Africans.

Mr Mac drove from Salisbury to Bindura fort and briefed me on such a task. The South African Police (SAP) had indentified a target in the triangle where the borders of South Africa, Swaziland and Mozambique meet. For years, they had warned Mozambique that if she harboured the ANC, which was carrying out terrorist attacks in South Africa, then South Africa would hit out across the border. Our target was a houseful of important ANC men in Namaacha, just inside Mozambique on the Mozambique-Swazi border and the whole operation had to be utterly deniable. Mr Mac said the SAP wanted us to come to South Africa for a reconnaissance.

I took Ron Cook with me. He had been in 'A' Squadron in the British SAS. We drove 375 miles south, through Salisbury to Beitbridge on the banks of the River Limpopo which marked the Rhodesian-South African border. We left our vehicle in the Rhodesian police customs post where we met the SAP men. They came across routinely to coordinate customs matters. Hidden in the customs compound, we got into a yellow SAP van so no one could see us and were driven straight over the border into South Africa. No stamps, no passports. Secrecy and deniability were paramount.

They drove us 300 miles to Pretoria and put us in the Hotel Continental, all expenses paid. I have to say this made an agreeable change after life in Bindura and the rigours of Rhodesia under sanctions. I don't think Ron or I look like your average tourist and I can't believe the hotel staff were fooled for a minute, but they blandly served us very well as we tucked into steaks and a bottle of wine.

The following day, the SAP drove us another 275 miles to Komatipoort, a small town on the South African-Mozambique border some thirty-seven miles north of Swaziland. Here, in the SAP police station, we met a Colonel Slade and received a full briefing on the ANC target. Namaacha was right on the border triangle between South Africa, Swaziland and Mozambique, and only about sixty miles from the important port of Maputo on the coast, where Chinese ships docked with arms and equipment for the terrorist groups. We did not want to risk compromising our intentions by going too close and made a note of the ground as best we could. All round were hot, sun-baked hills, with dusty red tracks and thick burned-out knee-length grass.

Back in Bindura, Mr Mac heard our report, gave the go-ahead and we made our preparations. I had a team of eight, including myself as commander. We were equipped with non-attributable Soviet weapons and plastic explosive which had been captured during various camp attacks and could not be traced to Rhodesia or South Africa. Our civilian clothes, jeans and veltskoen (Chukka boots) and everything else we carried met the same rigidly deniable specification in case one of us was captured, dead or alive. We would go in completely 'clean'. After a week's training and rehearsals using pictures of the building supplied by the SAP and working on a similar building I found locally, I expressed myself ready. We drove back south in an unmarked civilian Mercedes truck. It was March and the summer rains poured down all the way.

The SAP met us at the border post, covertly ferried us across the border as before and we drove through the rain to Messina, a very hick little town just inside South Africa. We spent the night in the Messina Hotel which was like the Last Chance Saloon. As if to confirm this, 'Saloon' was engraved in curly lettering in the mirror behind the bar. We took the opportunity to stock up with sweets and chocolate. Rhodesia had had no decent sweets since sanctions began.

Very early next morning, we drove to Pretoria and straight on to Komatipoort to meet four SAP men. They surprised me by asking if we could do the attack at once. Our guide (the SAP 'source'), a black called Ramon, had turned up to say that the four key ANC men we wanted to hit were in the house and he was afraid they might move the following day.

We were tired after our fourteen long hours of driving in the truck from Messina but I agreed without hesitation. As the sun went down, we followed them for thirty miles bouncing over rough tracks through the grassy hills to a remote staging point they had already secured in some disused African farm huts about three miles from the border. We unpacked our gear, changed into green FRELIMO combat uniforms and totally blacked our faces and hands so we would look like black men. I must admit that I look rather convincing in this disguise, my nose being ideally flattened from too much fighting! We loaded several magazines for our Russian AKs and Beretta 9mm pistols, checked over the explosives, carried out some quick last-minute rehearsals, of cutting the border fence and our actions on the target, and generally talked over the whole operation. Then, at about nine o'clock at night, with Ramon leading, we started walking to the junction of the three borders.

We walked south in the darkness for three miles brushing through the long dry grass and crossed the border into Swaziland. Then we turned east towards Mozambique. We moved very carefully indeed. There was a guarded Mozambique radar station on one side and a Swazi border post on the other, with a road running parallel to the border inside Mozambique which FRELIMO used to patrol in vehicles. We opted to cut the fence between the two guarded posts but I held the patrol back in the grass, to watch the fence for a while, to feel 'at home' in the place before we moved. Sure enough we saw a Land Rover pass along the road. Then I signalled the move forward. Keeping alert to the chance of more border patrols, we reached the fence and worked fast. First, we tied the tensioner wires together to stop them springing apart, wrapped the cutters in hessian and then cut a hole. After we had all come through we wired it together again so no one would notice.

Inside Mozambique, Ramon walked unerringly through the thick grass towards the lights of Namaacha in darkness a half a mile away. When we reached the slums on the edge, he led us through the back streets to the target. Plainly, Namaacha had once been a pleasant colonial town of attractive flat-roofed two-storey villas surrounded by gardens but, since the Portuguese had left, the place had become a pit. It stank. The gardens were overgrown, we passed empty swimming pools filled with chickens, garbage was strewn everywhere and pools of untreated sewage lay in the dirt roads.

As we picked our way through the narrow streets we used our Passive Image Intensifier Night Observation Devices (NODs) to see ahead through the darkness. We spotted two guard positions, one at either end of the town and we avoided a FRELIMO army barracks we knew was on the outskirts. Otherwise, we encountered no one else. If the occasional black saw us in the shadows he probably took us for FRELIMO troops. Anyway, I doubt any of them wanted to get involved. In a Marxist state, civilians are not encouraged to be inquisitive.

In the centre Ramon stopped at a street corner and pointed at our target. The house was an old Portuguese colonial villa with terracotta tiles on the roof and it had been built back into the sloping garden so the wall of the house at one end was higher than at the other. After a final check, peering up the darkened streets, I motioned the guys forward. As rehearsed, we split into three groups. The four men with the bunker bombs containing $1\frac{1}{2}$ lbs of plastic explosive moved to their allocated windows round the villa, two men covered the door and I waited with Frank Tunney. Checking my watch, I blew a whistle. The bunker bombs sailed through the windows and the guys jumped back out of the way. Four seconds later the bombs erupted, blowing out the walls at each end and the roof partially collapsed on either side of the door. Deafened by the blast, I dashed forward with Frank to lay a huge 44-lb satchel charge. The first charges were to kill the occupants but this second charge was to rub it in, as a warning to the ANC. However, one of the four ANC was still alive. He started shooting at us with a Tokarev pistol when we ran through the door and I never heard him, still deafened by the bombs. Fortunately, Frank shot him. Then we laid our charge, pressed the percussion igniter and ran for it as hard as we could. I had chosen a thirty-second delay to give us time to run clear. We legged it through the streets and just before time was up, Steve Cleary shouted, 'Down! Take cover!'

We dropped as the villa blew up in a shattering roar which shook the ground and should have woken all Africa. For minutes, it seemed, pieces of smashed terracotta tiles and brick splattered down all over the town like rain.

We scrambled to our feet and withdrew, at speed. People started popping out of houses to see what had happened and Ramon called out, 'Don't worry, everything's fine!' He told them we were a FRELIMO patrol looking for the bombers which seemed to do the trick. As we left, we dropped pamphlets all over the place telling the locals that the bomb was the work of the Mozambique National Resistance, RENAMO, and exhorting them to join at once! This was the idea of the SAP and seemed to me to stretch credibility rather.

We were all dying of thirst when we reached the border fence. The night was warm and we were literally soaking with sweat after the excitement of the attack and our dash back to the border. We were all dreaming of the water which I had asked the SAP to provide for us on our return.

No one could have missed that bomb, yet the border guards never reacted, nor did the FRELIMO burst out of their barracks to chase us. At the fence, we hid in the long dry grass watching the same Land Rover cruise along the patrol road as if nothing whatsoever had happened to spoil the calm of a hot African night. After it passed we slipped through our hole in the fence and jogged back over the hills to our start point.

We arrived sweating, dirty, blackened with the stinking camouflage cream and desperately thirsty. And all the SAP could offer was beer. They had heard the explosion and were delighted. I suddenly realised they genuinely thought, 'Surely real men want to drink beer after such success?' This, as I found later, was typical of the macho South African psyche.

We drank the beer, because we were gasping. And, naturally, because our bodies were deficient of fluid, we got drunk. Very quickly. The SAP approved. So, there we were, miles from Rhodesia, standing about blackened, hot and stinking on a remote South African hillside a couple of hours before dawn, talking to a group of South African policemen who were ecstatic that we had, as the Special Branch called it, 'deployed' four people into tiny pieces. And everyone was pissed.

Finally, the police saw we really did need water to clean off the black stuff before going back to the streets of Komatipoort. While we stripped off our uniforms to change back into jeans and shirts, they found two battered old galvanised tin baths from somewhere, fetched water from a nearby stream and we did our best to wash off the black. But cam cream is impossible stuff. Glazed with beer and not having any soap, no amount of scrubbing helped. We cleaned the easy-to-get-at bits, but we still looked like a troupe of the Black and White Minstrels or eight black and white stand-ins for Rudolf Valentino, with dark mascara rings round our eyes, up our nostrils and stuck in the crevices of our ears.

This seemed to satisfy our SAP friends but I cannot believe that the long-suffering staff at the Hotel Continental in Pretoria were duped when we rolled up later that day.

The hotel staff watched impassively as eight of us stamped through the foyer, still reeking of sweat, our ears and eyelashes streaked with black, as rough a crowd as any, with bent noses, cropped hair, bulging muscles and big Jim McGuire's arm covered with a huge peacock tattoo. 'All right, mate? How's it going?' we called out cheerfully and breezed into the lift.

'These are tourists,' announced our policeman friend.

The hotel staff smiled blandly, as before, and checked us in. Such is South Africa. I expect the SAP used the hotel a lot, so they must have known we were up to something. Anyway, they never blinked when we ordered a large number of bottles of real Scotch whisky, which, like the sweets (which we ordered too) could not be had for any money in Rhodesia. We showered, which was glorious, and ate ourselves stupid on a huge spread of steak, lobster, crayfish and wine which would have fed the population of Swaziland for a week. The SAP picked up the tab, which for all eight was enormous, we passed through the customs into Rhodesia, all deniable and secret again (and so did our drink), and finally reported back to Mr Mac. He was more cheerful than ever, especially when I gave him a bottle of real Scotch. Rhodesians never liked to admit it, but the proud Rhodesian 'sanctions imitation' of whisky was, frankly, disgusting.

'Call the chaps into my office,' said Mac McGuinness, grinning broadly. When we were all gathered in front of him, he said, 'You've done well. Mission accomplished and no one any the wiser. The South Africans are very pleased and wanted me to give you this.'

With that he reached into a briefcase on the floor and pulled out wads and wads of money. The highest denomination in Rhodesia was $10 and he counted out $1,000 for each of us. He said, 'Look on it as a bonus. But if you'd rather have it in South African rand, then just say.'

At once eight packets of money dropped back on his desk. He grinned widely. At that time in Rhodesia, no one needed telling that Rhodesian money was worthless abroad, even had we been allowed to take it out of the country. He reached into his briefcase again and gave us each 1,200 rand instead. I opened a building society account in the South Africa Bank, and went to see Jane for a couple of days' leave.

These bonuses were a common feature of Special Branch life. I doubt it was widely known but there was an incentive scheme, call it a production bonus if you like, for killing terrorists. Quite simply, if you were out on patrol or ambush and killed up to five guerrillas, you got a $50 bonus, whereas if you killed six or more you got $100. I imagine most people will be rather shocked by this, except possibly my old blue-rinse lady in Salisbury who wanted me to 'get one for her' every time I went on patrol.

Now, the human mind is both devious and never satisfied. The incentive scheme, like most others, had loopholes. A liaison officer called Bob Perch saw a way to cash in. On ambush, he took no prisoners at all and killed as many as possible. Let us, for example, say two. On his return to Bindura he only declared one, for which he was given $50. The other one he stuffed in a deep freeze which he acquired specially and kept in his garage. The next day he claimed another successful ambush, defrosted and handed in one dead terrorist, at $50, thereby gleaning $100 instead of $50.

I can hear your outraged voice, 'This is insane!' You would be right. Bob Perch went berserk one day and threw a hand grenade at the police.

Communist terrorists were also criminally commercial. As the war worsened, so did the poaching of animals for profit. The poachers were black terrorists 'on leave' making some extra pocket money on the side, or 'genuine' black poachers who joined ZIPRA or ZANLA to be on the safe side. This, incidentally, is no different to the IRA protection rackets in Northern Ireland, for example taking a levy from the black taxis or the builders working with Belfast City Council grant schemes, which makes them no different from Al Capone.

Special Branch produced information about a group of poachers in the southwest. The SB source was a very thin, sixty-year-old black man who said the poacher-cum-terrorist lived just inside Botswana on the edge of what was known as the Tuli Circle. The Tuli Circle was a bulge in the border line which arose from the historical arrangements made between the first white settlers and Chief Lobengula who was the last Matabele king. Lobengula agreed to let the settlers build Fort Tuli and take land all round in a circle with a twenty-five-mile radius. Later when borders were fixed between Bechuanaland (as Botswana was then known) and Southern Rhodesia the circle remained and provided the poacher with a salient into Rhodesia where the circle came back to a straight line near the Shashi River.

The moon was up and full when we set off through the trees and scrub towards the border with our elderly black 'source', but soon the sky darkened with clouds and it started to rain. I found a place to cross the Shashi River but the water was up and we had to force our way over, chest deep, holding our weapons high above our heads. Inside Botswana, the rain poured down as we sloshed on through the soaking trees towards our target. We were still some way off the poacher's hide in a cluster of village huts, making slow progress in the pouring rain and darkness, when the old black man in front of me disappeared down a big hole. We dragged him out but he was howling with pain. Then he sat down and flatly refused to go on, forward or back. No amount of cursing helped. I had to abort the patrol as he was the only person who knew where the ZIPRA poacher was living and we had to carry him back to Rhodesia. The rain never let up and we were pretty tired by the time we reached the Shashi River. By this time, the water was a black raging torrent swollen by the downpour of rain. I cast up and down the bank for the least frightening place to cross and we plunged into the water. This was the last straw for the old man who began flinging his skinny arms and legs about in terror. Like a good many Africans, he could not swim. We were soon exhausted, washing about in the darkness, fighting to hang on to him and trying not to drown ourselves, till we noticed the old man's fearful thrashing kept him afloat to such a degree that we just gave up struggling, flopped all over him and used him as a flotation raft!

Amazingly, the old feller was persuaded to go back and they got their man. Steve Cleary took the patrol as I was training Auxiliaries elsewhere at the time. I only mention it because they were rather pleased to be carrying new Rumanian AMDs for the first time. These were Russian AKs cut right down and they certainly looked the part. The wire shoulder butt folded round, the barrel was reduced in length almost to the gas port and a huge muzzle brake, like something off a tank, was fitted on the end. However, when the shooting started in the dark, Steve opened up with his smart new AMD and was immediately blinded by the muzzle brake which blazed like a flame thrower and sounded like a huge 12.7mm heavy machine gun. Not good kit for covert work!

Back in Bindura, I soon had cause to involve Jane more closely in what I was doing. We had married, on 26 January 1979, and were living in a villa near the fort. Like all civilians, Jane saw the security situation worsening, but as a nurse she saw more than her share. There were an increasing number of victims of road ambushes brought to the hospital, on one occasion a bus full of blacks had been shot up, and she had lost friends on the civilian Air Rhodesia Viscount which had been shot down with a SAM-7 by ZIPRA terrorists. Her friend, a nurse who had trained with her, was one of those who survived the crash only to be murdered by other ZIPRA who found them injured on the ground. It is perhaps not surprising that she smoked a lot and then got bad-tempered about once a month trying to stop!

I set about training a group of one hundred UANC men on the outskirts of Bindura in some farm buildings at a place called Retreat

Farm. The house and a barn were used as barrack rooms and another barn was turned into a cookhouse. The training was basic infantry work with a counter-insurgency lean to it; covering subjects such as individual weapon handling and battlecraft, section battle drills, fire and movement, radio procedure, immediate action drills and contact drills. We fired on ranges near by and practised every technique we needed to operate against the ZANLA terrorists who lurked in or near most villages by then. I found the Auxiliaries keen, enthusiastic, and their leadership intelligent, though communism had left a com-missar-like attitude in their senior ranks. Lieutenant Sam was shadowed by a political adviser.

When the training was finished I was told to take my band of Auxiliaries to guard Keep Three which was one of the new protected villages about three-quarters of an hour's drive from Bindura near Mzura. Rhodesian Keeps were an attempt to copy a plan which had been very successful in the Malayan Emergency, when over 600,000 Chinese squatters were given freehold land of their own and 'New Villages' to live in. This encouraged them to support the government and provided the security forces with the added advantage of being able to separate the civilians from the terrorists. However, in Malaya, the British were able to staff, fund and man the Keeps so that the concept worked. In Rhodesia, the Internal Affairs Office had responsibility for Keeps and the plan suffered from a lack of all these crucial elements.

I was not at all keen to go to Keep Three, or any other, but SB officer Brian Pym explained to me that, because Special Branch had overall authority for 'tame terrs', we might be able to win back the 'hearts and minds' of the blacks in the protected village and develop some sources of intelligence among the terrorists in the bush around.

If I was reluctant to start with, when I drove down the dirt track through savannah woods and grass to the Keep, I was totally appalled. I found 1,800 black men, women and children squatting about in utter squalor in a ring-fenced village of mud huts with rotting that-ched roofs. The Africans just sat about in the dirt, with not a sign of a man between the ages of sixteen and sixty. They seemed beyond the stage of being able or willing to help themselves and at the mercy of ZANLA terrorists roaming the bush around.

Keep Three was in a worse condition than San Antonio di Zaire in Angola had been and some of the awful scenes of starvation seen on television recently are reminiscent of it. These people certainly gave up without leadership but, given the political decay in Rhodesia in 1979, they were well down the list of the regime's priorities and I wonder if some whites would be much different elsewhere under similar pressures.

The Internal Affairs Office supervisor never turned up so I set about organising the place myself. I could see it had been well set up originally, so there was hope. First, I deployed my Auxiliaries on patrols into the surrounding bush to drive off the ZANLA guerrillas and prove to the people inside the Keep that we had the upper hand. Then I turned to the Keep itself. In order of importance, I discovered six youngsters with Kwashiorkor, the terrible condition affecting small children suffering from severe nutritional protein deficiency, which gives them dry skin, de-pigmented hair and the awful swollen bellies which have become the hallmark of African famine. I drove them straight to see Jane in the Bindura hospital for blacks and she presented them to the doctor immediately. Two were beyond help and died but the others were saved. Next, I realised that my own medical skills were quite inadequate to deal with a problem of this magnitude (remember the goat?). So I appealed to Jane again. She agreed to come at once, and, having qualified as a nurse with an 'A' grade in Community Health, she was a great help with her advice.

Plainly we needed a medical centre and supplies. I went to the army, posed the problem and asked for medicines. The quartermaster in charge of the stores said, 'It's no good, Sergeant McAleese. You're only allowed one trummel of kit. Standard Platoon Medic Kit. One box only. Those are the rules.'

'Fine,' I replied, saluting smartly, and went straight round to his stores where I looted as many boxes as would fit in my truck. I took the best part of twenty boxes I found lying about there. One Platoon Medic Kit was sufficient for only forty people and I had 1,800 desperate people in the Keep.

Jane emphasised that the blacks needed protein. She rang up a local company called pro-Nutro which made a milk protein supplement for children, and asked for all their rejects, such as the punctured bags which could not be sold commercially. They offered them at cost. I persuaded the Special Branch to cough up $600 from their seemingly bottomless account and we drove off with a truckload.

At the same time, I set up a creche for the children in the Keep. This probably sounds rather charming, but there was a good reason. In Africa, the women feed the men first, before the children, so when, as here, there was little food, the kids went hungry and got sick. So, I fed the kids at the creche, telling the older children, who were not more than fifteen years old, to make sure they fed the small ones. It was really very satisfying to see the way they perked up at once and began behaving like children again.

I got more enthusiastic than ever as things improved and looked round for further ideas. Fortunately Bindura was an important citrus growing area, with acres of orange trees and I had noticed a lot of ground-fall oranges in a place called Mozoe. For only $200 this time, we picked up enough to last a full week.

Next, I called a meeting of the headmen on the verandah of the wood house where I lived with the other SB men, and we discussed the feeding arrangements. The Keep was a protected village and everyone had to eat in one fenced-off area, about the size of a football pitch. The idea was to control the food so that they could not give it to the terrorists, or, if ZANLA threatened them, they had an excuse for not being able to supply food. However, the place was a serious health hazard. All 1,800 people had their meals here, among a jumble of filthy, stinking grass huts and shelters. There was no running water, no sanitation and no cleansing. I persuaded a doctor called Sandy Kirk, who had been my best man at our wedding, to condemn the place, and, quite by chance, one night the feeding area caught fire and was burned to the ground.

'What the hell happened to the feeding area?' demanded a young white man who came rushing down from the Internal Affairs Office as soon as they heard it had burned down. I had seen neither hide nor hair of any of them till then.

I watched him strutting up and down with his arms crossed over his chest in my little office in the wood house, and my blood began to boil. I asked him, 'D'you want to know the truth?'

He nodded arrogantly.

I lost my temper and snapped, 'I fucking burned it down! And I'll tell you something else. There are people here suffering hardship because pricks like you won't do your fucking job and run the Keep!'

Seeing the expression on my face, he backed off rapidly through the door and vanished across the verandah shouting, 'I'm going to report you to the District Commissioner, see if I don't!'

I did not see him, or anyone else from the Internal Affairs Office, again.

We rebuilt the eating area. By various means, I obtained sand and cement and we made concrete washing places, with gradients and drains. We piped water in and kept the place clean.

Now that the basics had been fixed, I turned to other ideas. I obtained some white paint and had my Auxiliaries paint the houses in the Keep. This spruced the place up, but again there was another reason. When our patrols were out at night, they could see who was moving about in the Keep much more easily against the white walls of the houses than against the dark wood.

I organised daily football matches to give the Auxiliaries and young lads in the Keep something to do. I got blue and red football strips from Bindura and they played every afternoon.

In the mornings, I made the villagers sweep the ground round the Keep with a patrol of Auxiliaries. This kept them busy, kept the place clean, gave them a sense of pride in their village, and my black Auxs could report if they saw any tracks of people creeping in and out of the Keep at night. These UANC Auxs had been doing their stuff among the people, persuading them to give up support of ZANLA and that we were on their side. This had the desired effect. The headmen approached me, their confidence buoyed by all that was going on, and said they had heard that some ZANLA hiding in the bush wanted to talk. This was exactly what the SB had wanted and all the work seemed to be paying off. I knew that the local ZANLA leader, Teddy Natsango, was away in Mozambique for resupplies, so I gave the headmen a quantity of cigarettes to pass on to the guerrillas and waited for developments. Maybe, some of Natsango's less committed terrorists would come in while he was away.

Some days later, a black headman came to my office in the wood house and announced that there were four ZANLA men at the back gate waiting to talk to me.

'Great!' shouted two SB officers who by sheer bad luck happened to be with me at the time. Ignoring my pleas not to get involved because they were not known by the local people, they ran over the verandah and charged through the Keep to the back gate. Word travels faster than the average SB officer, so the four ZANLA were alerted in time and they legged it back into the bush before I could intervene.

There were no more contacts by ZANLA and I wondered if the people trusted me after that. However, we carried on. All the important things had been done in the Keep and now the villagers wanted a church. We made a wood frame structure, complete with a spire and covered it with long lengths of hessian (courtesy of the quartermaster's stores again) which I made them dip in a mixture of sand and cement, giving the building a wattle and daub finish which dried off hard. We painted it white. Our church was no bigger than a large room, but everyone, especially me, was very pleased with it. I can also say it was a Catholic Church. Roll on Father Brett.

I knew we had won over the villagers when the men came to me and said that ZANLA had laid a mine on the dirt track leading to the Keep, just for me. I went to have a look and skirted the place every time I drove in and out until a suitable period had elapsed for me to have the engineers lift it without ZANLA blaming the villagers for telling me about it.

The terrorists did not give up easily. They tried again and this time their approach was more devious. Again the villagers let me know. One morning, they called me over to one of the gates of the Keep. ZANLA had done a beautiful job! They had taken a Chinese POMZ-2 stick grenade and buried it in the ground just under the gate leaving a fragment of the top visible. This was the fuse, which they had attached with a string to the bottom of the gate. Open the gate, pull the fuse, and bang. It all looked very straightforward, but it was a little bit obvious and I was instantly suspicious. Sending the others back to a safe distance, I circled it and had a good look. Then I approached the bomb, knelt down and began brushing away the earth around it with my fingers. I worked very carefully indeed because these Chinese fuses only need a 2-lb weight to set them off. Soon I revealed some of the pineapple body of the grenade and saw that the fuse was a MUV-2 with a three-second delay. Still suspicious, I worked deeper and saw the real danger. Underneath the first grenade was a second. This had an instant pull-type MUV fuse tied to the first grenade. If you fell for their booby trap and lifted the first grenade thinking that was all there was to it, you set off the second beneath it and died. I disconnected the second grenade, took them both away and blew them.

Shortly afterwards, just before Christmas 1979, I was called away from Keep Three to train a new bunch of Auxiliaries at Retreat Farm again. I arrived, formed them up on parade in ranks and I can honestly say I have never seen such a motley collection in my life. Every second man had a pair of mirror sunglasses and the British sergeant major who talks about 'mixed orders of dress' has never seen anything like this! One man wore a black tanksuit held in place with bright yellow socks up to his knees, another had a purple shirt and a yellow cravat, there were jeans, T-shirts and hats of every colour and shape. Their weapons were as varied. I found out the SB had rounded every unemployed free-loader and 'tame terr' in every barracks and camp in the region and sent them to Retreat Farm for me.

'This,' I said to myself, 'is not on!'

I raided the stores in Bindura again for shorts and khaki T-shirts, paraded this motley crew again and stripped the lot naked. I issued them with two pairs of shorts and two T-shirts each. A Greek called

Maggie Christo ran a shop like Aladdin's cave from which he supplied the Special Branch with all manner of odd things. He supplied me with boots. I persuaded Mr Mac to use more SB cash to pay for some very smart camouflage uniforms of my own design to be made up by a local tailor and soon the men began to look the part. At my suggestion, Mr Mac obtained some very impressive helmets I had noticed being worn by the police who guarded the nickel mines near Bindura. They looked similar to helmets worn by German troops in the Second World War. I gave them to the largest of my recruits, some of whom were huge men, and they looked splendid in these helmets and new uniforms. I made them my Military Police section to mete out discipline to the rest as necessary.

The next two months were spent training and they shaped up well. By the time we had finished, I had fifty keen black soldiers ready to start operations. We were to be used to fight ZANLA in the area, to take the pressure off the regular battalions of RLI and RAR in the Fire Force.

I found that discipline round the country was beginning to collapse. Of course, regiments like the SAS, the RLI and the RAR remained solid until the very end, but elsewhere the command and control of operations had begun to fall apart and I certainly found this the case in the places I was deployed with my new Auxiliaries. The terrorists were everywhere and total anarchy was galloping over the hill.

I tried to make sure we were deployed on operations based on good intelligence from professional Special Branch officers, like Mac McGuinness, but increasingly this was not possible. One SB man called Steve sent us to ambush a crossroads in the Matepatepa area which he was certain was used by terrorists. We approached the crossroads on foot through the scrub in darkness and pouring rain and I just didn't feel right about it. I changed course and stopped at a local police station. I asked the station sergeant on duty, 'Anything going on in the area tonight?'

'Yeah,' he replied, waving his hand at his operations map. 'Guard Force are ambushing the Matepatepa crossroads tonight.'

I was furious. If we had carried on as planned, we should have walked straight into the Guard Force ambush. I turned my black Auxs round and we walked back to base where I left them to clean up. I set off at once to find Steve. He was, naturally, in his billet stretched out in his bed. I burst in, dragged him off the mattress and demanded an explanation. He apologised. He promised to 'get it right the next time'.

He did not. On a Thursday evening, I was sent with a reaction force of twenty-five of my Auxs to observe an area near Keep Three over the weekend, with a view to attacking ZANLA if we saw them, which was highly likely at that time. Just after lunch on Friday, the comms went dead on my radio. Lying hidden in bushes with no radio, no support, and no casevac, I felt this was no way to treat the black Auxs. I left the radio with the others and took one man with me. I washed up in a stream to remove the black cam cream, or as much of it as possible, and we hitched back to Bindura. I should imagine that the driver was terrified when he saw us emerge from the bush. In Bindura, I marched into the ops room only to be told that Steve had pissed off for the weekend. And it was a long weekend.

This was no way to treat men in the field. Without hesitation, I took two trucks and brought the Auxs back in. Typically, when Steve got back after his weekend, he just shrugged.

I should add that by this time Keep Three had once again degenerated into total chaos. I regretted it, but I suppose I always realised this was inevitable. Rhodesia was a country in its death throes.

I teamed up with an ex-RLI officer called Mike Webb, who was on contract to work with the Auxiliaries. He suggested we use my Auxiliaries in another area, where they came from, because they might know where to look for terrorists and to show a good example. So, we moved across Mashonaland to a small town called Mudzi north of Mutoko and here things were really bad.

Mudzi was smaller than Bindura, one main street and the bare necessities, and a great deal more rural. Around, the savannah was characterised by dongas, which were small hills standing out of the landscape, and the area had become virtually a Liberated Area in Mao Tse Tung terminology. ZANLA did not actually control the region, but whenever a truck left base, the young black boys called Mugibas who kept watch passed the word and within minutes a flare would shoot into the sky alerting every terrorist for miles around.

Understandably, morale was rock bottom in Mudzi base. The local SB were on their own, without the discipline of the regimental system, unlike the RLI or SAS, and matters were beyond recall. One ground coverage officer called Trevor, dressed in the usual SB fawn shirt and shorts with veltskoen shoes, used to sit in his office and play 'darts' by firing his 9mm pistol at the dartboard on the wall opposite.

We did a lot of patrols in this area, characterised by long night approach marches on foot, to avoid being seen by the local Mugibas. We went deep into enemy country where we manned observation positions to spot the enemy. Our first operation went well. At night, I took ten Auxs and we marched across country into a range of hills. By dawn we were hidden in scrub overlooking a group of huts. As the sun warmed us in our bushes, we watched a black woman about her daily chores going down to the stream to wash and mix meal. One of my black Auxiliaries nudged me and whispered, 'Boss, there are terrorists in the huts.'

'How d'you know?'

'Either she's got an awful big family or she's feeding terrs.'

'Why?' I had noticed nothing unusual. To me we had spent the day watching a typical African village scene, complete with chickens and dogs lying in the dust round the huts.

'She's been four times to the stream. That's not usual. She must be making extra food for the enemy.'

This was a glimpse of how the Selous Scouts worked, knowing the ground and the people so well they could read every action.

I considered the options. It would take too long to call for troops and the enemy might hear the planes or helicopters coming and run off. I decided to attack. I whispered quick orders, we simply broke cover and swept down onto the village.

We captured two ZANLA terrorists and returned to Mudzi where they were interrogated by Trevor. His technique was not clever.

He pointed at a place on the wall map and said, 'The terrorists with you came from here, didn't they?'

'Yes,' said the black man, eyeing a length of rubber hose Trevor was hefting in his other hand.

Trevor hit him with it.

He said, 'And were they carrying rifles with straight magazines or curved magazines?'

'Curved ones.'

Trevor hit him again. 'So, they were carrying AKs?'

'Yes,' replied the desperate black man, knowing that whatever he said, even agreeing with everything suggested by this mad white, he would be hit with the rubber hose.

Trevor nodded and hit him again.

At this, Mike Webb stepped in and took over. Mike's technique was more subtle and the black ZANLA terrorist was so relieved he told us the location of a camp which was occupied by ZANLA. One of my Auxs confirmed that he had heard the place was used by ZANLA.

The camp was thirty kilometres away and the only possible approach was on foot. It was a long, sweaty night march in full patrol gear and a light pack. We skirted villages and huts but we had to cross a bridge which I found manned by a small patrol of black Guard Force soldiers. We walked up silently and caught them unawares. They were lying loose-limbed on the earth floor of a small hut by the bridge smoking dagga and totally spaced out of their minds. 'You're smoking dope?' I asked incredulously.

'Er, yeah,' replied the black NCO in charge, the whites of his eyes rolling vacantly in the light of my torch. The germ of an excuse occurred to him. 'We're, er, testing it. To see if it can be used as evidence.' He grinned with embarrassment but made no attempt to hide the great pile of weed on the floor at his feet.

I shrugged. That was the way of things.

We crossed the bridge and continued our long march through the night. Shortly before dawn, Mike Webb disappeared into the shadows with a group of six Auxs to act as my stop groups behind the camp and, as light brightened the sky, I started the sweep with the rest. We advanced methodically but cautiously through the dry scrub, grass and trees towards the camp. It was deserted. We searched the make-shift huts and found little hides of clothes and personal belongings, but no ammunition. I guessed the place had been recently occupied and we all agreed that we had missed them by less than two days. We continued to search the area around and came across some huts near by where we flushed out several young men who were ZANLA lookouts or Mugibas. The first young black walked out of a dusty yellow hut and looked up in surprise at the line of soldiers advancing on him through the dried grass and bushes. He was no more than forty or fifty metres from us, we had all seen him, and yet to our great amazement he casually pulled a Chinese stick grenade from his trouser pocket, unscrewed it and tossed it at us, thoughtlessly, as if he were experimenting with it. It was the last thing he did. The grenade had hardly burst before the whole sweep line opened up on this young idiot and literally shot him apart. Mike Webb captured two others with more sense, trying to escape through the stop groups, and we returned to base.

These ops were not much different to the endless patrolling on minimal intelligence which the British SAS did in Borneo or Northern Ireland in the early days. By 1980, the extent of guerrilla infiltration into Rhodesia was such that the structure of the counter-insurgency operation was falling apart at the seams. There were some excellent professional Special Branch men but there were also men without the necessary training and police background who could not cope under such pressure. Without adequate supervision, their wildest schemes took shape and added to the increasing atmosphere of anarchy and unreality.

Mudzi suffered particularly and Trevor was not the only lunatic. An Internal Affairs officer, who was a tiffy, a mechanic, spoke Mashona rather well and decided on his own initiative to infiltrate the local people disguised as a black man. His plan was to pick up gossip and information about the terrorists. His problem was that his features did not lend themselves at all to this plan. However, ignoring all criticism, he blacked his face and arms and legs very thoroughly and set out on his own to join the villagers. He took a bus and sat down. The blacks looked at him very strangely but no one said anything. The bus rumbled on. A black policeman on duty in uniform got on at a stop, glanced round and walked up to the Internal Affairs officer.

'Hey, you're white! What the hell you doing on this bus?' he demanded in English. 'This bus is for blacks!'

'I'm a black man,' insisted the Internal Affairs officer in Mashona.

'No you ain't,' said the policeman, pointing at the man's head. 'You got red hair.'

'I'm telling you I'm black,' said the Internal Affairs man, sure of his disguise.

Exasperated, the black policeman replied, 'Then, if you'se a black, I'll treat you as a black.' And he gave the Internal Affairs officer a sound beating, threw him off the bus and sent him back to Mudzi on foot.

I might mention how this lunatic ended up as it illustrates just how seriously the system of law and order and democratic values was threatened at that time. He had a friend nicknamed Steptoe and these two Internal Affairs officers went to Salisbury for a day's leave. They got completely drunk, emerged from the bar, climbed into their truck which had two GPMGs mounted on the rear, and drove back to Mudzi machine-gunning blacks on the road as they passed. They were given ten and twelve years. On reflection, I suppose it is possible that their imagined experiences with Special Branch undercover work at Mudzi made them believe they could do what they liked, and made them think they were above the law.

Rhodesia's political situation worsened. The world refused to recognise the new black majority under Bishop Muzorewa. Robert Mugabe's ZANLA and Joshua Nkomo's ZIPRA were too powerful and could not be stopped militarily. At Mrs Thatcher's first Commonwealth Conference in August 1979, she agreed with Australia, Jamaica, Nigeria, Tanzania and Zambia that Nkomo and Mugabe had to be a part of any settlement. She agreed to set up talks leading to 'genuine' black majority rule and new elections. For their part, the terrorist leaders Nkomo and Mugabe were persuaded by other black African leaders (like Kenneth Kaunda of Zambia) to fall in line with these proposals. The black Front Line states were not keen on the successful Rhodesian cross-border operations which were becoming increasingly ambitious and seriously threatened their countries' vital infrastructure, such as bridges, railways, and oil installations. In March 1979, the SAS had attacked the Beira oil depot on the coast with considerable success. New Rhodesian elections were eventually set for March 1980.

During this period, I was moved about with my Auxiliaries from place to place and everywhere the security situation was grim. Without coordinated intelligence we tended to mount operations on the scantiest of information and ended up going out hoping to stumble on some terrorists by chance. They were certainly there, in droves, but the tribal villages were increasingly under the control of ZANLA terrorists and we constantly ran up against the Mugiba lookout system. This was particularly well developed round Mutoko, east of Bindura where the villagers sent out their children to clear tracks of our ambushes by walking parallel to the tracks, in the bushes. Of course, they walked straight onto us as we lay back in cover watching the track and at once set up a terrible caterwauling, 'The soldiers are here! The soldiers are here!' Within minutes we could hear the message being picked up and shouted across the valley. Nothing for it, we packed up and went back to base.

There was madness in Mutoko too. One day, a couple of Special Branch men there called me to one side and said quietly, 'We've got some gooks here. They're real bad bastards. Murderers. Take 'em out somewhere quiet, Peter, and deploy them, will you?'

Here we go again, I thought. Why is it people always think I am a pathological murderer? I like fighting, I like soldiering, but I am not the sort who just knocks people off for the fun of it. Bluntly, I told them, 'If you want to kill them, do it yourself.'

They acted insulted but tried me again. 'Listen, Peter, these bastards killed a couple of men in the RLI!'

'Then get the RLI to do it,' I said and walked out. Rhodesia was falling apart.

Bindura was the same. I took my good friend Dr Sandy Kirk out to the range one day to show him how explosives worked. He used to help me with medical training and supplies and in return I satisfied his curiosity about demolitions. The place for dems practice was at the back of the gallery range butts, in a secluded wooded area where the explosions would cause no harm. One day, I set out several charges for him on the dry ground, linked them in a ring main – a circle of detonating cord so they all go off at the same time – and set them off with a length of safety fuse. Sandy and I retired to one side of the butts and, after the explosion, came back to see what had happened. To our horror, a hand was sticking out of the ground where I had set one charge. Needless to say, the hand was black. The blast had blown away the earth, and beneath was the rest of the body in a shallow grave; one among several casually buried behind the butts.

No one was too surprised when I reported this to the Special Branch office at the police barracks. 'Oh, sounds like Phil Young has been up to his tricks again.' I would very much like to give his real name, but he was never charged and is still alive. Young was obsessive about slaughtering captured black terrorists. He had simply taken them off to the butts and shot them. Nothing was done about it.

Young's enthusiasm for killing the enemy led him to making a Q car. In theory, this was a reasonable response to the constant threat of ambush on the roads outside town but the elements of overkill and absurdity were typical of the times.

The Rhodesians developed a variety of such vehicles, with armoured sloping sides to deflect the blast of a mine and soft tyres to give minimum low ground pressure (remember the Russian TM mines which set off with only 26 lbs of pressure). They filled the tyres with water to absorb the energy of the explosion. Young's idea was not merely to survive but to give the black terrorists a blasting as well and, typically, he overdid it. He took a police Land Rover, kept its canvas back so it looked perfectly normal from the outside, and fitted bullet-proof armour inside. Inside, he concealed twin machine guns mounted to fire on automatic, several grenade-lobbing devices and twin cannons under the bonnet to fire out the front. The whole device worked electrically, at the flick of a switch near the driver's seat. Young used this 'Rover as his private vehicle and one day parked it in the Bindura Country Club car park in the centre of town and slipped inside for a beer.

In the back of the Land Rover was a can of petrol he had managed to acquire (petrol was scarce) but he had foolishly left it sitting on top of the batteries which powered his Q car arsenal. After a while in the heat, the metal can short-circuited across the terminals. Suddenly, the unmanned Q car exploded into action, shattering the peace of Bindura. The top flew open, the machine guns rose majestically through the roof firing on automatic, the twin cannons roared at the front and grenades sailed out in all directions, exploding all over the place. The car park was turned into a shambles, cars were riddled with shrapnel and shot to bits but, amazingly, no one was hurt. Everyone thought it was a big joke and forgot all about it.

Africa casts its spell on white and black alike. Or, maybe in the death struggle of cultures and politics there is always space between the great battles to hide a multitude of terrible sins.

The annual Bindura ball suffered too. All the whites who were anything in Bindura went. There were 1,200 whites so numbers dictated the ball had to be in the Bindura school hall. Bindura etiquette demanded black tie and long dresses, while the security situation obliged the men to arrive tooled up with Kalashnikovs and FNs. Ben van Schalkwyk, the hotelier who ran the Bindura Coach House Hotel, arrived in a natty tuxedo and dickie bow tie toting an FN rifle. The festivities started at a pace, huge volumes of alcohol were consumed, temporarily driving away Rhodesia's grim reality, and the dance floor heaved to the sound of tunes like Abba's 'Money, Money, Money' and 'Keep the Home Fires Burning'. Even the poor woman nicknamed the Kiss of Death inveigled some new men onto the floor. The name arose because she had been married to three men all of whom had been killed in the war and word was that she was looking for a fourth. Sober, men avoided her like the plague, but at the ball that year nothing seemed to matter any longer.

Of course, the opportunity was too good to miss and out in the darkness on the edge of town, a couple of ZANLA fired off their magazines in the general direction of the school. At once, pandemonium broke out at the ball. The men left their women standing on the dance floor, grabbed their weapons and poured out of the brightly lit school hall into the darkness.

'They're over there!' shouted one.

'No they're fucking not. I saw tracer that way!'

Within seconds all these drunks in dinner jackets were pouring out a fantastic weight of fire all over the place, and, because most carried Soviet weapons like the AK and RPD, a tangle of green tracer patterned the darkness over Bindura.

Elsewhere in the town, the Guard Force heard the racket and tumbled out of their barracks. They were not top-line troops, but one look at the green tracer flashing over Bindura convinced them the town was under heavy attack on every side. Their commanders were grimly determined Bindura should not be the first town to fall to the hated ZANLA and immediately despatched fighting patrols to defend the place at all costs. Cautiously, the patrols advanced through the dark streets towards the unseen but obviously very powerful enemy, using the American technique of reconnaissance by fire, shooting at everything which made them jump.

At the ball, the increased noise of firing convinced the revellers that matters were almost out of hand. Bow ties were loosened in earnest and someone went for more ammunition.

In the garden, a terrified dog skulked under a bush while inside the school hall, an old lady was slumped drunk in an armchair singing loudly at the top of her voice, 'Land of hope and gloree, Mother of the freee ...'

The battle went on for hours.

In the morning, when the party-goers were sleeping off their hangovers, a police patrol found the little pile of AK empty cases which had started it all off. ZANLA, if they had a sense of humour, must have laughed till they cried. Bindura looked as though it had been attacked by stormtroopers, with bullet strike on walls, smashed windows, shattered doors, and riddled cars, but, once again, with the luck of the devil, no one was hurt.

The Bindura school achieved prominence a second time, during the March elections. The British had rushed through their new plans for Rhodesia and soon Bindura was visited by British Army officers for the first time in years, and a British bobby, complete with peaked helmet. These were men of the 1,300-strong Commonwealth Monitoring Force who were charged with supervising the elections to ensure fair play, British style. I must say they looked very weedy, white and British compared to the bronzed, muscled, bush fighters of Bindura.

Robert Mugabe had no intention of allowing this golden opportunity slip away. Here was his chance to be democratically elected in the eyes of the world. There had been a sort of ceasefire since 28 December and in the new year his ZANLA (now ex-terrorists) had been forming up in camps supervised by the Monitoring Force. Mugabe instructed them to make absolutely certain that all the blacks voted for him in the areas they had infiltrated, which by then was all northern, eastern and southern Rhodesia, no matter what techniques were necessary. ZIPRA did their best to do the same in the western areas.

The most appalling stories of intimidation emerged from the bush. Lord Soames, who was the interim Governor, was faced with cancelling the elections. He let them go on. Later, he said, 'I believed that Robert Mugabe was going to win anyway, and you must remember this is Africa ... They behave differently. They think nothing of sticking tent poles up each other's whatnot and doing filthy beastly things to each other. It's a very wild thing, an election.'

Amazing as it seems in retrospect, I am told that many Rhodesians did not believe that the communists, Mugabe or Nkomo, could win. Somehow they believed a Seventh Cavalry would come charging over the horizon to save them and maintain Bishop Muzorewa in power. ComOps and Army HQ certainly maintained this bubble till the bitter end, to the chagrin of the security forces (particularly the SAS who were actually in position in Salisbury waiting for the code word to assassinate Mugabe).

Of course the Rhodesians did their best to fix matters too. Don't go thinking the blacks were the only ones busy rigging the election. In Bindura, the Special Branch did their bit. On 3 March, the voting took place in the school and a Special Branch group took over a house. Acting in the greatest secrecy, they barricaded themselves in, covered all the windows with thick mattresses, on the pretext that they wanted to prevent anyone using powerful directional microphones on the glass panes to hear what was being said inside, and methodically set about fiddling the result.

A German observer of the elections said, 'If this election is fair and free, then I am a Chinaman.' He was right. While the famous British bobbies stoically sat out in the heat watching the blacks and whites sliding little pieces of paper in the slot at the top of the voting boxes, the Bindura Special Branch were hard at work in the gym unscrewing the bottom of these boxes to get at the papers. No one seemed to have noticed that all the boxes were wood and the bottoms held in place with only four screws.

The calm of voting day in Bindura was disrupted only once when a ZANLA-inspired black began pointing at the house windows and shouting that the whites were rigging the votes. He was quickly suppressed by the Rhodesian police and dragged away. No one else was allowed near the house and the SB sweated on through the night, but the result was beyond their control.

At 9.00 a.m. on Tuesday 4 March, the Marxist revolutionary Robert Gabriel Mugabe was declared the winner, with fifty-seven out of the hundred seats taken by his ZANU and ZANLA. Within a year he had declared his intention of setting up a one-party Marxist state.

The white Rhodesians were shocked to the core.

The SWAPO base outside the town of Quamato, Angola, before it was attacked by the South African Defence Force in February 1981 (*Al J. Venter*).

Hitting the ground running into contact as we attacked Quamato (*Al J. Venter*).

Checking a captured SWAPO guerrilla for documents at Quamato (*Al J. Venter*).

A SWAPO guerrilla surrenders to South African forces (*Al J. Venter*).

Removing identification papers from a dead SWAPO guerrilla (*Al J. Venter*).

Teaching an SADF officer how to make a decent curry in Ondjiva, Angola.

Leaving the South African army.

Zero-ing rifles in preparation for the attack on Pablo Escobar's villa, Colombia 1989 (*Dave Tomkins*).

Planning the attack at the flat in Cali (*Dave Tomkins*).

The final dress rehearsal at La Gagua training camp (*Dave Tomkins*).

The wreck of the Hughes helicopter shortly after we had crashed into the mountainside (*Dave Tomkins*).

The Gunmaker's Arms, 1993.

The witchhunts and purges started very quickly. Mugabe's ZANU were now the majority party and they started trying to find out who had been giving them a hard time in the bush. The SAS, Selous Scouts and of course the Special Branch were prime targets. Black men seem to be more unpleasant to other black men and it was no surprise that our Auxiliaries were under pressure at once.

I was in the office in the fort in Bindura and the phone rang.

'I want to quit,' said one of my colour sergeants, called Sam, his voice oddly quiet. He was phoning from Retreat Farm and close questioning revealed that my band of black Auxiliaries were in a state of near anarchy. By then, they consisted of all factions in the war: SEPs (Surrendered Enemy Personnel) from ZANLA and ZIPRA, Sithole's ZANU PF and Muzorewa's UANC. Using their new-found power, Mugabe's ZANU/ZANLA were using the well-tried communist technique of denunciation to terrorise the people and consolidate their position. The existing rank structure and discipline was seriously threatened by three junior ranks who were bullying the rest. Worse, many of the Auxs feared that they would be hounded all the way to their tribal villages even if they left the unit.

The poison of this made me mad with fury when I thought of how all these men had so enthusiastically committed themselves to our training and fought well on some very tough and dangerous operations. They were good men and they had worked damned hard in difficult terrain during extraordinarily difficult political times. Tough measures were called for.

I rang the farm and told Alec Lennox to find some excuse to gather the men on the square, without their weapons. Billy Chambers and I jumped into a Land Rover and drove out to confront the three ringleaders who were led by an enormous six-foot-four black called Israel. We arrived and Billy, who was himself a big man, stepped briskly over to Israel who towered over us all with a smug expression on his face. Without warning, Billy shattered a knobkerrie stick on his skull and floored him. I had all three arrested and jailed in the cells.

Here I must confess, like a (not so) good Catholic, I was so angry at the insidious and underhand way that Israel and his two henchmen had bullied and terrified the others that I decided to kill him myself. He had, after all, betrayed the others. At gunpoint, I ordered him into the back of a police Land Rover with a lockup in the back and drove him out to a secluded place on the Shashi Pass between Bindura and Mount Darwin. I left the road at the top of the steep climb, pulled into some trees and dragged him out of the back of the Land Rover. Crying, pleading and begging me not to kill him, he crawled on his hands and knees towards me, his face streaming with tears. Disgusted, I levelled my Beretta pistol at him and prepared to squeeze the trigger.

A flood of memories came back. Of Old Miles's anger killing Germans in the First World War, of the maniacs killing each other in Angola, and of all the murders I had come across in Rhodesia. In retrospect, perhaps I had been sucked into the unreality of Rhodesia in those days, because I knew there would have been no comeback for killing him. By the grace of God, I hesitated at the last moment. The act of killing the man would have been so easy. Pulling the trigger would have been a simple thing to do of itself, something I had done numerous times on operations, but this was murder, without question, and I did not want murder on my conscience. I lowered the Beretta and ordered the big blubbering bully back in the truck. We drove back to Retreat Farm.

The lesson was not lost on the Auxiliaries for a while, but circumstances were beyond small incidents like that and soon the ZANU comrades fingered another two Auxiliaries called Saul and Eddison. I arranged for them to move out to a small place called Sinoa but ZANU tracked them down and they had to come back to Bindura. These two were ZANLA SEPs and the triumphant ZANLA wanted to settle old scores with people they reckoned had been traitors to the cause. Later, Saul disappeared but Eddison was captured by ZANLA and tortured to death. Life is all a question of perspectives but the victor calls the tune.

Another black man, called Lazarus, who worked for the Special Branch, was a Matabele and had been trained in Russia for eighteen months before changing sides and working for the Rhodesians. He was caught by ZANLA in their post-election purges and taken outside Bindura to the mines. They tied him down, ripped open his stomach with a knife and filled his intestines with burning coals.

It was the end. I spoke to Mac McGuinness who agreed to disband the whole group. He gave them three months' pay each and they dispersed very rapidly to hide in their tribal areas.

I lost track of them, but I do know that Mugabe used the new Zimbabwean Army's 5th Brigade, incidentally still with a good many white officers, to eliminate all opposition to his plans for a one-party Marxist state. Primarily, the 5th Brigade worked in Nkomo's areas of support in the Matabele lands, where they destroyed ZAPU and ZIPRA. Estimates of the numbers killed vary between 100,000 and

150,000. There were very few reports of this in the Western press which was still intellectually blinded by its support of Mugabe's glorious fight against the Rhodesian whites-only regime. One lone voice was the editor of the London *Observer*, Donald Trelford, who did write about the massacres taking place after a visit to Zimbabwe in 1984. On 15 April, he published an article entitled 'The Agony of a Lost People' but the call was not taken up by other journalists.

Did no one care what happened in Zimbabwe any longer? The war had cost some 30,000 lives, mostly black, and yet, true to African form, more died in the settling of scores after the war was over. The pity is that the blaze of world media attention during the war died away when the Africans got down to the serious and murderous business of staying in power.

The media had switched their attention to South Africa.

I recognised that my time in the country that was now Zimbabwe was finished but the final straw was hearing my name being broadcast by Radio Maputo. Several young men I had trained had been captured on cross-border operations in Mozambique and obliged to tell all.

'The Forces of the Glorious People's Republic must find Mr Peter!' crowed the Maputo radio station six hundred miles away on the coast of Mozambique. 'He has been training the enemies of the revolution!' For four days, they plugged their line, including an identifying reference to my Dobermann dog.

'The search goes on for Mr Peter!' they shouted over the air.

The incident focused my thoughts. The political situation was fraught with dangers for people like me who had not merely fought against the new black government when they were guerrillas in the bush but had served in special forces. Guerrilla propaganda always paints special units as 'criminal' because these units work on specific intelligence and are more successful than regular infantry units. The Rhodesian Special Forces Group had been spectacularly successful, man for man, though fighting what was ultimately a losing battle, and we could not expect any favourable treatment from Mr Mugabe's new regime, many of whom had been on the receiving end of our operations. What focused my concern was Jane who was pregnant with our first child. I saw no future for us in the New Rhodesia, now called Zimbabwe. I handed in three months' notice and we departed for South Africa.

— 8 —

High Standards are the Only Ones Acceptable

All the business of war, and indeed all the business of life, is to endeavour to find out what you don't know by what you do.

ARTHUR WELLESLEY, DUKE OF WELLINGTON

Joining the South African Army was a no-nonsense affair. I decided that at thirty-seven years old I was more use to 44 Parachute Brigade than the South African Reconnaissance Commando, their special forces unit, and, in June 1980, I went straight to Hallmark Buildings in Pretoria to sign on. The board examined my British and Rhodesian service record and interviewed me carefully. There was no covert surveillance of my private life, as in Rhodesia, nor the defensive arrogance typical of the British SAS, as in, 'You don't know nothing but you'll learn it all with us, lad!' The South Africans are accused of being humourless and intense, but they are committed and straightforward too which is not a bad start for an army.

Without further ado they signed me on as Number 80021355 in the South African Defence Force (SADF) and gave me the rank of colour sergeant. I was posted to 44 Parachute Brigade at Murray Hill, forty kilometres outside Pretoria, and within a month, Colonel Breytenbach promoted me to sergeant major. He wanted me to work as chief instructor for Captain Botes and our job was to raise and train the first regular Pathfinders and form No. 1 Pathfinder Company. This, I felt, was a job in which I could really use all my knowledge and experience and I can honestly say I started the most satisfying period of my soldiering career.

Jane and I were given an apartment in the Hotel Pretoria, a grand name for a SADF families hostel, where we had our own flat but ate in a communal dining room. Community is a powerful concept in South Africa.

HIGH STANDARDS ARE THE ONLY ONES ACCEPTABLE

A truck came by at 7.30 a.m. every morning to take me to the camp. During the last few months of chaos in Rhodesia, my fitness had slipped and I decided to run along the road to camp ahead of the truck. I made a race of it. Every morning I tried to increase the distance I ran before the truck caught up with me. The fitter I became, the quicker I pounded along and my best distance was eventually seventeen kilometres.

Murray Hill at the time was nothing more than a tented camp on sloping grassland beside some old farm buildings, with a stream running through the camp from a small reservoir. Colonel Breytenbach, a brother of the South African poet Breyten Breytenbach, was the commanding officer of 44 Parachute Brigade and he energetically set about building up his command to prepare it for the fighting on the Namibian-Angolan front. His technique of cutting across red tape and bending the rules attracted a good deal of criticism elsewhere in the South African Army but he gave us the backing we needed.

Captain Pete Botes and I were told to start picking men for the first selection course for the Pathfinders. He wanted it based on an SAS selection and said, 'Make it hard!'

We rustled up twenty-three people to begin with, from all over the world. There were Italians, Belgians, Germans, Rhodesians who, like me, had come south after the loss of their own country, Canadians, a British public school boy called Roy Kaulback, an American banker who was bored of banking, Hungarians, and a Russian who made the South African Special Branch totally paranoid.

Colonel Breytenbach told us to find an area to train in and we ended up at a place called Mabalique, which was tucked right up in the northeast corner of the country, on the border with Zimbabwe. The camp was remote, reached on a dusty, dirt road through tall, thorny trees and tough grass which grew up to the gate through the fence bordering the Kruger National Park. This was a double wire fence separated by a thick planting of spiky, cactus-like sisal plants, impossible to walk through, and it was said the sinews would even foul up tank tracks. From there, the vegetation softened down gentle rolling grassy slopes to the winding flat banks of the River Limpopo, as Kipling described it, 'great, grey, green, greasy' and 'all set about with fever trees'. Our camp was on a pimple of high ground about three kilometres from the park gate overlooking the river. The nearest town was a small place called Pafuri, in the corner of the Zimbabwean, South African, and Mozambique borders, and its only claim to fame was that it had been used on location to film *The Wild Geese*. Further away was a spa town called Tshipise.

Needless to say, the living conditions in our camp were primitive, though the place had been used as a camp before. There were two concrete buildings, the kitchen was made of wood and the rest was tented, so we were constantly improving the place as time went on.

The Pathfinders are the vanguard of any parachute unit and I really worked hard to make our people the best. Colonel Breytenbach and Captain Botes made sure we had the necessary support and I organised the fullest training I could devise.

Our routine was tough but intensely satisfying. We started the day at 4.30 a.m. with a cup of tea followed by a seven-kilometre run from the camp down to the Kruger Park gate in the sisal fence and back. I was by now so fit that even at my advanced years, only three others could beat me. I have always worked on the principle that I should never ask anyone to do anything I could not, or would not, do myself. After a shower and breakfast we went to the range where we trained hard for the rest of the day on the whole spectrum of subjects: shooting practices, section battle drills, contact drills, ambushing, live camp attacks, medical skills, demolitions and so on.

We fired every weapon we were likely to encounter and threw literally hundreds of grenades in realistic bunker and trench clearing practices. We acquired a box of new Spanish Star automatic pistols and I ran a CQB (close quarters battle) course for extra interest. These pistols were terribly unreliable. Sometimes several fell apart in a day, but we were so involved in our training that when they broke up – usually the slide would shatter – the men just dropped them in the bin, picked out a new one from the box and carried on firing.

We did an awful lot of night training, such as reconnaissance patrols, movement by night and map reading, ambushes and contact drills. We also had to man a picket every night on a hill outside the camp in case of guerrilla incursion. The security situation in South Africa was worsening and now, with Robert Mugabe in Zimbabwe, the African National Congress had another sympathetic communist border to hide behind.

We worked very hard for five months and became thorough in every aspect of our employment. In all my soldiering, I have never seen such a level of training and competence as there was among even the average member of the Pathfinders in 44 Parachute Brigade, but my enthusiasm began to wear the men down!

One morning I woke up at Reveille, at 4.30 a.m. as usual, had my cup of tea and started to feel rather groggy. I shook myself and marched out on muster parade with the men lined up in three ranks. When I came to attention to present the parade to Captain Botes, my legs buckled and I nearly fell over.

'Have you been taking drugs, Sergeant Major?' demanded Captain Botes in a shocked voice.

'No, sir!' I replied, trying to stand up straight.

'Have you been drinking?'

He watched, amazed, as I wobbled about in front of him.

'No, sir!' I said, furiously trying to get a grip of myself.

'Well, what the hell is wrong with you?'

'I don't know, sir! Permission to lie down, sir!'

'A very good idea, Sergeant Major!'

I wobbled off the parade and spent the rest of the day on the camp bed in my tent trying to understand what had happened to me. The men took a most gratifying interest in my well-being and kept me supplied with cups of coffee and Coca-Cola. For five days, I suffered, wobbling in and out of my tent as I fought to stay with the training programme.

Hazily, I began to piece together various remarks I was overhearing among the men, like, 'He seems to be perking up a bit!' and, 'Time to hit him with another dose!' and I realised the whole thing was a scam. The bastards had grovelled about feeding me with all these drinks just to keep me heavily tranquillised with Valium!

I was not the only one to suffer the combined humour of men from so many countries. Captain Pete Botes was very popular and a good soldier, but he was seriously Afrikaans and had a particular obsession with the fauna and flora of his country. One day, someone backed a truck into a small tree outside his tent and knocked it over. He flew into a rage, muttering about rare plants and damage to the environment and the men were rather taken aback. Next day he came out of his office to find the tree had been fitted with a medical splint and bandaged exactly as instructed during the medical lectures. Bemused, he stared at the tree and went off scratching his head.

After five months we returned to Murray Hill and I made a recce of the Drakensberg Mountains for a suitable place to hold our selection process for non-Paras. You might wonder why we did not select the men before training them so thoroughly, but we were building up the Pathfinders from nothing and we had to wait that long before we had enough men to work with. Anyway, Colonel Breytenbach had no intention of losing the failures, who he planned to post into non-combative roles in the brigade, as drivers or clerks in HQ.

Jane had given birth to a boy, Billy, on 1 November. I was delighted. Life was really looking up. Also, we had a place of our own, in a South African army quarter. Faced with an influx from Zimbabwe, the South Africans had put up mobile homes, which sounds grim, but in fact they were very nice indeed, spacious and extremely well appointed. We had nothing ourselves, but we moved straight into the quarter and lacked nothing. The South Africans treated all the ex-Rhodesian servicemen very well, and we lived comfortably for a charge of only 15 rand a month.

Jane got a job in the military hospital and we settled down to our own lives much as we had in Bindura. She was always very supportive; tolerant of my single-mindedness and the endless stream of friends who came to visit. One day, when I was running selection, the cook in Murray Hill failed to get up in time to give us an early breakfast which we wanted before driving into the Drakensberg, so I took all the eggs, bacon and sausages and we trucked off to my house where Jane cooked breakfast instead, for two dozen.

I ran the first selection in the Cathedral Peak area and we decided to make it short and sharp. We had already seen these men over all the previous months and formed a good assessment of their capabilities, so a final five days would set the seal. All ex-SAS and Selous Scouts were in theory exempt from this selection but I took part in it because I was their sergeant major. I wanted to show them we had all been through the same mill. We started with a twenty-four-hour march in full patrol gear, with rucksacks and a 82-lb ammunition box which I added as the sickener or 'embuggerance' factor. We carried that box up and down the hills for about forty kilometres and it was a real ball-breaker. It was a terrible weight, an impossible shape to carry and rubbed your shoulders bare. We slept out at night, as I had done for the Rhodesian SAS selection. This is a fine hardening process, and I have often wondered why the British SAS truck back to camp at nights during their selection.

We left our ammunition box behind after that first day, but the marches continued relentlessly. The Drakensberg are an impressive range of grass-covered mountains rising to 15,000 feet. One day we marched up hill and down dale for thirty-two kilometres with 50-lb loads. Next morning, the guys groaned aloud when I told them we were going to march all the way back again, and very scenic it was too! The South Africans are obsessed with runs, so we finished off with a short 2.4-kilometre run uphill in full gear and rucksack. We lost a few during this, as you may imagine, but the majority were determined, fit young men and we finished with seventeen good soldiers.

One of the men came in from a march between Champagne Castle and Cathedral Peak which had taken him sixteen hours and I said, 'What took you so long?'

Understandably annoyed, he said, 'I bet you couldn't do it.'

'Give me your rucksack,' I snapped and did it in twelve hours, a time which remained unbeaten for a good while. I was very fit then.

We divided our new men into two sections, one commanded by Sergeant Major Dennis Croucamp, an ex-Selous Scout who was excellent on recce work, and returned north to Mabalique. Meanwhile, Colonel Breytenbach was pushing the army 'system' to employ us on the Namibian border with Angola, so I set about perfecting our live camp attack training. I wanted to get the men used to the reality of live fire and the blast of shrapnel overhead. For example, as we crawled up to the start line for a camp attack, which I had put right on the edge of the safety distance for mortar bombs landing on our target 'enemy' camp, I would be counting the number of high explosive mortar bombs landing in front of us. At a pre-arranged number, say eighteen, the mortar team would switch without a break to firing smoke bombs, and as I counted the burst of the last HE round, I shouted, 'Stand up!' and we began to advance, using 'fire and movement' into the camp while the smoke bombs continued to drop ahead of us. It was good realistic training and it was to come in very useful indeed.

In January 1981, after some Christmas leave, Dennis Croucamp took twenty men up to the Angolan border and I followed with another eight in February. We were attached to 'C' Company of the 1st Para Battalion for an operation on a small town thirty miles over the Angolan border called Quamato. This was at a time when South Africa was vigorously denying it had anyone inside Angola!

My new enemy was SWAPO, the South West African People's Organisation, which was the liberation and nationalist movement for Namibia. Like other African guerrilla movements, SWAPO was communist, trained by Russians and East Germans and supplied by the Soviets. SWAPO claimed to represent all Namibia, but, like the other African liberation movements I had encountered, SWAPO was recruited tribally. The majority of SWAPO recruits came from the Ovambo tribe which occupied the northern half of Namibia and made up 46 per cent of the population. Now I had come full circle in Africa. SWAPO guerrilla bases in southern Angola were supported by the Marxist MPLA which I had first come across during the chaotic days of January 1976 when I was in Holden Roberto's FNLA.

Then, in 1976, SWAPO was an emergent and weak force of about

2,000 men, but once the Portuguese left Angola, it grew rapidly in the fertile communist ground of Marxist Angola to over 10,000. More important, SWAPO was able to transfer its bases from Zambia, which were well out of the area of their interest far down the Caprivi Strip, to communist Angola and infiltrate Namibia directly over a long frontier. By the time I joined the South African Army, the security situation in Namibia was beyond the control of the South African Police and was firmly in the hands of the South African Army.

All this may sound similar to the problems which had faced Smith's Rhodesian regime, but South Africa had three great advantages; it was not completely surrounded by land frontiers, it had a much larger white population (4 million among some 20 million blacks in 1976) and it had economic strength. The South Africans were horrified by the prospect of a double threat from terrorism, from the ANC in the east, through communist Mozambique and Zimbabwe, and from SWAPO in the west, through communist Angola. The government took special measures. It doubled the length of its national service to twenty-four months, recruited Asians, coloureds and blacks into the army, and developed its own arms industry. The result was to produce a standing army of some 70,000 men with a total mobilisation of 400,000 available by calling up the Reserves, the Citizen Force and local 'home-guard' Kommandos. Of these, about 30,000 to 40,000 were employed in Namibia at any one time.

And South Africa took the offensive. They had considerable business interests in Namibia and, rather than let SWAPO keep the initiative, with the usual round of terrorist attacks on police stations, bridges and small towns, the SADF struck out at specific SWAPO bases inside Angola and kept the problem at bay. This was a similar strategy to the Claret operations in Borneo and the Rhodesian cross-border camp attacks, like Chimoio and Tembue. Because of its size, South Africa was not so severely affected by the international pressure which had hampered Rhodesia's strategic decisions. There seems to be no doubt that cross-border attacks to punish terrorists in their resting places and training camps is an essential ingredient to winning a counter-insurgency war. When I came back to Britain, I wondered at the situation in Northern Ireland. Of course, this brand of military action is nothing without the political will to see it through.

Cross-border attack does not mean invasion. In 1975, South Africa tried conventional military invasion and found it did not work. The SADF was obliged to withdraw from southern Angola, after a spectacularly successful attack, for very similar reasons which had made the Israelis quit Lebanon. They realised they did not want the ground they had captured and that just pushing back the border did not prevent terrorism. Instead, the SADF employed an effective combination of supporting Jonas Savimbi's UNITA inside Angola; encouraging anti-communist resistance among tribes like the Ovimbundu and Chokwe which were hostile to the Ovambos and the Angolan Government; and sudden SADF strikes against SWAPO camps in Angola. Our attack on Quamato was one such strike.

Quamato was a town about thirty miles inside Angola, a miserable cluster of single-storey buildings dotted round a dusty main street, painted in typical Portuguese pastel pinks and greens, lying heavy with neglect in the flat sandy scrublands of southern Angola. Intelligence said that SWAPO and FAPLA (the armed wing of the MPLA) were stationed there. We flew to the forming-up point near the town in Puma helicopters and advanced into the town only to find the place was deserted. I noticed two things. There was a strong, sweet smell of human occupation, and washing was hanging out to dry, some of it still wet. That meant the enemy had been there that morning, and fled, probably hearing the beat of the heavy Puma rotor blades, or maybe SWAPO had lookouts nearer the border. As if to confirm this, our pilots informed us that they had seen plenty of uniformed enemy moving out north. 'C' Company was ordered to advance and flush them out.

We found them, all right. About seven miles north of the town, all hell suddenly let loose somewhere at the front. The ground was flattish and sandy but obscured by thorny trees and scrub bushes and out of sight ahead the forward elements of the Paras had stumbled across a heavily defended SWAPO and FAPLA camp. The firing was intense, tearing through the branches above us, and stoppped the leading platoon dead in its tracks. I happened to be near the front, crouched down with the platoon officer and heard the company commander's voice on the radio. He was further back nearer the town and said we needed to keep up the momentum of our advance to get a foothold in the camp.

The young platoon officer, called Lieutenant du Plessis, turned to me and said, 'Do you think you can break in there?'

'Dear Lord!' I said to myself, staring at the bushes for a moment where a horrendous volume of fire was ripping the leaves off the trees just over our heads. 'Why me?' I thought. The front sections had taken casualties and were pinned down on one side of a wide open clearing about 150 yards across. Both sides were busy shooting shit out of each other, trying to win the firefight. Plainly, on the other side was a full-blooded SWAPO camp with all the trimmings; trenches, underground bunkers, heavy machine gun positions, anti-aircraft guns, and beyond I could hear the hollow thwack of their 82mm mortars coming into action.

Crouching, I moved forward in cover of bushes to look at that short piece of open ground between us and them. It seemed like a mile across. I considered zigzagging across or doing it in bounds of fire and movement, and then decided that the best way was just to storm across in a straight line. I said to the young National Service officer, 'Can you give me as much cover as you can, lay down a heavy base of fire support? We'll cross as fast as we can.'

Du Plessis agreed and I called up my Pathfinders for some quick orders. 'Now we earn our pay!' I said urgently, crouching down. In my excitement, my quick attack orders tumbled out in short staccato sentences. I watched their faces and felt proud. I knew how hard they had trained. I could feel their confidence and the momentum of the attack building up. My hand stabbed this way and that. I pointed out the ground, the place where I wanted to force a way into the camp, the location of supporting fire from the other Paras, and I finished with, 'We've done this a thousand times before in training, now it's for real! I'm asking you to put yourselves in my hands. Follow me!'

And we charged straight over that open ground. God knows, I've never felt bullets cracking round me like that, but we lost no one and killed six enemy as we burst into their first line of trenches. My grandfather, Old Miles, told me about being on the receiving end of heavy fire in the First World War, and SWAPO certainly poured out a heavy volume of fire. I could feel it in the air round us, but, thank God, it was not effective.

We held on in these trenches and supplied covering fire for the follow up. A 'Valk' of twelve Paras (half a Dakota-load) charged over the open ground behind us into the SWAPO trenches on our right. Immediately hand to hand fighting ensued in which two South Africans were killed but they held on.

We took another bunker. I threw a white phosphorus grenade inside, stepped aside as it exploded and suddenly a black SWAPO soldier burst out covered in flames. He was understandably agitated and very aggressive. I aimed to shoot him with my South African Galil but the bloody thing jammed! Without hesitation, I swung the Galil and started to beat him up with the butt, to stop him shooting me, till thankfully someone behind me leaned over my shoulder and shot the man dead. These South African Galils, called SA R-4s, commonly jammed with double-feeds (when not one but two rounds are picked up from the magazine) because they used different metals to the Israeli Galil and overheated with heavy use. We certainly gave them heavy use that day.

More Paras poured in behind us and we tried to fight our way through the camp. It was enormous and well defended and we got bogged down as darkness fell. Our helicopter K-car gunships could no longer support us with their 20mm cannons. To my fury, we were ordered to pull out. All that effort for nothing! The young platoon officer had no alternative. Orders were orders, but as we withdrew, the enemy realised what we were doing and went completely crazy. They opened up with everything they had, pasting us with mortars and we could hear the thudding racket of large calibre ZU 23mm anti-aircraft machine guns winched down for use in the ground role. We lost another man killed and two wounded on the way out and Lieutenant du Plessis was hit in the back with shrapnel near me. I picked him up and carried him out of the firefight on my back.

We retreated, or as the military prefer to call it, withdrew, several miles back from the SWAPO camp to Quamato and dug trenches on the edge of the town. It had been a long dangerous day and all for nothing. I must admit I was angry at the waste. We had lost three dead and five wounded in 'C' Company for no gain. I was so fired up inside the camp that I had wanted to dig in right where we were and fight on the next morning, but I said nothing.

The problem was that SWAPO were a tougher enemy than ZANLA and ZIPRA had been in Rhodesia, and the South Africans could not afford the political and social criticism of losing too many men in one day. They had to pursue their aims with a very wary eye on casualties, however committed the white population may have been to fighting terrorism.

Later, another officer, Lieutenant Taylor, told me that he had written me up for a bravery citation. Nothing ever came of it, and later Taylor was himself killed. I mention this only because I have not hidden anything in this account and by now you will have made up your own mind about whether I invent things or rot. I would have been very proud to have received an award, especially for Jane and my little son Billy, but the fact that I was not accepted made no difference to my feelings towards the South Africans. They treated us foreigners well and fairly, probably because they were a bigger, more established state than Rhodesia had been and possibly because the Paras were more straightforward and honest about other men's performances, being regular troops, than the SAS. Of course, they aways made fun of us, calling me, 'Fucking Sotpeel', 'Sotty' or

'Roineck' as a term of affection, meaning that us foreigners had only one foot in South Africa because the other was still in England and our balls in the ocean, but we always got on well.

Perhaps this was because I felt that I blended into the regular army system here better than I had elsewhere. I had a rank which I could handle, I felt I was functioning properly and had something to offer. Also the South African Army, with a standing strength of 70,000 men, was much bigger than the Rhodesian Army had been, where the regular combat units were only the RLI, the SAS and the Selous Scouts, totalling some 3,000 men, excluding the two battalions of Rhodesian African Rifles, the Rhodesia Regiment and all the part-time call-up men.

At six o'clock the following morning, the SWAPO enemy camp was given a thorough softening up. We waited in our trenches watching Mirages screaming overhead to neutralise the mortars and 23mm anti-aircraft ZU-23–2s with bombs and rockets. Once the anti-aircraft guns were out of action, sixteen Alouette gunship K-cars swooped in with their 20mm cannon and they really pounded the place. The racket carried on all morning, reaching us quite clearly over the trees beyond the edge of town. At midday, we flew in Pumas to attack again.

My Puma touched down in a clearing among the low scrubby trees and we had no sooner jumped out than we were under fire. We caught sight of four FAPLA men hiding in bushes trying to load an RPG7 to fire at the Puma and blasted them. One died immediately and the rest stuck their hands straight in the air. By contrast to my experiences in Rhodesia, these men were made POWs and taken back for interrogation, more use to Intelligence alive than dead.

We advanced in a sweep line through the dense trees towards the camp and spent the rest of the day clearing one line of trenches after another. The K-cars had really shot the guts out of SWAPO but we still went through our drills, attacking with covering fire, firing, doubling forward, firing again, grenading the trenches and underground bunkers, firing into them to make sure the enemy were dead, consolidating and moving on.

In the darkness of one deep bunker, I was nearly caught out by the enemy's old trick of pretending to be dead. As I moved cautiously inside, shining my torch about, out of the corner of my eye I spotted the glistening skin of a black SWAPO guerrilla behind me. There was no time to turn my body. In an instant, I swung my pistol up and over my left shoulder and shot him three times.

That evening the Pumas lifted us out altogether and flew us back to a South African army base in Ondangwa, a large town sixty-three kilometres south of the Angolan border.

Quamato had been a good start for the Pathfinders, but Colonel Breytenbach ordered me back to 'The Republic' to train another batch of Pathfinder recruits. The turnover was too large and he needed more men. This was partly the South Africans' own fault, as they signed men on for only one year. By the time their training was up, they had precious little time for operations, and most men, given the chance to leave the army, behaved like soldiers anywhere and quit. After all, the pay, about 300 rand a month for a trooper, was no incentive to stay. Even Captain Pete Botes left, because there was no career planning for his future in the army.

Some of the men may have found the South African Army rather more formal than the Rhodesian Army, where most of us came from. The regular cadre of the SADF were the senior ranks, staff sergeants and above in the Sergeants' Mess, and captains and above in the Officers' Mess. Many of them did not like to see troopers and privates in the Pathfinders with five or ten years' service who did not jump to attention for them. They were used to dealing with young National Servicemen and Reserves. For example, a South African sergeant major never queued at the camp barber's for a haircut; he just walked in and whoever was sitting in the chair with his hair being cut had to leap out of the way at once and wait till the barber had finished with the sergeant major. In all National Service armies there is a confusion between true discipline and just fucking the men about.

The South African sense of humour was rather straight-laced, with a strong religious bent, so there was uproar when they saw a mannequin's hand stuck up outside one of the Pathfinder's tents with condensed milk dripping off it and a sign which read, 'Hand jobs available within'. The mannequins, by the way, were part of a deception plan. When patrols went out in a truck to be dropped off near the border, they hopped out in cover of some bushes and the driver's mate, riding shotgun, stayed behind to set up a row of these mannequins, wearing natty camo hats set at a jaunty angle, to make the locals think the truck was still occupied.

On another occasion, the Pathfinders encouraged a young officer to blow up the reservoir at the top of Murray Hill camp. Lieutenant Brown was a very self-obsessed young Permanent Force engineer officer who became fascinated with mosquito larvae breeding on the water in the warm weather. He decided the only solution was to blow a breach in the earth bank of the dam and release the bad surface water. He also wanted to impress the Pathfinders. They thought this was a wonderful plan and egged him on no end. They sat about in the sun on the grassy bank of the reservoir while Lieutenant Brown sweated buckets digging holes in the earth bank, rammed in pounds of plastic explosive, tamped and blew it, sending up showers of earth and newly planted trees. All afternoon, explosions shattered the peace of Murray Hill and officers all over the camp wondered what sort of training was going on. Guy Gibson, as the Pathfinders had by now christened Lieutenant Brown, after the Dam Busters' pilot, slaved on and his breach grew bigger and bigger. Finally, a little water trickled over the top. Exhausted, filthy with earth, but triumphant, he turned to his audience and said, 'How's that then?'

'That's great, sir. Great!' said the Pathfinders, thoroughly entertained. 'But why didn't you just let out the water with the valve gates over there, at the side of the dam?'

They wandered off, leaving him shell-shocked on the earth-spattered grass bank among a wreckage of tree stumps with water pouring through the cratered, muddy breach. The commandant was not amused.

The new selection course started and an ex-British SAS officer called Major Alistair McKenzie joined the SADF to reorganise and formalise the Pathfinders' training. He preferred to run selection along modern British SAS lines, reducing the weights carried on the hill marches and studying the timings carefully. He also cleared out the nooks and crannies in the brigade where the inevitable freeloaders were hiding. He wanted professional standards and did not care how unpopular he made himself. I admired his attitude and I think we got on well.

Of course the first lot of Pathfinders complained that the new course was not tough enough, echoing that typical refrain beloved of all specialised units, 'Selection isn't as hard as it was in my day. There's no 82-lb ammo box to carry for a start!'

However, the men continued as committed as before and Alistair McKenzie went up to Angola to see what the Pathfinders were doing on operations. While he was there he blew a road culvert. Shortly afterwards, he left the SADF.

Colonel Breytenbach was posted to a command on the Namibian-Angolan border and we had a new commanding officer called Colonel Frank Bestbier. Within days, he decided the Pathfinder Company should be transferred lock, stock and barrel to join the Reconnaissance Platoon of 32 Battalion. This was the best of the South African infantry battalions, as it was permanently posted on operations and filled with experienced men. It was composed of retrained anti-communist black soldiers, who had been in UNITA and the FNLA, and was used extensively to conduct 'search and destroy' sweeps in enemy areas and to conduct attacks on the Angolan economic infrastructure.

Colonel Bestbier called me to his office and asked me to train groups of Citizen Force Territorials on their National Service, at Murray Hill, and then take them on operations in Angola. I readily agreed. This gave me the best of both worlds, training at home when I could see Jane and my son, and taking the men I had trained on operations. He let me select my training team and I chose four men from the Pathfinders: Derek Andrews, Terry Tagney, Chris Rogers, and Jock Philips.

The South Africans called their Territorials up in companies of about 200 strong, and my first group went on operations for two terribly uneventful months during which 2 Para skirmished with SWAPO and FAPLA inside Angola, through Namacunde to Ondjiva. The only thing I can remember about this trip was the convoy out, back to Namibia. I was in the cab of a big 'Kwevoel' six-wheel truck and we were towing a trailer stacked with Commandant Montagu Brett's company office equipment, plus items Brett had liberated to make life comfortable during our stay in Angola. Only fortune dictates that a whole line of vehicles passes down a road before one finally sets off a mine. We drove over a mine on the very culvert which Alistair McKenzie had blown before. Fortunately, the cab passed over the mine which exploded under the wheels of the back axle, blasting the trailer up and forward in a huge arc till it crashed down on top of the truck above us in a shower of paper files, chair legs and typewriter keys which fluttered down like sycamore seeds.

The Territorials were so keen to get back after their stint that the column carried on.

'You stay here, Sergeant Major,' said the officer in charge of the convoy. 'You've got twenty-three men to guard the broken truck and I'll get them to send out a recovery vehicle as soon as I reach the border.'

I was not impressed. Recovery might take hours, and I had heard on the radio net that HQ reckoned SWAPO were converging on the area.

I inspected the damage. The two back wheels of our 'Kwevoel' were smashed, but the other two axles, the engine and the winch at the back seemed all right. So I took the wire from the winch, pulled it up and over the whole truck, across the underneath of the trailer, attached it to the front of the trailer and started the winch. The wire strained alarmingly but it gradually winched the trailer upwards in a big circle off the top of the truck till it toppled over and bounced back onto the road. We straightened it out and limped south to Santa Clara on the border that same night.

Operation Daisy was busier. Special forces Recce Commando units had reported heavy concentrations of between 1,000 and 1,500 SWAPO in the Techematet area inside Angola, near Cassinga, and a big combined airborne-armoured operation was mounted. The East Germans trained SWAPO as conventional troops rather than terrorists living among the civil population and they were heavily armed. The South African politicians allowed the SADF to strike at SWAPO camps with all the force they could muster, and concealed the SADF's real impact by constantly denying cross-border operations. Operation Daisy was the deepest penetration of Angola since 1975.

The SADF armoured cars, called Rattels, looked rather top-heavy with their 'Eland' gun turrets, but were born out of necessity and suited the environment. They were wheeled, for the sandy flat country, fired 76mm or 90mm shells, and had a distinct advantage over others because they carried not 46 rounds, which is normal in a European armoured car, but 200 rounds. They were to drive to the target while the Paras did a parachute drop to pin down the enemy till they arrived.

We were training a Para battalion at the time, in 44 Para Brigade and the battalion filled six Hercules C130 aircraft. We were dropped at night, about 2 a.m., over the sandy, scrubby dropping zone (DZ) at an operational jump height of 500 feet and as usual I was wildly fired up with excitement as I jumped. When I stripped off my parachute on the ground it made a stirring sight to see and hear the other big aircraft trundle overhead and watch hundreds of parachutes floating down. Our DZ was just off target so we could reorganise without having to fight the enemy at the same time, and, as sergeant major in charge of DZ rallying, I spent a very busy two hours running round in the darkness gathering the men together in their fighting formations, including one plane-load which was dropped off line. I was pleased with the time, and the whole battalion was ready for action, with the leading companies moving off the DZ as dawn lightened the sky.

Each company had a a different area, and was to find the enemy by advancing to contact. Each one had a group of my Pathfinders, to lead the advance and navigate. I was with 'C' Company. Midmorning, we stood among scrub bushes and trees and looked across a wide, dried-up swamp, called a flay. These flays become very soggy in the wet season and tall grasses grow thickly, but then it was dry, open and caked hard. The company moved across in bounds, one platoon covering another onto the slight hill on the other side of the flay. In the lead, I breasted the top of this hill and spotted movement in more scrub and trees seventy metres beyond. I ordered Corporal Sean Wyatt to keep his eye on the place while a platoon moved into a sweep line behind us. Suddenly someone fired their rifle by mistake. In answer, the enemy opened up on us from their cover in the trees. Everyone fired back and Sean loosed off his 40mm grenade launcher at the leaves we had seen twitching. We assaulted across the open ground. Moments later, as we fought into the trees, we discovered the grenade had hit a man right in the chest. Of course everyone else had fired too so they all claimed a hit. And what a hit it was! The dead man turned out to be SWAPO's second-in-command of logistics. Of course, he was rather beyond interrogation but there was a goldmine of information in papers we found in a leather pouch on his belt. Strange how the communist system lets itself down in these wars with its obsession for keeping details on its members and their activities.

The second day, the sweeps continued with sporadic contacts all over the area of operations under a baking hot sun. It would be no exaggeration to say we walked and skirmished over sixty-five miles or so in these two days. As sergeant major, I had a lot of chasing about to do and I must admit I began to feel my age! We were promised five litres of water per man per day, but it did not always reach us. I made every man parachute with extra water canisters, but that supply was long gone. I also ordered them to carry a trauma pack each. The drips carried were usually 0.9 per cent normal saline. Giving sets were also carried which could be connected via a plastic to administer the fluid. The drip bag and giving set were packed ready for immediate use, with the needle fitted to the tubing and three strips of sticky tape ready to attach the set to the arm. Casualties could be given the contents of their drip without delay and it was also handy because you could drink the fluid if you went down with heat exhaustion.

That day, I suddenly passed out on the march during the afternoon and woke up to find the doctor sticking a needle in my arm to fit me up with my drip. It was strange to feel burning hot one minute, with the sweat pouring off me, and suddenly cooling down as the drip slipped into my veins the next.

The SADF realised they had a serious heat exhaustion problem.

Their answer was typical of the universal sense of emergency in South Africa at that time. They stripped a Coca-Cola factory of its two-litre plastic bottles to fill with extra water and choppered in crates to the troops.

Heat, rationing and water supply were always important features of any operation in this dry, sandy and barren area, as was the disposal of rubbish and soil. On Operation Daisy, I recall being able to smell the pungent sweet stench of the latrine pits hundreds of yards away as we walked through trees into the base camp. Not enough quicklime (even cement can be used) was being sprinkled on the excrement every day. On another operation, we dug a tin pit where we threw our rubbish and scraps, and there was so little food anywhere in Angola that I reckon every bloody dog in the country was in this tin pit at night, howling and fighting in rival packs. We could not get a wink of sleep. Finally, Derek Andrews lost his patience. He set up a Claymore anti-personnel mine over the pit and soaked the place in petrol. That night, the howling began as usual until suddenly there was an enormous explosion, an eyeball-searing ball of flame which lit the dark trees around, and we lay on the ground listening to the the sound of shrieking dogs fading at speed into the night. For days afterwards, we saw nothing but bald, hairless dogs with charred eye-lashes wandering about in a daze. For a while at least, we slept fine.

Fresh rations are always vital to troops in the field living off tins. When we were resupplied with bags of vegetables, mainly potatoes and cabbages, the South African National Servicemen simply did not know what to do with them. I took charge and instructed the cooks how to make bubble and squeak. The troopies thought it was delicious and we lived on it for days.

Another operation, Carnation this time, pushed FAPLA and SWAPO back from Ondjiva altogether. Now we could fly straight from the Republic and air-land inside Angola at Ondjiva which became a staging base for our attacks further inside Angola. The South Africans gave Ondjiva to UNITA to control, treating the area as liberated and turning Mao Tse Tung's own communist principle of a People's War on its head. This allowed the SADF to penetrate deeper into Angola and attack SWAPO bases further away without worrying about the areas near the border. Also, regular SADF troops were not tied down protecting captured areas, as had happened in 1975.

Ondjiva at that time even used South African currency. This was a pity because my Pathfinders and I were digging trenches on the edge of Ondjiva airfield and we discovered a large box which contained no less than 60 million Angolan Kwanzas! Presumably this treasure was being used to finance SWAPO. In theory, the official rate was, as far as I can remember, 32 Kwanzas to a pound Sterling, but in practice no one wanted Kwanzas and we treated it like Monopoly money. I divided up the loot among the men who went round like children with great wads of paper money, like Kelly's Heroes, played cards with it and argued about who was richer than who.

As always, when operations were uneventful, boredom set in and standards began to slip. Only a couple of months of operations is not enough to turn National Servicemen and Territorials or even regulars into experienced combat troops, and maybe the intrinsic anarchy of operations loosened discipline too. Whatever the cause, men started to sunbathe by their trenches in Ondjiva, lounging about bollock naked on the sand. I did not agree with this at all. I went round picking men up for being improperly dressed. One of their officers called Lieutenant Peter de Klerk objected. He was a student at Cape Town University doing his National Service in 44 Para Brigade. He said to me, 'I think you're being too harsh on the men, Sergeant Major.'

I looked at him standing there in just boots and yellow underpants and replied, 'I don't think so, sir. We're on operations.'

'But this is South Africa, land of sun.'

It was the land of shorts as well, like Rhodesia had been. At this point, our conversation was interrupted by shouts of alarm. A Soviet BRDM armoured car was tearing across the airfield behind. It was actually a UNITA vehicle, but Lieutenant de Klerk thought it was attacking the position. He grabbed a RPG7 anti-tank rocket and the last thing I saw was this absurd-looking young officer sprinting after it dressed only in boots and yellow underwear!

There was nothing wrong with the spirit of these young officers, even if their military professionalism was at times a little relaxed. In fact, Lieutenant de Klerk joined us later on the training team.

Ondjiva was a wreck by now, with few civilians left who could stand the constant battering and looting by FAPLA and SWAPO. Our battalion commander, Commandant Monty Brett, said, 'I can't have my men sitting on the ground!' All the shops were empty, so he ordered us to liberate vital items from the town, for the proper comfort of the men in the field. Among other things, the Town Hall yielded some rather fine old colonial Portuguese furniture: a set of high-backed chairs and the long table from the council chamber.

Major Jet van Zyl, the company commander, gathered us under

the tent shelter he used as a briefing room and gave us orders for our next operation. We were to attack Evale, a town about forty miles north of Ondjiva and sixty-five miles inside Angola. After two days preparing our rations and ammunition, we drove north in armoured Buffel troop carriers and four-wheel Samil-29 trucks to form a HAG. This was Afrikaans for a helicopter administration location, like the Rhodesian Forward Air Field (FAF), and contained everything, including bulging bladders of AVGAS, fire-fighting bowsers, boxes of ammunition and a medical first-aid post.

The plan was for the Alouettes and Pumas to lift us from this HAG directly into the attack. Van Zyl's briefing gave us to expect about eighty SWAPO, commonly called Garden Boys by the South Africans, so we all expected a good day's jousting, as firefights with the enemy were termed. It did not work out quite like that.

I was left in charge of the HAG, much to my annoyance. Even back there I knew things had gone wrong. When the first lift went in, they found not 80 Garden Boys but 300 Garden Boys, with some rather large tools. Like 14.5mm and 23mm HMGs, 82mm mortars and a call on Soviet T54 tanks at Mupa. In addition, they were well trained and stiffened by large numbers of East Germans. Our choppers ferried the troops in and when they returned to my HAG, we picked up the pilots' shocked radio messages, relayed back via a rebroadcasting station in a Bosbok light fixed-wing aircraft orbiting high above us. The pilots reported very heavy resistance and seeing white faces and East German uniforms in the defensive trenches and among the houses of the town. This was confirmed when our ground troops joined battle on the edge of Evale. The ground comms radio buzzed with reports of heavy machine-gun fire and being accurately pasted by the enemy 82mm mortars, which were almost certainly being organised by the East Germans. Within half an hour, we had suffered ten wounded. The Alouette helicopters flew in under fire to lift them out and landed back in the HAG peppered with holes. I could tell things were grim. I detected a feeling of panic and felt very frustrated being left out of it.

Major Jet van Zyl came down in his command helicopter to refuel in the HAG. Over the noise of other choppers landing, I shouted at him, 'Sir! The guys are having trouble. They're National Servicemen up there and not many with experience. Can I join them, to see if I can help?' I was fired up and at my most persuasive. I hated seeing them coming back all shot up and not being able to contribute.

'Yes,' said van Zyl without hesitation. From his position in the air, he had seen the battle was getting out of hand.

A big Puma took me forward hugging the tops of the trees covering the flat savannah landscape. Ahead, I could see the low rooftops of Evale where the sky was filled in all directions with streams of green and red tracer and white vapour trails of SAM missiles being fired at the Alouettes and the noise of battle was fearsome. Nearer the edge of the town, we saw an Alouette K-car lurching and dropping through the air towards us. We learned later it had been badly shot up when the pilot landed to pick up the crew of another K-car which had been destroyed on the ground by enemy machine guns as it tried to rescue some wounded Paras. The pilot was later awarded the Honorus Crux Gold, the highest South African bravery award. His Alouette was heavily over-loaded with Paras and the crew from the other K-car and I gestured at him to land wherever he could. Our Puma set down beside him and we took the men, with the wounded and one dead Para, off the Alouette so it could limp back to the HAG.

Back in the HAG, I shoved all the casualties, by then one dead and seventeen wounded from the company of eighty, on our one Puma. The pilot only just made take-off.

After only an hour, the Paras claimed to have killed forty-eight but their own casualties were politically unacceptable. We had failed to enter the town and our commanders decided to withdraw until the armour closed up. I must admit I found it strange they never had the armour there in the first place, because Paras on their own never have enough firepower to overcome the sort of well-organised and well-defended positions we found at Evale.

A withdrawal is always difficult, especially after hard fighting which introduces its own strain of chaos. A sharp explosion went off in the HAG, which I believe was someone accidentally firing a 40mm grenade launcher, and a young National Serviceman in a truck started screaming, 'Mortars! Mortars! Incomers!'

Men began to panic. The young National Serviceman in the truck went on screaming hysterically and I did what anyone does to someone with hysteria, regardless of rank. Without delay, I hopped up to the cab and slapped him a couple of times round the face. He quietened, his face white, but things were still on the brink, with men driving about and pushing and shoving. I found Major Jet van Zyl in the mêlée and said, 'Sir! With respect, the attack belongs to the officers, but the withdrawal is ours! Permission for the NCOs to organise this withdrawal, sir?'

He looked at me a moment, at the open space in the trees around us, at the choppers coming in and out, at the piles of stores scattered round and his men running about in all directions and said, 'It's all yours, Sergeant Major.'

He and the other officers left me to it and I restored order. As the Para sections were choppered back from the fighting round Evale I calmly lined them up on a track. When the whole company was accounted for, we embussed in trucks which HQ had sent forward for us and trundled back to our camp.

At the same time, the Russian T54 tanks from Mupa were driving into Evale on the other side of town. We had nothing to stop them. South African radio intelligence confirmed a heavy East German presence so we left them to it. South Africa's fight was with SWAPO, not with the East Germans. Also, the East Germans could fight.

As the end of my contract with the South African Army grew closer, I decided I must do one more operation and one more parachute jump. I have never agreed with those soldiers who think there is a time when they can hang up their boots and coast along in an easy job to their retirement. The sentiment, 'I'm running down to demob,' is bad enough among cooks, drivers and medics, but in specialist parachute units it is nothing short of disgusting.

My last operation with the South African Army took place on Mupa, some 100 kilometres north of Evale and 200 kilometres inside Angola. The SADF attacks into Angola penetrated deeper and deeper, continuously forcing SWAPO to increase the safe distance between them and the border they had to cross into Namibia. We were allocated to a composite group of 32 Battalion and Paras from 44 Brigade. We were flown in by Puma helicopters to 32 Battalion's area of operations to attack the Mupa FAPLA/SWAPO administration base. To preserve secrecy, we were dropped off some distance from the enemy camp and began the approach march.

I found this excruciatingly painful. I had twisted a knee ligament on a parachute jump not long before and it started to play me up. The South African Army were very good with their medical support, knowing full well how vital it was to let soldiers know they would receive instant care if they were wounded, and they employed doctors down to platoon level on operations. Our company had four platoons, so we had four doctors with us. One of them looked at my knee and said straightaway, 'You should be casevaced for this.'

I shook my head. 'Just give me some painkillers, Doc. I can't call in a chopper just for me. I'll wait till we attack the camp.' There were bound to be other casualties then.

We marched twenty kilometres that day along narrow winding tracks through the flat countryside. The grey dusty earth was trodden hard by countless people, local tribesmen and enemy soldiers. On each side, soft knee-length grass grew among the savannah scrub and low trees which stretched for miles in all directions. We stopped and lay on the ground in a defensive position for the night and by morning my knee was worse, stiff and painful. The doctor gave me a painkiller called Deloxene and I carried on, determined to see the operation through. It was not to be.

At dawn, we continued to follow these narrow tracks through the flat bush and trees. I was at the back of the company and almost 100 men had passed along the track when I heard a soft roaring explosion a couple of men in front of me. One of the soldiers had stepped on an anti-personnel mine. Some of the men near him started to run and help but I roared at them, 'Stop! Stand still!'

I had seen this situation many times. The enemy laid these AP mines in the line of march on the track itself, which was only about eighteen inches wide. There might have been others not set off yet. One hundred men had walked past this mine and quite possibly there were others they had not trodden on as well. I also knew the enemy very rarely doubled the booby trap with other mines laid out to the flank of the track, to catch people bypassing the scene of the first explosion. I moved several paces directly away from the track through the grass, turned at right angles and walked carefully along parallel to the track, very carefully looking through the grass ahead of me to look for more mines. Then, when I was opposite the wounded man, I turned at right angles again and came in towards him.

His foot had gone. There was just a torn stump of bone and sinew. No blood. The flesh was cauterised by the fire of the explosion. I felt terrible physical sympathy looking at him. He was so young, no more than nineteen. His life had been utterly, irrevocably changed. He stared at me, his eyes wide in shock and cried out, 'I'm an athlete, Sergeant Major. I'm a Springbok!'

I knelt down beside him and held him in my arms. There was nothing else I could do.

I shouted for everyone to search the track immediately round them in case there were more mines.

The young man in my arms began to cry. He was thinking of his career as an athlete. Gone like his foot. In an instant. Happily, he could feel no pain, yet. While the others cleared the track, I could do no more than hold him tight in my arms, like a son, while the tears rolled down his sweat-stained cheeks, and he gazed at the ground, bemused, shattered by what the mine had done to his life.

The doctor came up as soon as he could, moving on the cleared ground, and then someone at the back of the column shouted the alarm. An enemy vehicle was coming.

Our track had just led us across a road and the rear party could see a large Soviet ZIL truck trundling up the road towards us about a mile away.

I lost my temper. The pain of sympathy for that young Springbok turned to fury. I ran back down the track to the road and rapidly deployed the guys at the back of our column in immediate ambush positions. They ran and hid in the scrub at the side of the dirt road. Someone had dug a trench at the junction of the track and the road. There was a large tree beside it. I hid behind the tree and waited, seething with rage.

It's no good ambushing vehicles from the side of the road because the target is too fleeting. When the ZIL truck came up close, I stepped out in full view in the road and blasted the cab head on with my Galil, smashing the windscreen and raking the three enemy MPLA inside. As it passed, swerving and slowing up, I shot another enemy soldier sitting in the back.

The guys in their immediate ambush positions finished the truck off, pumping a fearsome weight of fire into it as it rolled past them to a stop. One enemy soldier jumped off with an RPG rocket which he fired off into the bushes. The rocket hit a water bottle on the belt of one of the South African soldiers. He was lucky. I suppose the water absorbed most of the energy of the explosion but a chunk was blown off his arse.

Now we had two badly wounded men and we needed a chopper casevac as soon as possible. When the Alouette arrived, I went back too. I hated to have to admit it, but my knee was excruciating. They flew us back to a HAG at Nehone, still 100 kilometres inside Angola, where I experienced the South African painkiller called Sosogen for the first time. This stuff is one step off morphine and has to be taken with Stematol to stop being violently sick. I was lying in the medical tent waiting for the Stematol when I felt the analgesic flooding inside my body and I was violently sick. The only container available was a mess tin and I can tell you it was inadequate to the task!

My last parachute jump in my remaining few weeks of service was equally full of foreboding. I joined a basic free-fall course being run for another group of trainee Pathfinders and had a malfunction. I dived from the Dakota at nine thousand feet and after thirty-five seconds' free-fall, I set up in the frog position to deploy my parachute, slightly head up to ease the shock of opening and pulled the handle. Nothing happened.

I beat the parachute pack with my elbows, hit it and kicked it with my feet. Vital seconds ticked past. I hurtled towards the ground. 'Nothing for it,' I thought automatically. 'Go for the reserve!'

Suddenly, before I had time to move, the main parachute popped open, deployed perfectly and I floated to the ground like a feather.

You must always get back on a horse after a fall. Parachute malfunctions do occur from time to time, and I went straight back to the jump centre for another parachute, strapped it on my back and went up in the next lift for another jump. I did not want to leave the army with a bad feeling like that. This time, it went fine and I felt back on form, but maybe in retrospect I should have taken the warning there and then.

Maybe, but then I'm not very good at giving up like that.

9

A State of Emergency

Saint Michael, patron of parachutists, protect us always.

My life seems to have been a series of violent swings from one extreme to another. Since things had been going well, perhaps I should have guessed I was due for a fall. However, I left the South African Army on a high, a warrant officer with a good report, which is given in Appendix C just to show the sceptics back home! I had managed to save some money for once, a remarkable feat for me, and Jane and I were really at peace with each other, happy with little Billy and our prospects. I hoped to get a new job with reasonable pay. A tall rather serious South African friend called Mark Adams, who had known me from Rhodesia days when he was an officer in the RLI (and on the Chimoio raid) and later served a shorter time than me in the SADF, recommended I join the company he was working for.

This was COIN Security Group (Pty) Ltd, a big South African security company based in Jan Niemand Park in Pretoria. The name was deliberately chosen to be the acronym for COunter INsurgency and at first glance it was all there; uniforms, ranks, armoured vehicles, weapons, badges, even medals. COIN supplied manpower, static and mobile guards and guard dogs to protect installations like factories, shops, stores and banks. In the increasingly uncertain atmosphere of South Africa, this was profitable work.

The managing director, John Bishop, interviewed me. He was a dark-haired man, always meticulously groomed with a penchant for good clothes and his greatest skill was in choosing the right men for the job. He had started COIN only a few years before with a dozen guards; when I joined there were about fifty and two years later there were nearly thirteen hundred. With such rapid expansion he needed men to handle his 'troops', the guards, and realised from his own National Service that the army could provide them. He had been a National Service corporal in the South African Army and been promoted year by year in the Territorials after each annual camp. By the time I met him, he liked to be called 'Major'. I could see that he deliberately cultivated a military image, but that seemed rather appropriate for a security company and he was enthusiastic about having me join the team. So was Yvonne Lottering, an attractive blonde woman in her thirties who was his marketing director and partner.

They offered me a job, and I accepted. A security company seemed to be the closest thing to the army, and at the relatively young age of forty-one, I didn't want all my past experience and the whole motivation of my life just to be wiped out when I walked through the camp gates for the last time into civvy street.

I set out to serve this new entity with the same enthusiasm I had displayed in my soldiering. I found the company very gung-ho, which I liked. John Bishop wanted to hear all the opinions of new men like me. We had some really constructive meetings about the constant expansion problems, and I felt we all had a common interest in getting on with the job. COIN was expanding rapidly and there was no time for unnecessary paperwork, office minutes, memos and reports.

Jane and I went to live in a rented company house in Jan Niemand Park. The house was a spacious bungalow with big rooms in a quiet residential road called, tellingly, Lamerwangerstraat. A lammerwanger in Afrikaans is a griffin, the symbol of 44 Parachute Brigade. In fact, several old army friends lived close by, from 44 Para Brigade and Rhodesia days, and life was looking up. Jane found a nursing job in the Huis Luzetta old people's home, also in Jan Niemand Park, close to home, and we settled into the local community well. I even began going to church with Jane every week. There is still a lurking vestige in me of the Catholicism of my early childhood, deeply implanted by the iron discipline of Sister Loyola and Father Brett, but I enjoyed the church for its sense of belonging to the community. The South Africans are very strong on religious background and social conformity. Belong to the club and you can go to heaven!

Every day I went to work in my Dihatsu Charade company car which I was paying for by instalments, and I worked long hours. We were on the go all the time, running round meeting clients, managing the guards and checking installations. South African businesses needed no persuading of the importance of security. Nelson Mandela was still in prison and the still-illegal African National Congress was increasingly active, with tremendous international support. Car-bombs, shootings and riots were common. In this atmosphere and having just left the army, I saw nothing strange about the way we always addressed each other by rank and the other deliberate parallels with army life.

My expertise has always been motivating the people working for me and the 'Major' gave me a job which entailed behaving as a sort of sergeant major over the black guards in an area. I discovered that the lower the rank in civvy street, the grander the title, so I started as a 'Senior Operations Commander' which we called SOC, copying the army's obsession with acronyms. In practice, as SOC, I was a general dogsbody for an operations manager. Between us, we kept the company's static guard operations in Pretoria running smoothly; including personnel, pay, discipline and guard rosters, timings, routes, locations on factory sites, and so on.

Most of our guards were from the black homelands, like Venda, Bushbok Ridge and Bophuthatswana, and they worked bloody long hours. In theory, they were supposed to work twelve-hour shifts, six days a week, and take one week off in seven. Most people who have worked shifts of twelve on, twelve off, would agree this was hard enough, but in practice they worked harder. All nattily turned out in their smart uniforms, these blacks did nearer fourteen hours on duty, adding the extra time for driving them to work and back, and signing on and off. Also, the company was so busy that the guards were commonly kept on the job seven days a week and their week off was cancelled. They were in no position to argue, apartheid or not. They needed the work to send money back to their families.

Under the DomPas (Domicile Pass) system, homeland blacks were not allowed by law to bring their families with them to the city, so the company provided living accommodation which was very basic. In Pretoria, they lived in a rectangular building made of concrete blocks and they slept on bunk beds, built into the walls like racking, three high to the ceiling. In Johannesburg they were racked four high to the ceiling. Sounds rough, but there was no point providing beds or movable furniture because the blacks always stole it and ran away. Also, the company had to pay a tax on each bed-space so our 400 blacks used the 'hot bed' system, to conserve space like sailors in a submarine. Two men shared one bunk bed: 200 were on duty while the other 200 slept. It's not surprising they were exhausted and I was constantly sweeping up the problems caused by men literally falling asleep on guard or going absent in desperation.

'Your guard was not on duty!' one client shouted at me. 'I came to the premises in the middle of the night and he wasn't there!'

I quickly worked out a system for dealing with this sort of complaint. I called it the toilet trick. With a deference I had not employed since talking to Sister Loyola as a boy, I inquired politely, 'When did you visit the premises, sir?'

'At 02.34 hours,' shouted the man. 'I noted the time exactly!' They always did that.

'And how long did you stay, sir?' I knew civilians like to check up on people, but they do not care to hang about in the middle of the night when a warm bed is calling. There doesn't seem to be any point. It was a crucial part of my ploy.

'Oh, I don't know. About ten minutes, I suppose.'

'Did you look in the toilet while you were there?' Crux question.

'Er, no.'

'Well, I'm sure the guard was on duty, sir, and don't you think it's possible that he was in the toilet?'

'Maybe.'

Then the ace. 'I mean, sir, even black men have to use the toilet on a twelve-hour shift.'

Grudging acceptance.

This excuse worked particularly well if the client was British. Whereas the South Africans had no interest whatsoever in a 'kaffir's' urinary habits, British clients retained some vestige of fair play in this vital biological regard!

Mind you, the black guards had little interest or pride in their work even though it provided them with a wage they could not earn anywhere else. Guards certainly got very tired, but they took every excuse to skive off. If we needed more than one on an installation, they decided among themselves who would stay awake while the others slept, got drunk, smoked dagga, or simply went absent.

The 'Major' was tireless in trying to control these lapses of discipline. He introduced fines. Every time a guard was found asleep, he had to pay a fine of 5 rand. I can still recall one black who was caught so many times that after six weeks' pay had been taken into account against his accumulated fines, he owed money to the company!

Guards going absent were a real problem. Clients were always furious, so the 'Major' also introduced a system of reserve guards who could be held back and used to fill the gaps of those who went absent on duty. The 'Major's' enthusiastic plan was that we could merely replace the missing man with another when we were called out, as our great selling line was that we were the only security company which drove the black guards to work ourselves, to make sure they got there. That was fine in theory, but in practice, when the reserves were stood down waiting for a call out, they got drunk or went absent too.

I became very good at crisis management. I pacified endless angry clients after some drama caused by the guards not doing their jobs, and the number of clients continually increased in parallel with the worsening internal security situation in South Africa. In September, President Botha announced a new constitution giving limited political power to Asians but nothing to blacks. At once, the ANC stirred up violent rioting in five townships outside Johannesburg in which twenty-nine died, including the Mayor of Sharpeville who was hacked to death, doused in petrol and burned. This sort of thing is bad news for everyone except security companies and COIN expanded. We were always under pressure and I enjoyed that. I found the work absorbing in that first year. It was new to me, I liked the man-management aspects and the hours were long. At least, I worked long hours. To start with anyway, we ex-army men were appreciated and I was quickly promoted to operations manager, responsible for all static guard work in the Pretoria area.

I was so busy with the job that I had little time for my family. Jane and I hardly saw each other. Somehow, this kind of commitment works in the army, where operations and even training exercises demand twenty-four hours a day. Service families seem to accept the whole-hearted commitment required of their men, but I had not yet realised that the civilian work ethic operates with a subtle difference. I did not get the chance to appreciate this before fate intervened to stop my life getting too comfortable.

In October 1984, the 'Major' suggested I do a demonstration parachute drop on the COIN annual open day. I agreed at once and found some 44 Para Brigade free-fallers to make up a team. I was delighted to get back to something I really enjoyed. I was to jump in with a COIN pennant flying from my ankle and enthusiastically organised some practice jumps.

On Sunday 7 October, six of us assembled at Wonderboom airfield near Pretoria and everything went wrong from the start. We were jumping with civilian equipment and, as I had no parachute of my own, so I borrowed a square from an ex-Pathfinder. As I walked out to the aircraft, the pin popped out and one of the others stuffed it back in with the 'chute on my back while the Pilatusporter, a short-take-off-and-landing plane, took us up to 9,000 feet.

Nothing matters as you leap out of a plane into the emptiness of the slipstream high over the earth. The moment of commitment is totally absorbing. No matter how many jumps you have done, every jump is a thrill. I was first man out to act as base-man in free-fall, so the other three could close in on me to form a four-man link up, or star. On exit, my goggles flew off. On the way down, my altimeter, which was supposed to stay strapped down at my chest, worked loose in the slipstream and flapped its way up where I could not see it.

Two others came in and grabbed me to form our star. I tried to see their altimeters. Normally, this is easy, just a question of looking across at them as you hang on to each other, but my eyes were watering so much without goggles, I could see nothing. Conscious that every five seconds we hurtled a thousand foot closer to the ground, I decided to pull at the same time as them. But civilian free-fallers pull lower than army free-fallers, because civvies pay for their jumps and want their money's worth. Every second counts, quite literally.

The others started breaking off to find some free air space to pop their parachutes. Once they were away, I took a last, routine, safety-check look-around as my hand went to pull the handle, and saw a man above me! I could not pull. I tracked away a little. Suddenly my altimeter popped up in front of my face. 1,200 feet! Too low! I yanked the handle out at once.

The parachute deployed instantly and I can remember to this day what happened next. Instead of the usual jerking halt and gentle safe swing under the canopy, I heard a series of terrifying snapping noises as several rigging lines broke under the opening pressure, like huge rubber bands being cut. One side of the canopy collapsed immediately and the whole parachute started a sickening rotation with me swinging on the end, as if I were on some mad circus roundabout. There is no time to think of consequences in parachuting. You just act. Working instinctively, I fought with the risers and brake lines to get beneath what remained of the canopy and fly it. After two giant rotations, I managed to control the swing and get under the parachute but I was dropping too fast.

I looked up. Only four of the seven long cells were inflated. Less than half the parachute holding me.

I looked at my altimeter. Six hundred feet. Too low. No time to cut away this shambles and go for my reserve. I was dropping too fast. No time for anything! I had to ride it in. God, it made a noise! The loose material, rigging lines flying, rattled in the wind like a motorbike with no exhaust as I plummeted towards the ground.

Helpless, I looked down briefly. There was no way out of this. I was totally on my own, and maybe it was the Catholic in me, but I said quietly, 'Oh God, get me out of this one!'

I smacked into a deep, soft, ploughed field.

I broke up and bounced like a rag doll. It happened so fast but I was conscious of it all, as if in timeless slow motion. I could feel my right leg snap backwards under my body, crushing the bones and ripping the flesh. My left leg shattered at the thigh, and I felt the vertebrae in my back crushed between the impact and the force of my head ramming down onto my chest. There was blood and snot everywhere. Shards of my broken bones had ripped through my muscles and opened an artery which sprayed the white parachute as it fluttered round me. At once, it seemed to me, I started shaking with shock and broke out in a terrible sweat.

Jane arrived with the ambulance. She and little Billy had watched my parachute come down without any idea I was in trouble. Then, she saw the others running about shouting for the medics and jumped in the ambulance with them. I was conscious throughout as they lifted me very gently off the ploughed earth and I could hear, and feel, my broken bones grinding as they straightened my right leg. Jane sat in the ambulance and stroked my head over and over, to calm me and I kept saying, 'This time I've had it. I've really had it!'

She calmed me and they cut my parachute harness off my body with knives. God knows what my little son Billy thought seeing his father lying in such a mess, or when one child said, 'They're cutting off your dad's leg!' Billy was not quite four years old. He was silent for weeks afterwards. Maybe, he has never forgotten.

After a speed drive to hospital, I was put in an emergency ward in a bed surrounded by curtains, still conscious, and festooned with drips. By now, the pain was really building up. No morphine is allowed before an operation and I was feeling extremely sorry for myself. In the next door cubicle, I could hear groaning and someone muttering in Afrikaans and I wished he would shut up! I stared at a large yellow object sticking out over the top of the curtain rails. Suddenly, the nurses busy round him opened the curtains trying to make space for him and I saw he had a huge chunk of a glider's wing stuck inside his chest. I thought I was in a bad way, but I will never forget the sight of this guy being wheeled off to the operating theatre surrounded by nurses trying to stop that great section of yellow wing knocking on the doorway and tearing him apart.

My turn came. The surgeon, van Dyck, was a gentle man with a round face and the kindest expression in his blue eyes of any man I've seen. You notice that sort of thing when you are all broken up and meet your surgeon for the first time. He bent over me, put his hand gently on my head and said, 'If you come out of this theatre with both your legs, then look upon it as a bonus.' What a bedside manner, but I was past caring!

When I came to in a crisp bed in the intensive care ward, I remembered what Jane had said about plaster casts when we were in Rhodesia. As a nurse there, she had seen a lot of gunshot wounds. She said that if the surgeons left a leg in an open cast it meant they were trying to save the leg, but that most of the cases she had seen with open casts ended up with the leg being amputated.

I lay surrounded by five drips, glistening plastic tubes, stretched out and unable to sit up. My legs hurt. I wriggled my toes. I could feel them, so I guessed I still had legs. Then I remembered that amputees sometimes imagined these reactions. I had to look. Struggling, I could just twist my head and, to my horror, I saw my right leg lying in an open cast.

Dr van Dyck came to me the next day. He looked as kindly as ever. He examined me and stared at the open cast on my right leg, the one which had been so crushed under me on landing.

Bluntly, I said, 'You're thinking of cutting off my leg, aren't you?'

'Yes,' he said. That subtle Afrikaans bedside manner again. 'The bone in your lower leg is more or less pulped by the impact.'

'Well, cut if off!' I retorted harshly. You see, I have to admit it, the pain was terrible and I hated the feeling of helplessness.

He just looked at me and said, 'I don't think you should talk like that. We'll wait to see how you get on.' Then he moved on, followed by a starched procession of Matron and a cluster of nurses.

We are never as badly off as we think. An American friend of mine, an ex-Pathfinder called Dave Barr, came to see me. He had lost both his legs, on a mine in Xangongo in Angola. He tottered into the ward on his tin ones clutching a signed copy of Douglas Bader's biography, *Reach for the Sky*. This, of course, had become his role-model.

'Sergeant Major McAleese!' he boomed in his wild American drawl. 'I've come to see you as I believe you're in deep trouble!'

I nodded. There was no denying that.

He gazed at me with an intense expression in his eyes. 'I know you read the Bible,' he said, and I remembered how we used to sit about on the sandy ground in the bush during quiet periods on operations, with a brew of coffee, and talk about Catholicism, life and death. He said, 'It's written there in the good book, "If it offends you, cut it off!" I did just that with my legs, and look at me. I'm fine!'

With that, he swung round awkwardly on his tin legs and staggered out, teetering from side to side, a legless wreck! Was I going to look like that? But he was a good man and hard as nails. He had refused to give up free-fall parachuting. He jumped with his tin ones and learned how to land on his arse. In fact, one day, one of his legs blew off in free-fall. Someone found it in their back garden and returned it by post.

So, next day, I told Dr van Dyck to 'cut it off'.

He was a kind man and serious, for he knew I was vulnerable, lying in bed helpless and broken, and he replied carefully, 'I need to go away and think about this. I'll let you know.'

We resumed our conversation during his next visit. I noticed the excitement in his voice as he said, 'Peter, if you can stand the long-term pain, I think I can do something to keep your leg.'

I said, 'How long?'

'Two years, maybe two and a half.' Doctors are kind, but they are hard too. What a casual little sentence to describe so much misery!

I agreed. What else could I do? But there were times later when both Jane and I seriously wondered if we had done the right thing.

For twelve days I lay in intensive care being tended every fifteen minutes by a continuous series of wonderful nurses, drifting in and out of consciousness on a heavy dose of painkillers. My legs stayed on. At the end of this period, during a daily visit Dr van Dyck stated, 'He's stabilised.' And forthwith, I was taken out of this clean white haven and thrown into the general orthopaedic ward.

Here, I have to explain the South African hospital system because it, as much as my accident, was responsible for changing my life. All those complaining about the British National Health system pin their ears back and listen closely, and all those cheapskates who refuse to pay full medical insurance cover think again!

In South Africa, the State paid for all the expense of the initial emergency treatment, the operation and the intensive care, but as soon as you were moved into a general ward, you got the same level of nursing care, but you paid 20 per cent of the cost of everything. They noted down every single paracetamol and tissue. As I said, I was broken physically and, soon enough, financially.

This first time in hospital, in the orthopaedic ward, we were all in a bad way. We tried to control ourselves like good manly Afrikaners and not complain about the pain, but, come night time, everyone lay in bed in their own private hell and listened for the Midnight Express. I cannot describe the joy of hearing the squeak-squeak of that night-nurse's trolley which brought our painkillers. When the needle jabbed, I passed out at once and never stirred till morning when a nurse wiped my face with a wet face towel. I slept so deeply, it seemed like one second they were drugging me to go to sleep, the next beating me about the face with wet towels to make me up. It was like doing interrogation training on a combat survival course.

Jane was a great support to me, as a wife, and as a nurse. I imagine she will be less than impressed if I mention that she helped me with a rather vital suppository matter after leaving intensive care. I felt terribly embarrassed lying helpless on my bed, unable to relieve myself and hating to ask the nurses. With typical gentle determination, she organised the whole thing for me, told the matron she was a nurse, drew the curtains and, after thirteen days, what a relief! I apologise here and now, as those poor nurses carried on working on the ward when we were all desperate for respirators!

I left hospital only twenty days after the accident, because it was costing 100 rand a day for the bed alone. The ambulance men stretchered me into my house, dumped me on my sofa and walked out. I do not know how Jane coped, because I was completely immobile. It was not till much later that I could use a wheelchair which Mark Adams bought for me. I have no idea what happens to people in South Africa who cannot afford a wheelchair or do not have friends as I did. In the meantime, I got around on a garage trolley, of the sort used to slide underneath cars. I rolled and heaved my plastered legs off our bed, flat onto the trolley, shoved myself around at floor level with my hands, and could just drag myself back onto our low bed.

This was one of the most miserable times of my life. I had to accustom myself to being an invalid and I was not very good at it. I am a man who loves action. I like to take the lead and all of a sudden I had to learn how to ask people to do things for me. I was bored and intensely frustrated. I took ages to come to terms with my injuries. I never have, really. I still hanker to be the man I was before my accident.

Our marriage was under pressure at once. With typical calm common sense, Jane put Emelda and Billy in a creche and carried on working, because we needed all our income to pay medical bills, while I was stuck at home. I had never taken the advice of Captain Harrington-Spear, Royal Anglian, all those years before, and found a hobby. I was bored, helpless and almost incapable of movement. Even as I mended, I resented being stuck in my wheelchair and hated my crutches. I frequently lost my temper and threw my wheelchair across the room. Not only did we have to come to terms with my injuries and pay huge medical bills, but Jane and I were simply not used to having me moping about at home.

I went back to work as soon as I could, ten weeks after the accident, on a stretcher in the back of a TUV truck. Of course, the 'Major' was delighted at this show of gutsy determination. This was just the sort of attitude he liked to see among his employees. He was right to say I would be better off with something to occupy myself, as I was terribly depressed stuck at home. His remarks were encouraging. I felt the business needed me. Yvonne agreed, with a wide smile of 'Welcome back', though I have a feeling she was thinking more that if I stayed home, I was being paid sickleave for doing nothing.

Later, I learned to lever myself in and out of my car. I wheeled my chair near the passenger door, opened it and lifted myself and my plastered legs inside with my arms. Then I wriggled over to the driver's seat and finally leaned back to collapse the wheelchair and pull it in.

So, I went round Pretoria in a wheelchair, trouble-shooting for the company. I suppose I was driven by frustration and pain but I learned how to manage and delegate to such a degree that I was promoted, wheelchair and all, to branch manager. Now I was responsible for running armed bank guards as well as the static-guard business sector. With promotion came increased perception of the facade civilian security companies present when exposed to hard commercial realities. The company was expanding so fast that the armed black guards on cash-in-transit duty, responsible for moving huge sums in armoured vehicles from bank to business clients, wore imitation flak jackets. The jackets looked good but were actually made of nothing more protective than thick canvas. I guess it has changed now, but it was a good thing the ANC never found out. Maybe that kind of thing would not have mattered in the army, where doubtless we would have thought it was a huge joke, but it mattered in civvy street where it seemed to be a con, not so much of the black guards, but of the client.

I was determined to get fit again, but I was impatient. I started heaving weights in a gym, working on my upper body, but the screws holding the steel pins in my legs loosened and suddenly I had raging septicaemia. My leg swelled enormously and I had to go back to the hospital. I lay on my bed back in the orthopaedic ward gritting my teeth, my eyes watering with pain. I refused to admit how much it hurt, partly because I was stupidly trying to be manly and partly because of the cost. A nurse noticed and insisted I take pethidine. I sank into a trouble-free sleep which turned into drifting consciousness. I became aware of a really beautiful nun in a blue habit sitting beside me.

'I'm in heaven,' I said aloud.

'No you're not,' said the nun, smiling. 'I'm a health visitor.' She had noticed from my record card that I was a Catholic and she chatted quietly to me about charismatic faith and faith healing. My God, it was an appropriate subject. The pethidine wore off, my swollen leg felt as if it was about to burst apart, and suddenly it did just that, sending a geyser of pus from the broken skin above the pins.

I cannot remember the sequence of going in and out of hospital. I had ten operations on my legs over nearly two years. I was in and out of my bloody wheelchair, on crutches, back in hospital, had foot-long steel pins fitted, then taken out. Dr van Dyck was tirelessly patient with me, gradually pulling my right foot round straight, grafting bone he took off my hip to repair my pulped lower leg, and fixing it with bone props. Once he showed me an X-ray of how the bones were healing and I got enthusiastically over-confident. I went to answer the front door at home on crutches, and, as I stood talking to an ex-British Para called Bob Phillips, my leg suddenly collapsed in an 'S' bend, like soft spaghetti, and one of the pins pressed out through the skin. Back to surgery. My treatment went on and on for two years, just as Dr van Dyck predicted, so for fear of being boring, I will leave it at that. Suffice it to say, I had, and still have, my share of pain and I have nothing but sympathy for people in hospital.

Jane and I were constantly paying medical bills and my promotion with a little extra pay was very welcome. Our savings were eaten up very quickly, and still the State-run debt-collecting agency called Med Collect kept sending big, burly men to the house demanding we pay our bills.

'You owe the State money for medical aid,' said one, towering over me in my wheelchair. He was very official, and handed me a large invoice.

I sat and read every minute detail of my treatment and my mood changed to raging despair. Helpless, I tore the bill to shreds and flung it at him. The pieces fluttered about at our feet in the doorway.

He was appalled and shouted aggressively, 'You could get into a lot of trouble for that!'

I gestured at my legs and bellowed back, 'What more can happen? D'you want my bloody legs too?'

The visit ruined the day.

Actually, Jane and I did once seriously wonder if it would be easier to cut the bloody leg off! Just to hire the operating theatre cost 1,800 rand but I am forever grateful to Dr van Dyck who showed us unending kindness. He never charged for his surgery on my legs, but we had to pay for everything else. Faced with 20 per cent of the total, we were always broke.

Another problem was that I could not afford any post-operative care or physiotherapy. Actually, to be honest, I had one session. A very nice lady asked me to raise my legs off the bed to her hand, which she held out above me, and when I did that six times with each leg she gave me some good advice and departed. For which the State charged 20 rand. I could not afford it and I think I am still suffering the consequences. Other people who have had similar injuries say their time spent in physio learning how to walk again was as important as the operations.

My therapy was going to the office where I had to learn a new approach to my life. I had always been the sort who goes to the other person if there's work to be done, and at first I continued to do this in my wheelchair or on crutches, up and down corridors and so on. By the end of the day, I was exhausted. My arm muscles looked like Arnold Schwarzenegger's. I took a lesson from Mark Adams who had been made a COIN director by then and, like a typical officer, always seemed to have people come to him. I began to learn new communication skills along with the art of delegation. The 'Major' cannot have thought too badly of me, even crippled. He promoted me again, to area manager, and put me in charge of all the company's operations in Pretoria, Johannesburg and the Transvaal. This new post gave me responsibility for all the company's security operations: static guards, all bank cash-in-transit work, and now the armed national keypoint guards. These last were run on infantry lines, armed with .223 version of the M14 and shotguns, and they were used by the State to protect important installations, such as electricity stations, railway facilities and warehouses. They supplemented the over-stretched South African police and army.

On 20 July 1985, President Botha declared a State of Emergency as the security situation in the country worsened. In February that year eight had died in terrible riots in the Cape Flats area, in March another seventeen blacks were shot by the SAP at Langa township on the anniversary of the Sharpeville massacre, and hundreds of black suspects were arrested under the new Emergency Measures. Five hundred were estimated to have been killed in the previous twelve months.

My problem was that our national keypoint guards were treated much the same as the other guards. Most South Africans saw nothing in this, but I thought they really did work horrendous hours. Therefore they were ripe targets for subversion by black activists. During a period of rioting in the townships, they decided to go on strike. I was in the company offices, as usual, and heard about it on the company's radio network.

'There's a mutiny in the blacks' hostel!' crackled the radio in panic. This illustrated the white South African attitude, especially that of the ex-army types we had in the company. The black guards were not seen as 'strikers' but 'mutineers'.

I struggled into my car and drove off for another test of my crisis management skills. I was on crutches at this time and stumped into the hostel to find blacks and whites facing up to each other in the concrete sleeping rooms and everyone looking very nasty indeed. The company had formed an all-white internal 'police unit' to check on black guards. A group of these, in their dark glasses and American-style police uniforms, were confronting a crowd of angry blacks. Outside, the night sky was lurid with burning buildings, we could hear shooting and everyone knew that there was chaos out there in the city. Blacks were fighting blacks, killing them with burning tyre necklaces and everywhere the SAP were trying to enforce control with riot sticks, guns and arrests. Tempers in our hostel ran high.

The senior white COIN 'police officer' waved his sub-machine gun at the blacks as if he was dying to use it and shouted that all the blacks should be arrested for stealing Revlon makeup. 'Red-handed,' he bellowed down at me on my crutches. 'I found it in their lockers.'

A quick glance at the packets showed the Revlon makeup was all rejected stock. I told him, 'You can't arrest them for taking this stuff out of dustbins.' The blacks were always rootling about in the dustbins to see what they could find.

Disappointed, he paused. Then he perked up and shouted in an outraged and triumphant voice, 'But they are smoking dagga!'

'They always smoke dagga, don't they?'

Puzzled, he retired, trying to reconcile the truth of this logic with his President's new Emergency laws. Once I had defused the situation and made sure there was no immediate chance of slaughter occurring, I was able to talk to the Volkani Black Guards Union rep, a woman called Grace. I asked her, 'Why are you on strike?'

She shrugged carelessly. 'I don't know.'

Another black was only slightly more forthcoming. He said, ''cause we've been told.' This was equally compelling logic.

It was black nationalist logic. The ANC were busy creating unrest in the townships and the last thing they wanted was our national keypoint guards to take the pressure off the over-stretched army and police units. So ANC activists inside the unions tried to take us out of the picture with a strike.

My loyalty was towards the company, and, whatever the problems in the black townships, my job was to keep COIN in business. I found various posters in the hostel, a bizarre but typically African mix of religion and communism, of Christ on the cross and Karl Marx. I showed them to the security police who studied this sinister mix as if their worse fears had been confirmed.

'That,' they said in a tone of high moral indignation, 'is proof of nothing less than Christian Liberation Theology!'

They agreed at once to help. Having defused the strike, I posted all the guards to their installations on the divide and rule principle, and then sent the police out to several posts where five particular guards were on duty who were always causing trouble among the rest. The police simply arrived, slapped on the cuffs and marched them off, no questions asked under the Emergency measures, and we were back in business.

These sort of strikes occurred a good deal and I thought the blacks had good cause to complain. The company had one black in the management, a nice man called Michael Kgabo whom Jane and I got to know well. He often joined us at home with other friends who came round to see how I was getting on. He had been educated at a missionary school but since the political system did not allow his wife Agnes to join him and live with him, because he was black, he ended up finding another woman, which broke up his marriage. I do not pretend to know about the origins of apartheid, but it caused a lot of problems.

Having been educated at missionary school, Kbago was dedicated to being a good, upright member of the community, but South African society abused his dedication, using his commitment to work but spoiling his life and that of his wife through stupid regulations. Of course, a good many of the guard force were idle by anyone's yardstick, let alone Kbago's, but the apartheid regulations did not encourage them to give their best. In Rhodesia, my black ex-guerrillas worked hard on operations with me, on equal terms and through equal dangers, and I don't think much of any system which condemns a man before he's started, because of his colour or creed.

I was normally the man the management used to handle strikes on the ground, as I am not afraid of having things out face to face with the men. I learned a lot about man-management, and dealing with black grievances in the particularly trying conditions of South Africa during the State of Emergency at that time was no easy task. It began to wear me down. One aspect I found hard to bear was pretending that we were an army unit, and not accepting that we were quite simply a company in the civilian market place with a manpower product to sell.

In between operations on my legs, I spent a lot of frustrating time at home. I do not suppose I made very good company and the strains on our marriage worsened, keeping pace, you might say, with the increasing trouble in South Africa. However, life was not all bad news. We kept open house for army and ex-army friends and had numerous reunions which we both enjoyed as old friends passed through. Jane never complained at people being in the house so much. She was always busy cooking and looking after them, she was extremely supportive of me during this period and I was delighted when she told me she was expecting our second child.

Having friends round was a mix of emotions, plain good fun, a desperate Celtic-inspired wake for my old army life, and a release from my current troubles. I had been through every grade of pain-killer, morphine, Omnopon, pethidine, Sosogen, Deloxene and par-acetamol, and finally drink. There were always friends who came to see how I was and I drank with them through sheer frustration.

One Sunday during the State of Emergency, a crowd of mates from 44 Para Brigade came to take me to a reunion in my wheelchair. I was not feeling too crisp, but they brushed aside my reluctance, promised Jane they would look after me, and drove me to a house in Hillbrow, in Johannesburg. The guys parked me in my wheelchair in the sitting room and the party began. Several beers later, the front door bell rang and Ossie Overall went to answer it.

A South African policeman stood on the doorstep and raising his voice over the racket of the tape player, he said, 'The neighbours have complained you're making too much noise.'

'Fuck off,' said Ossie pleasantly.

The policeman took a long hard look at the beer we were drinking. There is a terrible streak of old-fashioned self-righteousness in South Africa and the Afrikaner does not approve of drinking on a Sunday. He said, 'Do you realise there's a State of Emergency on, and the people who come after me may not be so reasonable?'

'We do. Now fuck off.'

Actually, there was no law against drinking in your own place, it was simply that the South African police did not approve. The policeman went away, Ossie shut the door and the party continued.

An hour later, we were sitting there still singing army songs and drinking, when suddenly to my amazement a gas grenade shattered the street window and burst on the carpet near my feet. I spun my wheelchair to escape to the back of the room when another grenade came through the back window. Within seconds, toxic white CS gas filled the room, police smashed through the front door and charged all over the house shouting, 'It's a drugs raid!'

'You've come to the wrong place,' burbled Ossie as he was man-handled away. 'There's no drugs here. We're all alcoholics.'

Amazingly, the police were not wearing respirators against the gas and brought a sniffer dog with them. I can only surmise its mere presence justified their drugs allegation.

While this battle took place, I sat in my wheelchair, choking on the CS gas which hung thick in the air, and totally ignored. Dismissively, one policeman explained why as he dragged off one of the guys. 'We don't arrest spastics.'

What misery. I could not stand, let alone walk, and there were stairs front and back which I could not manage in my wheelchair. I was a prisoner. For an hour, I sat coughing in the wreckage in the sitting room.

Then, to my immense relief, all the guys came back, shouting with laughter. Down at the police station, the SAP had routinely offered them Admission of Guilt forms which they all signed at once, and, still drunk, they had all been released to sin again. Such is the South African system.

The party carried on. Inevitably, because this was South Africa during the State of Emergency, the police raided us again. In strength. More CS gas grenades sailed through the windows, hordes of camou-flaged officers poured into the house, beat everyone up and dragged them off to the police station. Once again, I was totally ignored.

I spent the whole night slumped in my wheelchair in the smoking wreckage of the sitting room feeling terribly sorry for myself. When some of them were finally released and came back to rescue me on Monday morning, I was totally exhausted.

The South Africans must have wasted a lot of energy trying to stop people drinking on Sundays but they seem to have been driven by the Afrikaner mentality. Illegal shebeens sprang up all over the place. On another Sunday, on my crutches this time, I was in one of these with Pete Donnelly, an ex-Pathfinder, when Pete said, 'What's that funny noise?'

We could hear a harsh burring noise on the other side of the front door, and, as we looked, a chainsaw burst through the wood, carved the door in half, and as it fell apart into the hall, several fanatical-looking policemen in black overalls burst in, all carrying buzzing chainsaws. They paid no attention to us at all, so we carried on drinking out of their way at the bar, while they charged all round the house carving up all the furniture. Minutes later, they ran out, leaving the place looking as if someone had blown it apart with a satchel bomb, and all they said to us was, 'Drink up and leave!'

The pseudo-army facade of the company began to get me down about the same time the 'Major' and his partner Yvonne veered away from their enthusiasm for recruiting ex-soldiers. This was probably due to the expansion of COIN and their realisation that army men do not necessarily make good businessmen. Anyway, there were various little signs which told me my future in the company was not as rosy as I had been led to believe.

As the company expanded, there arose an obsession with paper-work, reports and request forms. Of course, all these had to be managed, so people were employed solely for this non-productive work while the likes of me went on seeking new clients and keeping the old ones happy; not an easy job as you have seen. One new paper-merchant of this type stood over my wheelchair one day and lectured me in a superior tone on how experienced he was. He ended by saying, as if I were a wet-behind-the-ears youngster, 'Don't you realise? I was a policeman!' He neither knew nor cared about me or, it seemed, anyone else.

Here lies the rub. Security companies are full of ex-soldiers because they think it is the next best thing after service life. They think all the things they enjoyed about the army, like the camaraderie, the safety of the structure, knowing your place, the emphasis on sports and fitness, the training and the action, can be found in civilian security companies. Well, it can't. The civilian world is, well, just different.

In fact, I find it sad that some of the finest things that motivate a soldier in army life, like loyalty to the unit and self-sacrifice, can be (but are not always) a distinct disadvantage to him as a civilian. There will no doubt be an outcry among civilian managers and employers reading this, but let them honestly answer a couple of questions.

Who in civvy street really has a true interest in your promotion and career development? Does the company, or your boss (whose job you may want and he knows it) or is it really a case of looking after Number One?

And second, who is employed body and soul for twenty-four hours a day but only paid for eight? The soldier is, but not the civilian.

The ex-soldier goes on thinking like a soldier when he becomes a civilian. I found the transition painful, and concluded someone was cashing in on my soldier's attitudes and taking advantage of me. Sadly, I don't think my case is unusual.

I was not pleased when Mark Adams told me that several people who worked under me in my area were being paid more than me. Did all those hours I was working overtime count for nothing?

I think the last straw was when Jane went into hospital to have Catherine. It was Saturday 20 July 1985 and I was out, as usual, driving round Johannesburg after working hours checking keypoints and guards at their installations. Quite by chance I pulled up on top of a hill and listened to the company radio network.

'Call for Papa Mike,' crackled the radio. 'Your wife has been taken into hospital in Pretoria.'

At that moment, I suddenly realised I was in the wrong place.

I had been so obsessed with my own work that I had ignored Jane at a very important time for her. I dropped what I was doing and raced in my car to the hospital. I was too late. I missed the birth. I arrived just afterwards and saw Jane with her tiny baby in her arms looking really quite beautiful. I was over the moon but at the same time miserable. Here was this woman who had done everything for me, looked after me when I was ill, helped me through all the highs and lows, cooked and washed for all the lines of friends who called on us, understanding me so well and finally having my baby. And what had I been doing? Mucking about on some routine job for a company which was a pale facade of the armies I had served and fought in and which couldn't care less.

There were other things. There always are when a person decides to leave a country. One was hearing my little son calling a black man 'kaffir'. He had picked it up somewhere as it was not a term I used. Of course there are lots of slang words like that, which have never meant anything to me because my feelings for someone have nothing to do with their colour. However, I suddenly realised Billy was going to grow up attributing something fundamental to such slang and I asked myself what sort of society did I want him to grow up in, with what sort of ideas?

Jane went back to England with the three children.

Almost at once, the company showed its true colours. The 'Major's' partner Yvonne served notice she wanted me out of the job and our house. I was prepared. I had learned a few things about civilian life during the previous two years. When I told them I was going, I left my car, which by that time was three-quarters mine, at the company's garage and quit the house which was immaculate. I had completely repainted all the rooms as new and given all the furniture to a neighbouring Afrikaans woman who had cleaned every nook and cranny. The final pathetic indignity was the company man who was sent round by the 'Major' to collect the keys of the house. He found me sitting on a packing case in a house empty of everything except memories, and later boasted that he had been obliged to strangle me to take the keys off me. I suppose he thought the lies would do him some good at work.

I joined Mark Adams at the Palms Hotel and was enjoying a drink to celebrate freedom again when the 'Major's' brother tracked me down. He said, 'Yvonne wants me to say you've got four days to apologise and we'll forget you ever wanted to leave.'

Actually, I liked him, but he had wasted his journey.

Briefly, in drink, I reflected on the previous two years, the start of my civilian life. God, what a thing is retrospection! I've never feared the future, as I've no fear of death, but God spare me the pain of regret.

I drank up and left Africa.

10

Guardians of the Myth

'But I don't want to go among mad people,' Alice remarked.
'Oh, you can't help that,' said the Cat, 'we're all mad here. I'm mad. You're mad.'
'How do you know I'm mad?' said Alice.
'You must be,' said the Cat, 'or you wouldn't have come here.'

LEWIS CARROLL, *Alice's Adventures in Wonderland*

I had been away for ten years. I came home with a wife and three children to find the United Kingdom changed. After seven years of Mrs Thatcher's government, people were pleased to be called British again but bureaucracy still ruled.

We lived with John Carey, a good friend from Parachute Regiment days, and his family, near Birmingham, so I put our names down for a council house and Jane tried to get a job as a nurse.

The council said to me, 'Where are you living now?'

'With friends. But only till we find somewhere of our own.'

'So, you're in a house already?'

'Yes, but it's not our house.'

'Ah yes,' he said, cunningly triumphant, 'but if you're in a house, you don't need one from us, do you?'

What can you say?

I don't know what we would have done without the kindness and support of John and Julie Carey who looked after us all those first difficult months. You really find out who your friends are when you are broke and have nowhere to live.

Jane went out to find nursing work and ran aground on the monolithic National Health Service. Officials refused to recognise her qualifications from Rhodesia, though I am sure the medical standards of the Rhodesian health service were as good as anything in British teaching hospitals. However, Rhodesia had lost and was now Zimbabwe. The Andrew Fleming Hospital in Salisbury, Rhodesia, had become the Parirenyatwa Hospital in Harare, Zimbabwe, to which she wrote for confirmation of her papers. While she waited, she found a job in an old people's nursing home pending confirmation of her nursing status. Finally, the Zimbabwean health authority confirmed her qualification but the British NHS then decided not to accept it. She lost her job. Desperate, she asked what on earth she could do to convince them she was a qualified nurse and they told her to write to the South African hospital where she had worked. Four months later the answer came back and the NHS graciously accepted her as a qualified nurse. To cap it all, another organ of British bureaucracy then chipped in to say she couldn't work anyway because she was born in America and did not have a work permit.

During all this time, I found it impossible to find a job. The security firms in England which cater for ex-soldiers like me did not want a man on crutches.

John Carey suggested I went on the dole. He drove me up to Smallheath in Birmingham where he was the publican at the Gunmaker's Arms pub and left me at the Social Security office. What a humiliating experience. I queued for ages with a roomful of others from the district, all Pakistanis and Indians, and all I could hear round me were incomprehensible conversations in Pushtu, Parsee, Arabic, and Hindi punctuated by that single vital word, 'giro'.

English instructions to sign on were at the bottom of a list of foreign hieroglyphics. I filled out a form, signed and felt like a beggar. The dole staff were surly and antagonistic. They assumed that since I had come from South Africa, I must be rich and they were cross because I wouldn't admit where I had hidden my money. Maybe they felt like that because of the strong anti-South African feeling at that time, influenced by the campaign to free Nelson Mandela and the anti-apartheid movement, or perhaps the British just think that hot sunny countries are some sort of paradise where everyone is well off.

Finally, I got a sniff of a job with KMS, a security company in London. I had been in touch with the company, through a good friend called Joe Lock, but I was given to understand that they did not like 'my mercenary past'. That was an unfair label if ever there was one, and based, I hope, on ignorance rather than knowledge of the facts. However, my sister Molly rang up from Hereford, where she lived, to say that Norman Duggan was trying to contact me from Uganda. Then David Richards, an ex-SAS officer who had recently left the army and joined KMS, called to arrange an interview with the company in London.

I felt terribly self-conscious. After two years with my wheelchair and crutches, my legs were wobbly, I was unfit and overweight. In complete contrast, David was tall, elegant, fair-haired and really rather athletic. He met me at the door of the offices and said with enthusiastic bonhomie, 'How's it going, Pete?'

'Fine, fine,' I said, sucking in my belly and shaking hands like a man.

'Good. Let's go and have a brew,' he shouted, disappearing up the stairs three at a time.

'Yes, yes, of course,' I growled, hopping desperately after him. At the top, out of breath, I stuck out my chest and tried to slow things up, walking about like a short, fat, John Wayne.

'We have a team of five guys on the Uganda job,' David explained, lounging in an executive chair. 'The contract is with Brussels and they look after official EEC visitors who go to Kampala. God knows why, but the EEC make substantial grants to Uganda and they want to keep track of what happens to the money. One of the guys on the team called Dougie Measham, who you may remember from "G" Squadron, is sick, we need someone to take his place for ten weeks and it means leaving tomorrow. Can you do it?'

'I think I can spare the time,' I said casually. I needed the work so badly, I would have crawled to the airport on my hands and knees, there and then.

I flew out to Kampala and Norman Duggan met me at the airport. We had not seen each other for over ten years since those ludicrous days with John Banks. He took one look at me and said bluntly, 'Pete, if I had known you were in such bad physical shape, I'd have said you couldn't come.'

I swallowed it. I needed the money. Actually, Norman was always a bit of a physical prima donna but he was right. My legs were still giving me trouble, and still do, but I set about training again. After ten weeks, I could do a whole twenty situps! It may not sound much, but I was delighted. I had never thought I could, and I kept going. Once Norman realised why I was in such bad shape, he was a great encouragement. We used to play badminton as best we could every day and gradually my fitness began to return. In the event, my contract was extended for a five-month tour and I managed to regain my alertness, balance and fitness. I even managed to beat Norman at badminton a few times by the end. Better still, I took six inches off my waistline. In some ways, this exercising replaced the physiotherapy for my legs which I had never had in South Africa.

The job was really rather boring. We grandly called ourselves an armed response team but in simple language we were minders and drivers for the EEC officials visiting Kampala. We kept one man in the office, three with the officials and one was always on leave. Uganda is rich in farming land and the EEC grants were to help rebuild the country which was in a dreadful state of corruption and decay after a series of selfish and destructive post-colonial leaders. The EEC money was for agricultural buildings, new coffee plantations, dams, digging new wells, water pumps and so on, and the officials were required to supervise how the money was spent. We had to make sure everything ran smoothly for them, and during the whole time I was there we had no trouble.

Don't misunderstand me. I am not complaining about the job. I was very pleased to have it at all and I think I did it well. I worked hard, got fit and did my best, but there is no getting away from the fact that bodyguarding is relentless, boring routine, even for the busy teams who look after a VIP like the US President or the Saudi Arabian oil minister. In Uganda, we were doing nothing more complicated than driving round some nice and rather naive chaps from the EEC and the biggest threat was of being robbed by a drunken black soldier.

The Ugandans had these EEC chaps weighed up. We drove them out to a farm in the countryside to see how European money was being spent. On arrival, we found a heart-warming scene of large numbers of black men grafting away digging for all they were worth. Our EEC officials were suitably impressed, asked a few learned and technical questions and we left. Whereupon the black men downed tools and forgot all about the hole till the next visit. We saw the place often and nothing happened between EEC visits.

Uganda was in a terrible mess. The British granted independence on 9 October 1962 when the exchange rate had been 25 Ugandan shillings to the pound sterling, leaving a beautiful, rich and stable country. When I was there twenty-four years later, the official rate was about 900 shillings while the black market rate was 33,000 shillings and the place was in ruins. We used to go out to buy the week's groceries with a quarter of a million shillings in our pockets.

Kampala must have been a beautiful city once, but was now the epitaph of so many decayed post-colonial African towns I had seen. It had become a shambles, with potholed roads, broken vehicles just rusting away where they had finally ground to a halt, decaying buildings, garbage in the streets, poverty, high unemployment and equally high street crime.

Of course the British were blamed, but we did not cause the misery which afflicted Uganda. Tribal Africa caused that. After independence in 1962, there were endless coups and counter-coups, each one followed by arrests, torture and murders. In February 1966, Milton Obote seized power, followed by Idi Amin in January 1971. Amin's terrible dictatorship is well documented. He placed members of his Kakwa tribe in all the senior government posts, threw out 50,000 Asians in 1972 and is reputed to have eliminated 250,000 Ugandans by June 1974.

One mass grave in Idi Amin's notorious Luera triangle had become something of a tourist site and occasionally we had to take our EEC visitors to see the piles of skulls on display. The Ugandans made a big show of blaming the 'others' for these atrocities, but I have seen enough slaughter in Africa to wonder if the circumstances leading to such terrible things are ever truly in the past in Africa.

In March 1979, Amin's rule was so outrageous that the Tanzanians invaded to overthrow him and make Yusef Lule the new President. Lule promised a return of the rule of law. He did not last. In 1980, Obote seized power again, was himself deposed by Tito Okello in July 1985, and finally in January 1986 Yoweri Museveni took over with the People's National Revolutionary Army.

Ugandans must have been utterly fed up with the thieving and depredations of one army after another. One wonders if there is a link between the size of an army and the chaos in a country. Under British rule there were 1,800 soldiers, mostly men in administrative jobs, and 6,000 police, and the country worked. Since then, armies have rampaged over the country and the latest, Museveni's personal powerbase, the NRA, is 40,000 strong.

An army this size in a country as bankrupt as Uganda is a scandal. The NRA was badly paid, poorly equipped and ill-disciplined. However, President Museveni wanted to do something about it. He must have read a book about the Duke of Marlborough who insisted his army had proper boots for his victorious marches back and forth across Europe during the wars of the Spanish Succession. Museveni must have decided what was good enough for the Duke of Marlborough was good enough for him and his troops must have boots too. He rang up the Belgian Bata shoe company in Kampala and demanded, 'I want boots for the NRA.'

'We don't make army boots,' was the reply. 'We only make Wellington boots here.'

'That'll do fine,' said the President, doubtless impressed with the name of another famous British general, and Bata produced 40,000 rubber wellies for the Ugandan army, all in different colours for different regiments; for example, blue for the Signals and red for the Military Police.

On the first anniversary of the People's Revolution, Museveni ordered a grand parade and full dress review of his troops. I have never seen anything like it. For several hours, the bemedalled President stood grinning on the saluting dias while his personal band played the famous military march 'Scipio', over and over and over again because it was the only tune they knew, and rank after rank of coloured wellies flicked in the air as his soldiers goose-stepped past. I do not know if the good President was trying to emulate the goose-stepping shock troops of Soviet Russia or the Nazi SS, but you just don't get the same effect with wellies.

Another time, Ugandan television showed a propaganda news report of the NRA storming ashore from Lake Victoria, still proudly wearing their wellies. We were not shown whether they had to stop once ashore, to empty them of water, but Uganda is on the Equator and we wondered at the smell.

Sometimes we took our EEC officials to the game lodge in the Queen Elizabeth National Park on the banks of Lake Edward in the Western Province and here was proof of the transient nature of Ugandan politics. The map on the wall of the lodge had been cautiously updated with tacky little name-tags stuck one on top of the other, as the lake had been retitled with the names of all the successive presidents since independence.

Everywhere was evidence of role-playing in the name of modern politics. At the airport, President Museveni made a televised speech to cheering crowds while near us his police were beating up co-opted Ugandans who were not cheering loudly enough. During another television broadcast, the President was making an important speech to his nation when suddenly a head appeared round the side of the picture on the left, wearing a baseball hat and peering into the camera lens. The President ignored the head till it was suddenly pulled away.

Corruption was endemic, and I believe it was encouraged by the influx of aid. For example, some supervisors of a project all bought status symbol Pajero land-cruisers, one each, which left very little for the project itself. A large open-air market outside Kampala was full of aid clothing (not made in Uganda) which, instead of going to the starving and poor, had been flogged off to the market traders for general sale. I found a tin of herring from East Germany in a shop and asked the man if he had any more. He showed me a crate.

Aid was as much part of the Cold War as arms sales, with the Eastern bloc competing against the West, each one trying to outdo the other. The Ugandans readily took everything on offer. In addition to East German herring, they received Soviet 'Hip' helicopters, two of which crashed at the airport where they were left to rot for want of repair, and communist China sent seven million hoes, enough for one between two of the population. This must have puzzled the Ugandans because in the past they exported hoes themselves.

I suppose some readers will call me a racist and accuse me of making fun of Uganda. My answer is that I treat all men equally, friend or foe, but that you cannot escape what goes on in societies as corrupt as Uganda was then. I imagine some black Ugandan politicians are trying to drag their country forward, but, having systematically destroyed the place over a quarter of a century, they have a long way to go and just pouring in aid is not the answer. Uganda is a beautiful country and I hope they succeed.

In the end, I stayed on the team a year until the end of 1987, when the group split up because a non-ex-SAS man was put in charge. There was no reason why a non-SAS man should not have been in charge of such a routine job, particularly when he had seen it going on for many months, but what irritated some people was that this chap pretended he was ex-SAS. He would cunningly say, 'I'm from Hereford, so let's just leave it at that.' This dishonest implication that he had served in the SAS was making good use of Joseph Goebbels' maxim, 'Good propaganda must contain a grain of truth.' Which was that he had lived in Hereford, though never in the SAS. He was a civilian mechanic and the sum of his military knowledge was based on having been a National Serviceman in the RAF. He gave himself airs and his appointment as team leader caused argument which filtered back to London where it made a poor impression. There was no question of excessive behaviour. While I was there for a year, none of us drank much at all. I for one felt better for it and enjoyed the self-denial. However, the London office decided to change the team and maybe they were right, after so long, to make radical changes to a small team like that. What was wrong was putting a weak man in control.

After Norman Duggan left the team needed good leadership, although there was absolutely nothing secret, exciting and dangerous about that job. In all that time there was only one drama, which happened before I arrived. An unfortunate Ugandan ex-soldier was shot dead trying to burgle an EEC house. I will never forget it because the guys who killed him never stopped talking about it during the long empty hours we had together. The trouble was that this and other not very interesting military events, like a parachute jump on Hankley Common in Surrey, seemed to be the most important war stories they had to talk about. I think they knew I had kicked around in Africa, but they were not interested, even perhaps a little jealous and embarrassed to ask, and carried on as if I had nothing to offer. I think that was foolish. Boasting is all very well, as long as you don't take yourself too seriously, but there is always someone else around with more experience than you. This is especially true in Africa with all the wars there have been there, and, thinking of all the Rhodesians and South Africans I had served with, I found it hard sometimes when some 'old SAS hands' carried on as though the British Army's experience of Northern Ireland was the height of soldiering and the only thing that mattered.

Actually, on reflection, I think it may be true that there is more blind arrogance in the SAS about other people's experience than in any other unit I've encountered or served in.

Perhaps we were too old for such a job, too set in our ways. The system was never questioned. Perhaps the system was not necessarily wrong, but it was not necessarily right either. For example, we carried 9mm Browning pistols and the Model 12.9mm Beretta SMGs, but we never practised on a range! This ran against the grain for me, and I made suggestions which fell on deaf ears. The arch-pacifist, Hermann Hesse, said in *Demian* in 1919 just after the First World War, 'The man who is too lazy to think for himself and to be his own judge accommodates himself to existing laws, such as they are, and has it easy.' We certainly had it easy.

I think that was the root of the problem. The job was undemanding and trivia became important. People would sulk if the security lights were turned out a few minutes late in the morning (even though they had been on for the previous twelve hours), one person was always grumpy at breakfast and refused to talk before he had had a cup of tea, behaving but certainly not looking like a Guards officer, and there was always bickering about who was in charge of whom.

I started an incident book in the office. The innovation was accepted and the man on duty used it to record and pass messages which came in by telephone or radio. One day, I logged a radio message and shortly afterwards another of the team called Pat walked in.

'I've just got a message on the radio which you'll need to know about for tomorrow,' I said to him and explained the detail.

'You must tell Norman to tell me,' he said. At this time, Norman Duggan was the team leader.

I took a deep breath and said, 'Pat, I am going to tell Norman, and I am also going to tell Norman to tell you.'

'Only Norman is allowed to tell me what to do,' he repeated petulantly.

'I am telling you, Pat,' I said with heavy irony, 'because you are standing here in front of me, and just in case Norman forgets to tell you himself!'

I found this attitude incredible. The man was forty-five years old, one of the super fighting men of the Parachute Brigade which the media so love to admire. What had happened to him? How had he changed so much from the time when he was a serving soldier in the British Army, when he certainly had all those qualities I have talked about before; commitment, loyalty, self-sacrifice and the willingness to get on with a job for very little reward?

Quite simply the answer is money. He and so many like him have become prisoners of the economics of modern special forces. Of course, you'll be saying, all soldiers have to wise up about pounds, shillings and pence when they leave the army. Blame the civvies. But the fault is not all civilian. The rot sets in before they leave the army. Long after I left, the British SAS were given special pay, to reward them for the extra responsibilities of special forces work. That may be proper, but whereas my contemporaries and I joined the SAS (and the army, come to that) for the life – the pay was appalling – there are now, without question, soldiers who join the SAS for money. Special pay in the SAS can typically mean a sergeant's salary is dramatically raised 30 per cent from £18,700 to £24,900 per annum. Most of them own houses now, which they could never have afforded in the past. So, instead of being committed to the life, too many are committed to large mortgages and when they leave they have to earn similar sums to maintain them. They are prisoners of their financial commitments, just like civilians, but they are flung out of their employment after twenty-two years and told to start again. Ex-SAS soldiers turn to these civilian security jobs, quite understandably, because they pay much better money and are much easier than driving trucks or digging holes or retraining to start a new career completely afresh.

Of course, everyone has to pay the bills, me included, but what I could not stomach was finding so many of them with absolutely no belief in what they were doing. I firmly believe if you agree to work for someone then you must be committed to that job lock, stock and barrel. I have always worked on that principle and always will. However, some of these guys were only interested in counting their money and totting up their expense accounts. They were actually not interested in the job at all. The real criteria now were pay and extras, not personal commitment, let alone risk. And God, what a pity. What a waste of good men. What prostitution! They are masquerading, pretending that they still have a devotion to duty (which in the civilian world means the job) whereas in fact they are saying, 'My loyalty, my dedication and my devotion to duty can be bought!' For that, whether civilian or soldier, there is no excuse.

Are these, then, the real mercenaries so beloved of the media? Set up and paid up by the British Government, then signed off, written off, and launched onto the civilian market?

11

The Colombian Adventure

'Get the boys ready,' he said. 'We're going to war.'
Gerineldo Maquez did not believe him.
'With what weapons?' he asked.
'With theirs,' Aureliano replied.

GABRIEL GARCIA MARQUEZ, *One Hundred Years of Solitude*

I can never resist a challenge. When Dave Tomkins told me in the Booth Hall pub in Hereford that he had met a Colombian Army officer who wanted an FARC headquarters attacked, I told him I would go and look at it.

Dave was an old friend from Angola days, a civilian without any previous military experience who had been wounded and shown a lot of guts. In June 1988, he rang up out of the blue and we met in the Booth Hall, an old SAS haunt in Hereford which is now boarded up. We had not seen each other since Angola, so God knows what he thought of the way I looked, but he was as ever a picture of studied elegance, tall, lean, tanned, his hair very grey and fashionably long. I was amused to see he had developed a habit of rather ostentatiously fingering various gold ornaments as he spoke: several large rings, a heavy bracelet and a medallion on the end of a thick gold neck chain which he pulled out through his open-necked shirt.

He explained the background. He had made good capital out of his contacts in the Angolan affair and become something of an arms dealer. During the course of business, he met the Colombian Army officer who had asked if he could provide some foreign soldiers to attack an FARC headquarters.

The FARC (Fuerzas Armadas Revolucionarias de Colombia) is a communist organisation which receives political support from Cuba, in the form of Cuban commissars who train and indoctrinate the

FARC military groups, called *frentes*. Over the years, FARC has carried out some dramatic attacks on the Colombian government, perhaps the most spectacular being the total destruction of the Justice building in the centre of Bogota, along with all the documentation on FARC and other anti-government groups. In accordance with Mao Tse Tung's principle of liberated areas, their control over the vast scrublands of the Llanos and the jungle further south is almost complete. They are so confident that they run big training camps where they openly fire weapons on jungle ranges, bring in local villagers for indoctrination and film shows, and drive about in Russian vehicles, all in broad daylight under cover of the jungle canopy. The Colombian Army and police enter the area at their peril.

'The army is fed up with the politicians,' Dave said. 'The Colombian government is trying to pursue talks with FARC, and the army is caught in the middle. Every time the army wants to attack, the government says dialogue is more important.'

'That sounds a familiar story.'

'So they want to teach FARC a lesson. They want to attack a place called the Green House, *Casa Verde* in the local lingo, where they reckon the FARC politicos have meetings. The place is about eighty kilometres south of Bogota, in the mountains. They want outsiders to do the job so the army can't be blamed.'

'Non-attributable.'

'Yes. The whole thing is very secret. This officer and three others have been taken away from their units, supposedly on a staff course, to handle the project.'

'I'm interested,' I told him. 'But I want to look at it first.'

This story rang true, especially the part about the army being piggy in the middle, but I had to be careful. Every year Colombia produces 185 metric tons of cocaine (see Appendix D), which converts to a street value of $44 billion US, most of which is controlled by Colombian cartels. This staggering figure excludes profits these drug traffickers make from marijuana and an increasing trade in the even more profitable cultivation of heroin poppies. It also excludes the profit made by Colombian cartels from trafficking cocaine grown south of Colombia in Peru and Bolivia. Legal national exports simply cannot compete. The World Bank values Colombia's legal production of coffee, bananas, cut flowers, clothing, ferro-nickel and coal, at a mere $5.8 billion US. Is it any surprise that the corruption of drugs infects every layer of Colombian society, and that most, if not all, important government appointments are affected by it? I wondered how the people backing this job fitted in.

I knew FARC was involved with drugs. An essential for all guerrilla groups is adequate finance. Like communist movements all over the world, FARC extorts local 'taxes' from tribesmen and villagers and they still kidnap whites from time to time, but their main source of funds is growing cocaine in the jungle and selling the unrefined base to the drug cartels in Medellin. This produces a cash flow which must be the envy of every dissident group in the world.

However, I have been fighting communism in one form or another all my life so the job sounded good enough to me and we flew out to Bogota to have a closer look.

We arrived on Friday 1 July, and stayed in the Plaza Hotel. Dave's Colombian officer, nicknamed Ricardo, arrived. A large, likeable man, well muscled but slightly overweight, he was dressed in a snappy grey suit with rather too much silver thread in the weave, his jet-black hair was smoothly brushed and he sported the typical neat South American moustache. After introductions and a short chat, he said, 'I must go now. I'll be in touch.'

We waited in our room for three solid days. The hotel staff must have thought we were a couple of gender-benders! Determined not to miss a phone call, we stayed in, lying on our beds, reading, using room service for a constant supply of club sandwiches and Cokes. We took it in turns to leave the hotel, just to get some fresh air and have a walk. Bogota is at 8,600 feet above sea level, usually overcast with grey smog, and sprawls from a soaring concrete and glass high-rise centre to filthy poverty-stricken barrios on the outskirts. Nearly five million people live there, on streets bursting with noise, murderous traffic and unbelievably filthy poor men, women and children who will try and sell you anything from a stolen gold watch to a single cigarette. We convinced ourselves we were being followed, and went into an absurd and elaborate counter-surveillance drill, cutting back and forth through shopping malls and supermarkets, certain there was a spy round every corner. The fact is, South America was new to us, there were no watchers and we soon settled in, suspicious still, but behaving less like a couple of trainee agents in MI6.

Finally, Ricardo appeared again, apologised and said, 'The men you need to meet aren't available yet, but I'll be back in twenty minutes.'

This was South American *manana*. We stayed confined to our room for two more days when Ricardo returned with three dark-haired, swarthy friends with the usual neat moustaches and wearing rather tight-fitting double-breasted suits. He introduced them as the others who were involved in the project.

One man said very little, but the other two were ex-army officers and supplied me with a full set of 1:50,000 maps and air photographs of the Suma Paz area. They understood when I asked to make a helicopter reconnaissance of the target. We flew from Bogota's old airport in a small Cessna, but bad weather typical of the valley forced us to land at an army airstrip in Villavicenzio where we hung about in the canteen and drank excellent Colombian coffee. Conversation was stilted, as we spoke no Spanish, and, as usual in these situations, revolved round the most impressive thing they could remember about their guests, which was the world-famous British obsession for 'fish 'n' chips'!

We took off in the Cessna again and were soon lost in a maze of mountains, flying in and out of cloud which clung to the dark green trees and thickly carpeted the mountain slopes below us. The Colombians excitedly pointed down, saying, '*Casa Verde!*' but, from the air, the jungle is like an endless field of undulating broccoli and, as there were no tracks or clearings, I found it impossible to orientate myself between the gaps in the clouds.

We tried again the following day with more success and flew slowly up the Sumapaz valley with huge mountains towering above the little Cessna on all sides, rising to the peak of Cerro Nevada at 15,048 feet. *Casa Verde* is hidden in trees near the top of the valley, on a distinctive plateau rising steeply above the valley floor. So I was not able to see the house itself, but I formed a good impression of the ground conditions for our approach and withdrawal. On the other side of the pass, the foothills gradually slope away into the flat river plains of the Llanos in Meta Province and the vast Amazon jungle beyond.

Later, in our room in the hotel, Ricardo and the others spread out a very detailed sketch map. At once I recognised the layout as a complete communist base. He described the principal locations, showing the secretariat and the training camp and casually mentioned that the main accommodation was built for 400 guerrillas.

'This is the target,' he said, his finger on the secretariat.

'Then where's the *Casa Verde*?' I asked, puzzled.

'Over there,' he replied pointing to a place on the map about six miles beyond the FARC communist camp.

'Well, which do you want me to attack, the *Casa Verde* or the secretariat?'

At this, they exchanged glances among each other and eventually said, 'Can you attack the *Casa Verde*?'

'Yes, certainly,' I told them. I wondered why there seemed to be some confusion about the mission, but put it to the back of my mind. I was happy to attack either place, but clearly the secretariat of a huge FARC camp was a different proposition to a few communists in the *Casa Verde*, and I wanted the mission quite clear before I started work.

They left and, using their photographs and maps, I prepared a full set of orders, and built a model of the *Casa Verde* based on their sketches. The house was small, a typical Colombian mountain farm-house of wattle and adobe with terracotta tiles on the roof. When I was ready, I was taken by Ricardo to an office near a large department store in Bogota. The other three men were there, all in civilian clothes, with an older man who wore a suit but had the unmistakable stamp of a South American general. I spread out my plans, set up my model, just as the Army School of Instruction tells us, and ran them through the whole plan.

I got quite fired up myself as I talked, visualising the attack, and, when I had finished, they exclaimed, '*Bueno, bueno!*'

The general asked me how many people I needed. The fees for all this were Dave's area, but I chose the most men I thought they could afford. Ten, plus Dave and I. Twelve men gave me flexibility in patrol numbers, two sixes or three fours, and extra firepower. All support, food, accommodation, training areas, helicopter air support and transport would be provided by them. They said they would think about my proposition.

At the time Dave was out of the country organising non-attributable military equipment to be brought in to do the job. The weapons were being provided by the Colombians. There must be more unsourced weapons in the country than people.

However, we had the basis of a plan and, after two weeks, relations with the Colombians were very good. One day, two of them arrived in great excitement, without Ricardo, and dragged me out of the Plaza Hotel for a long drive over terrible roads into the countryside in their Landcruiser, which is the status symbol of every successful Colombian. They kept pointing at the tree-covered hillsides and talking about, '*Sumapaz!*' and '*Bandidos!*' so I assumed we were on another recce and concentrated on the task. After more than two hours of bone-rattling terror while the driver played chicken with oncoming traffic, we stopped in a large but scrappy riverside town called Girardot on the Rio Magdalena, which looked like a Hollywood set for a Wild West movie, with tall facades fronting the single-storey buildings along the main street and dusty alleys between the houses at the side.

They led the way into a café and shouted at the owner who listened expressionlessly, nodding and wiping his hands on a soiled apron. He came back a moment later with *aguardiente*, the local firewater made out of distilled sugar cane. We sat drinking and I was ready for anything except what happened next. Suddenly, the café owner reappeared with a flourish and I found myself looking at a large plate of fish and chips.

My Colombian friends grinned delightedly. They had planned the whole, long day solely to please me, for a single plate of fish and chips, convinced I would be suffering withdrawal symptoms after so long away from my national dish.

Back in Bogota, word came that they had agreed to my plan and the numbers I wanted, and the senior army officers were satisfied with Dave's prices. I was told, 'Go and get the men.'

On Friday 22 July, I flew out of Bogota's Eldorado Airport, and went through Heathrow, London, to Johannesburg where I took a room in the Carlton Hotel. I had some friends to meet.

I chose men I knew well, whom I had trained and seen on operations in South Africa's 44 Parachute Brigade. I met them all individually to put the proposition in private, and not one refused. With Dave Tomkins and I, were Terry Tagney, Dave Borland, Dean Shelley and Gordon Brinley, all men who had also served in the Rhodesian Light Infantry, Gerry O'Brien, who had also been a French Foreign Legionnaire, Jock Moore who had also been in 15 Para Territorials in Scotland and the Rhodesian Engineers, Mark Griffiths, who had also been in 1 Para in the British Army, and Roy Kaulback, who had been to the famous Scottish public school, Gordonstoun, before seeking adventure in South Africa. The last man was Alec Lennox, for whom I had found a job training Auxiliaries in Rhodesia, which made eleven, as the twelfth never actually joined us.

They wanted to know whether I thought there was a connection between the job and the so-called drug barons, and I told them, 'This task seems as straightforward as anything in Colombia. I've been dealing with army officers, we've been to an army barracks and they produced photographs and sketches with army classifications. I'm sure the Colombian secret police, the DAS, are involved too, because my passport entry visa was stamped without any of the usual bureaucratic hassle and the DAS will have to help Dave bring in the military kit through customs. The whole thing is top secret but I really do think we're working for men in bona fide government agencies, and the bottom line is that we're attacking commies, or drug producers, or both.' That was good enough for them all.

I arranged a complicated flight plan for each of them to arrive in Colombia separately. The last thing I wanted was a milling crowd, like John Banks's recruits setting out for Angola with journalists asking to be taken on the coach which drove them to the airport. This operation had to be totally secret.

While I was doing this, Dave Tomkins was buying radio equipment. I returned to England and bought other stores we were going to need from an army surplus shop near Hereford; boots, rucksacks, carabiners, gloves, abseil rope, camouflage clothing, binoculars, compasses and so on. As a precaution, I kept receipts for all this equipment and, as a matter of interest, at no stage did any customs official in England or Colombia stop me at customs.

On Thursday 18 August, I flew back to Colombia arriving at 6.30 in the evening. I took a room at the Hotel Dan, and the others joined me over the next three days, flying in via Germany, the UK, Uruguay, Madrid and even direct from South Africa. We behaved like regular tourists during this time, going out in ones and twos to visit various sights in Bogota, like the Gold Museum and the famous church at Monserrate, 2,000 feet above the city at the top of a railway funicular. Standing overlooking the whole city, I thought this was not the first time British soldiers had fought for the Colombians. When Simon Bolivar fought to evict the Spanish and created Gran Colombia, including the present-day countries of Colombia, Panama, Ecuador and Venezuela, he had two battalions of British adventurers fighting with him, called the Battalion O'Neal and Battalion Ferguson. One of our Colombian friends told me they were filled with men who had been fighting in the Napoleonic wars. Anyway, they sounded plenty Celtic enough for me!

Once all the guys were together, Ricardo arranged for them to be bussed down to Puerto Boyoca, and they drove about 200 kilometres on winding roads through the mountains of the Eastern Cordilleras, dropping all the time until the road joins the flat river valley of the great Rio Magdalena. This enormous slow-moving river is a main artery of the country, flowing from its source high in the cold Andes 1,200 kilometres to the Caribbean coast. Halfway, at Puerto Boyacar, life on its banks is hot, sweaty and truly tropical.

I was busy in Bogota, organising maps and so on, and joined them by Landcruiser with Ricardo the following day. The Colombians had chosen a very discreet spot for our training. Our base was on a small island about 150 metres wide in the middle of an ox-bow lake hidden some way from the Rio Magdalena by thick trees. To cross to the island, you had to call up on the radio, and they sent over a boat. It was a four-minute ride over the smooth dark waters to the island.

It was rightly called Isla di Paradiso. We were catered for by a delightful couple who lived in a whitewashed villa with a low terra-cotta tiled roof which sloped over a verandah shaded all round with colourful bougainvillaeas and hibiscus. Wooden steps dropped off the verandah to the ground, and a barbecue and bar stood near the jetty. Our accomodation was in several similar buildings behind the villa.

They fed us very well, on rice and chickens, which until they were needed scratched about in the yard for food. A small black pig which rootled about by the house was destined for the pot too, but I grew very attached to this pig. By holding my hand up like a witch-doctor, I could make it lie down in total submission and, after I mended a nasty cut on its nose caused by a brass ring (I'd learned a trick or two since the goat in Aden) the pig followed me everywhere. Our South American couple thought this was very charming, but when it came to barbecue time I had to plead for my pet pig's life and felt very British.

'Don't kill this pig,' I pleaded. 'I'll get you another pig, but don't kill this one!' The little black pig was reprieved but what happened after we left I would rather not think.

We had no weapons yet so I started a fitness regime. Every morning we got up at five o'clock, took the boat over the water which was smooth as black glass at that time of day, and ran as fast as we could for seven kilometres along tracks through the trees. Each day we tried to cut the time down on the day before.

Our Colombian liaison officer at Paradise Island was an ex-sergeant major called Julio who had been in a Colombian detachment with the United Nations in Sinai, and we got on well together. Like me, he was always busy checking things, making sure equipment was in place and keeping an eye open for trouble. After some days, he took me to Puerto Boyacar in his Landcruiser. We pulled up at a seedy-looking hotel in the town, he led the way into the bar, and there I met a man called Henry. I have no idea if that was his real name, but that is what we called him. We sat down to tea. Henry wore a smart shirt and slacks and showed the exaggerated good manners of a celluloid villain. I discovered later that he was in charge of the peasant militia and took a very strong line indeed rooting out communists in his area. In other words, he killed them. We sat down to tea with a couple of Colombians in army uniforms and talked about the weapons I needed for the job. At this point, another person appeared and without ceremony dumped a large canvas toolbag at my feet.

'For you, my friend,' said Henry, grinning evilly. 'Take your choice!'

Puzzled but keeping my cool, I bent down and opened the bag. It was full of pistols. Fantastic, large calibre pistols. There were Smith and Wesson .357 magnums, Colt .45s, a 9mm automatic Smith and Wesson Model 59, and a truly massive .44 magnum Israeli automatic called the Desert Eagle. Every single one was chrome-plated. This is like the movies, I said to myself. What have I got myself into? I picked the Model 59, thanked Henry politely and Julio drove me back towards the island.

I reflected on the Israeli connection. Julio had spent time in Sinai, where he had had contact with the Israeli army, there was the Israeli .44 magnum automatic pistol which I knew had only just been produced by Israeli Military Industries, and there was a pair of slippers I had found in my billet on Paradise Island which were marked 'Made in Israel'. There was certainly an Israeli link through arms sales, but did it go further?

Some days later, Julio turned up with a Landcruiser full of German G3 rifles and I could see at once that they were all in extremely bad repair. In my ignorance, I put this down to the South American factor and told myself, and the guys, that at least there were plenty of them for spares. I amended our daily routine and wrote a programme of training similar to the one I had organised for 44 Para Brigade in Mabalique. We were up at five o'clock and after our run, a shower and breakfast, we started training at nine o'clock. To start thinking like soldiers again, we began with basic weapon skills on the G3, dry and live, followed by immediate action drills, fire and movement, battle skills, patrolling and navigation. There was scrub and trees on the island for dry training and small exercises, but we went over to the mainland for shooting practices and longer four-man patrol exercises.

I made them work against each other, one patrol tracking or ambushing the others in the jungle undergrowth, as I had learned to do with the SAS in Borneo, and I made them all do written military appreciations of various situations which we might face, on the way in, on the target, on the way out, and so on. We talked through all these, picking holes in each other's plans. Every day I put a different man in charge of the patrols, mixing them round, so everyone had a chance to demonstrate their version of command and influence the decisions, and also face criticism from the others.

There was method in this. I was not dealing with a group of men whose minds and attitudes were disciplined by the structure of a regular army. These men had all served in a regular army but now they were civilians, working solely for money, as true mercenaries. I had seen in Angola, South Africa and Uganda what can happen to regular soldiers left to their own selfish devices in the civilian world. The last thing I wanted on our job was bickering, because, by the law of that great scientist Murphy, it would happen at a crucial time when least wanted.

I wanted to bring all the gripes, complaints and feelings into the open, and iron them out, which we did. Finally, to set the seal on this process, I gave them all paper and pencil, and told them to go away somewhere private and assess all the others on marks out of ten in a variety of qualities which I listed for them, such as leadership, initiative, self-discipline, knowledge of soldiering, personal skills, weapon handling, shooting and so on. Later, we sat round by the barbecue and each one read out their assessments, so everyone knew exactly where they stood with the rest. Out of this came a well-understood pecking order, a rank structure or line of command which I felt confident would work when I was not around. I know this sort of democracy is out of the question in regular armies, though the Americans use something like it which they call 'bayoneting', but it worked for us. I hardly need tell you I came out top!

I had asked Henry when the operation was going to begin and one day, about four weeks into our training, we were on the mainland during a shooting practice in the trees when four very smart Land-cruisers drove up the track, gleaming with chrome fittings and one with a GPMG machine gun mounted on the roof. They skidded to a halt, hard-faced Colombians leaped out, all heavily armed with pistols and clean new Armalites, and immediately took up rather professional-looking protective 'bodyguard' positions round about, facing outwards. Two even carried 66mm Light Anti-Tank rockets slung over their shoulders. Two others ran off to one side where they rapidly set up communications with a radio. Rather impressed with the discipline of all this, I watched Ricardo, our liaison officer from Bogota, step down from a Landcruiser with another man, who was casually dressed in shirt and slacks, like the others, but his clothes were expensive. Everything about him spoke of command.

Ricardo introduced him, 'Mr Peter, this is one of the sponsors of our operation. Mr Rodriguez Gacha.'

At the time, his name meant nothing to me, but two things were perfectly obvious. He was not in the army and he was a big Mafia man. This confirmed the suspicions I had had all along that army officers, no matter how well motivated, could not fund the sort of operation we were doing. There was always a financier and in Colombia that means drugs.

For the righteous who are scandalised by my working for a Mafia and drug baron, it is worth explaining something more of Colombian society, which, it must be said with massive understatement, is rather different to our own quiet and structured life in Britain. Colombians live on the edge of violence, and always have. The country was born in violence. In the seventeenth century Spanish, French and English adventurers murdered each other up and down the Caribbean in their quest for the gold of El Dorado, officially encouraged by the kings and queens of Europe. The Spanish finally settled the northern coast of Colombia and set about murdering the Indians who stood in their way ably assisted by their priests who burned more Indians in the name of the Spanish Inquisition and for the good of their souls. Plenty more people died in slavery. This tendency to murder was maintained throughout the nineteenth into the twentieth century with ruling settlers fighting each other in endless civil wars. The last ended as recently as 1960, after sixteen terrible years called *La Violencia*, when rival Conservatives and Liberals between them killed some 300,000 people. In a land consumed with machismo, without doubt bitter memories live on. On top of all that, and in addition to the usual dose of South American corruption, the country nowadays is torn between the FARC communists, with all the typical violent communist tricks of indoctrination and terror, and the brutalities of the huge drug business. There are at least 15,000 murders every year, most drug related. In Colombia, there are no shades of grey on the fragile front line between life and death, and this violent history seems to have resolved itself into a straightforward conflict between the Right and the Left. The Colombian Army is basically right wing, and allows the local militia, a sort of home guard, to do what it likes as long as it suppresses communism. In other words, in stark Colombian terms, the army condones, at minimum, the support of the drug business as long as the worse menace of a communist takeover is defeated. So it was that our invitation and weapons came from the Colombian Army or militia while the cost of the operation was borne by Gacha.

Gacha behaved like a visiting general. 'How's the training going?' he asked me, speaking broken English. I briefed him, just as I had so many officers over the years past, and then he had a few words with the men, along the lines of 'Boots fit? Food all right? Getting the mail?' He looked a fit, tanned man and showed a serious interest in what we were doing. Then he left. His screen of armed guards piled back into their Landcruisers, never taking their eyes off the area round, and the cavalcade disappeared down the track in a cloud of dust.

Two nights later, we were relaxing on Paradise Island after the day's training, sitting under the stars round the barbecue fire, when Julio called me up on the radio from the mainland. His voice crackled, 'Mr Peter! Come over. I take you to visit. Bring your plans.'

Ricardo and I crossed the dark lake in our boat and Julio drove us in his Landcruiser to a secret meeting. The journey there took four hours. At the end of a long road through grazing land, we stopped at a luxurious Spanish villa with a wide verandah all round, ornate wrought-iron screens on the windows and whitewashed walls shining in the bright security lights.

Half a dozen bodyguards were standing on the verandah, one armed with a 66mm anti-tank rocket, and others lurking in shadows in the garden. Inside, we were taken to a spacious dining room with an enormous circular table in the centre. Suddenly, there was a tremendous noise of horses clattering up outside and a crowd of men burst in wearing classic South American gaucho clothes, ponchos, pointed riding boots and hats all spattered with mud. Everyone was shouting and laughing. Gacha was among them, in great form, and we shook hands. Beers were served all round, they lounged about on chairs and equally suddenly, they all fell totally silent.

'Tell us your plans,' said Gacha, his black eyes deadpan.

In an atmosphere of great seriousness, I detailed the plan to attack the *Casa Verde*. No one said a word till I finished and then they all burst out shouting, '*Muerto a los communistas! Bueno! Bueno!*' and stood up, their ponchos swirling, punching their hands into the air.

'We will set up a radio station and tell the world that *Casa Verde* is destroyed!' shouted Ricardo, wildly excited.

Rather detachedly, I observed this frenetic South American enthusiasm and noticed Gacha was not joining in. He had the most penetrating eyes. I wondered how many people he had murdered to get to his position. Suddenly, the room fell silent again. Gacha looked at me straight in the eye and said, 'Could you attack the secretariat?'

'How many communists are there?' I asked at once, remembering the same question in Bogota and realising this was what they really wanted us to do.

'Seventy men.'

'I'll do it,' I said, feeling their enthusiasm beginning to affect me too. 'But I need more men.'

'*Bueno!*' said Gacha. 'Go away and make your new plans and tell me later what you need.'

Whereupon, the place erupted again with ponchos, hats and shouts of 'Kill the communists! Kill the secretariat! *Bueno! Bueno!*'

I had obviously said the right things as it only took three-quarters of an hour to drive back, and I reached Paradise Island in great excitement. 'We are going to war!' I told the guys, and we all felt better with the news that matters were now on the move.

In a subsequent meeting with Ricardo and Julio, I said I wanted another twenty-five men to attack the secretariat, with all necessary ancillary equipment including helicopters, to which they replied, 'We will give you a number of our men to train up and you can select what you want from them, but we don't have any helicopters in this area.'

I knew I would have to come back to the problem of helicopters later, but training local men was all right. I had trained so many indigenous troops in the past, in Guyana, in Rhodesia with the Auxiliaries and in South Africa, so I agreed. It was obviously a cheaper option for them, but I was relieved too. Finding another two dozen men from Europe and South Africa would have delayed things terribly and might have blown the whole thing to the press.

Sadly, Paradise Island was too small for these developments and we moved. We drove for two hours on bumpy country roads north of Puerto Boyacar and turned away from the Rio Magdalena into the hills. I noticed there was a shack on every little road junction selling sweets and lemonade, although there seemed to be no one around to keep them in business. We stopped at one for a drink, and inside I saw the reason. Behind the counter was a smart new radio. All these little shops were part of a network which covered the whole area so that nothing could move without being reported.

Our road climbed towards the foothills, winding between grassy hills cleared of the mixed secondary jungle trees and palms until we came round a corner to find two bunkers, one on each side of the road, both in disrepair and unoccupied. I dismissed them as typical South American army show-pieces but when we drove into the small valley beyond, to find our new base, I saw bunkers above us on all the high ground around. Furthermore, when Dave Tomkins and I went for a walk to look for suitable training areas later on, we visited these bunkers and I found they had all been very well sited by professionals, and were mutually supporting, with at least two being able to provide interlocking fire with each of the others.

I was impressed. While we were up there, I was looking round and something caught my eye in the tree line near the top of a ridge of hills about three kilometers away. It looked like a man-made gap in the trees. Curious to know more, Dave and I walked up there, brushing through the grass and sweating in the hot tropical sun. We found a Bell 214 helicopter hidden under the trees. Enemies could not see it from the air, but we had spotted it from below, where only friends were expected to be. They had cut a tight clearing into the trees, enough to push the helicopter under cover on wood planks and left it covered with a silvery green tarpaulin. There were no houses near by and the unusual atmosphere was enhanced because there were no guards. Plainly, Gacha's people felt so secure in this area, the chopper was quite safe on its own. Perhaps there were more hidden in the trees beyond, which we never found. Anyway, so much for there being no helicopters.

Our camp was laid out among the trees in the bottom of the valley by a stream, where the scrub had been cleared and the grass cut. We lived in wooden huts with wriggly tin roofs covered with atap leaves, and Julio turned up to help us settle in.

I faced him and said, 'I thought you had no choppers?' watching carefully for his reaction.

For a moment he looked puzzled, wondering how I knew.

'There's one up in the hills over there,' I said, pointing.

At that, he just smiled, giving no explanation, and carried on with his work.

The fifty or so Colombians I had been promised turned up dressed in shirts and slacks and armed with a variety of weapons in reasonable condition, like Armalites, AKs and pump operated shotguns. I gathered them together on the grass near the huts, briefed them on our training programme and we started work. I must admit that these chaps, who came from all over the country, were keen, but they were very right wing indeed. Every morning, before we set off on our run, they would stand rigidly to attention on the grass and their squad leaders shouted at them from the front, '*Colombia patria mia!*'

The response came bellowing back, '*Colombia patria mia! Colombia patria mia!*'

Then they turned smartly to the right and doubled off on the run.

Our valley was at the end of the road, under the foothills of the higher sierras beyond, and needless to say there was another shop where the track peetered out in trees and scrub jungle. Now who on earth was going to buy anything from here? Of course it had the usual radio inside and we used to wave cheerfully at the man every morning as we ran past.

When it came to military training for these new men, I had to start with the basics. They looked good enough toting their weapons for the camera, but the cohesion of trained soldiers which I wanted for this operation was not there. We started with basic infantry training and individual jungle shooting lanes. There was nothing specialised about this. We were not training drug cartel 'hit squads', as various frenetic journalists later accused us of doing. For that, these Colombians did not need our help. With 15,000 murders every year, men like these grew up with guns as kids and it is the most ludicrous arrogance on the part of our press to think they need outsiders to tell them how to kill each other. Colombians have had plenty of grim practice at that, as anyone who looks for five minutes into their history will see.

In the first couple of days, I noticed Colombians coming and going to one particular hut in the valley near our billets and went to have a look. Inside, radios were stacked on tables and it served as base station for all the little shacks we had passed on the drive in, manned twenty-four hours a day. All in all, the area was well defended and I wondered at the reason for all this organisation. I was sure the set-up was not just for us, because there was an air of permanence about it, and I guessed at various possibilities; that Gacha or one of his family had a house near by which needed defending, or, more probably, that there was a cocaine laboratory close by.

I never found out, and our training never really got started, because, after only four days, Ricardo arrived in the evening and said, 'We have to move from here at four o'clock in the morning.'

I was not best pleased, especially when he could not say why, or where we were going. All these changes in the plan were beginning to affect the guys and changing tack all the time is no way to run an operation. However, we were all committed and the following morning we rolled out of our narrow wooden cots in the dark, trucked back down the dusty roads we had come on, and arrived at the broad muddy waters of the Rio Magdalena in the first grey light of dawn. The river was turbulent, deep and muddy, flowing terrifyingly fast, with great logs and trees bobbing swiftly past in the brown water. They squashed as many of us as they could into long thin wooden boats with outboards and I was relieved when we reached the opposite bank. Then we were led a short distance through some trees beside the river bank to a grassy airstrip where we sat down to wait.

There must have been some coordination in these arrangements because we had not been there long before the familiar shape of a Dakota appeared in the clear, early-morning sky, landed and taxied towards us. We all piled aboard, sat about on our rucksacks all over the floor and the plane took off.

All this may sound very adventurous, and it was, being taken round the country with a group of swarthy Colombians armed to the teeth, but we had no real idea what was going on. Nor, when I asked him out of earshot of the others, did Ricardo. However, some of the guys began to grumble and I gripped them very quickly. I told them to stick with it, whether they liked it or not. My earlier efforts to establish the right pecking order paid off, and they shut up. Frankly, they had no option. We were in the middle of Colombia, entirely in the hands of Gacha's militia. Besides, they were being paid, and at least Ricardo was still with us, so we could communicate with the others.

I found it very frustrating, having no map and no plan. Perhaps dogs feel like this when their masters take them in the car for a drive. They just follow on faithfully, or fatefully. All I could do was note the time, and stare down through the window at the craggy mountains passing beneath us. They faded into lowlands and then into flat, rolling cattle grasslands which spread to all points of the compass. After about an hour and a half we landed on a laterite strip beside the Rio Yuri, in Caqueta Province.

Once again, the organisation showed itself. The Dakota refuelled at once and took off, leaving us on the strip. Here, we were fed for the first time that day, with a mess of unappetising cooked maize, like couscous, covered by a thoroughly suspect vegetable sauce. There was more muttering. We all missed our nice couple at Paradise Island and the food deteriorated every time we moved base. Little did we know how much further there was to go.

Shortly afterwards three Cessnas landed. Feeling like mobile parcels by now, we were ferried south. Soon the grasslands gave way to jungle and after another hour and a half I saw the glistening silver reflections of a huge river meandering through the green carpet beneath us. The Cessnas turned and flew across another airstrip, hacked out of the forest by the river. Later, I worked out that this was the Rio San Miguel, and that we had flown about about 800 kilometres that day, deep into the inaccessible jungle of southeastern Colombia on the edge of the Amazon basin, as remote and in-accessible a part of the world as any.

We held off landing for several minutes, and I could see little figures scurrying about on the ground beneath, pulling aside coils of wire which had been tied across the strip to stop unauthorised planes landing. It was a neat trick, but quite who they were trying to keep from visiting them, I never did discover. There are many competing government departments in Colombia, as well as the militia and Mafia leaders, and the geographical diversity, with all the principal towns separated from each other by great Andean Sierras, only serves to enhance these power divisions, as it has always has done.

The man who met us was a very piratical figure indeed. He was large, muscled, and grinned hugely under a great wide floppy army camouflage jungle hat, tied up Australian-style on one side. He wore a filthy green T-shirt and army trousers. In the crook of his arm, he carried an SLR, with ammunition pouches filled with extra maga-zines festooned round his belt. A vast curving cutlass hung at his side, but for me, the *pièce de resistance* was his green wellies, which reminded me of Uganda. In fact, wellies in the Amazon jungle, which is always subject to flooding, are not so silly as they may sound. We christened him Mungo, from the film *Blazing Saddles*.

To my disgust, Mungo cheerfully announced our travels were not over and led the way to the riverside where he showed us several quite small fibreglass boats crewed by swarthy Indians manning the big outboards at the back.

'How far in these?' I asked without enthusiasm.

'Not far,' he replied, shrugging good-humouredly. There was no point pressing him. *Manana* again. Time and distance means very little in areas as large and remote as these.

As the afternoon faded, they ferried us all down the river in several lifts, and I went first. The Rio San Miguel was very wide, perhaps 200 yards across, and the banks were lined with palms and lianas hanging from the great jungle trees for mile after mile till we pulled in on the right-hand side at a muddy slipway above which was a two-storey wooden house on stilts, painted blue. The ground round the blue house was clear, sandy earth beaten flat and dotted with a few silver-barked trees. A sagging basketball net was strung between two trees.

By the time all my team and some of the Colombians had been brought down the river on the boats, it was evening. We were all exhausted having been on the move since three o'clock that morning and we were all very hungry. This was when we met Typhoid Mary.

'Typhoid Mary' was the cook. I never knew her real name, but that's what we called her because I can honestly say that of all the meals I have eaten over the years, she served the filthiest. She was ugly and unpleasant, a dumpy, black-haired Indian woman of inde-terminate age who smiled with a mouthful of rotten yellow teeth. Hygiene was not her strong point. Her 'kitchen' was a wooden hut, with a cutting table on one side and gas rings on the other. Dirt and the fatty grime of past meals were caked everywhere and the place reeked of smoke and the sickly smell of decay.

Her first offering, from a large battered aluminium pot, was truly awful and there was nearly a mutiny. She produced a sort of maize gruel with bits of 'meat' floating in it. Ricardo sat on a log just looking at his metal plate with doleful, shocked eyes, for he was a man who loved his food and I could see he was wondering how he would survive.

Fortunately, our attention was diverted at this moment by a strange sight on the river. Another of the small boats was back with a live cow in tow. The poor beast had been swimming desperately all the way downriver, dragged along by a rope tied to the boat, its head and wet nose just above the surface. The Colombians have a very casual attitude to life, especially towards those who are about to die, for this cow was fresh rations, Colombian style.

The Colombians pulled the animal, slipping and sliding, up the bank and a crowd of men surrounded it on the basketball 'court'. Quite possibly Typhoid Mary's meal had catalysed everyone's interest in this new source of food, as they all began shouting and arguing about the best way to butcher the animal. In the end, Mungo stepped over with a purposeful look on his face, put his SLR to the wretched cow's head and blew out its brains. The cow had scarcely dropped to the ground before its belly and throat were slit and several men were jumping up and down on its stomach. Others swiftly held buckets to catch the gushing blood. We foreigners sat on the verandah of the house, starving, and watched this grisly scene in amazement while Ricardo explained they used the gore to make a sort of black pudding. Before long, the Colombians had literally hacked the cow to pieces and there was blood, guts and limbs all over the sandy ground around. It looked as if someone had opened the cow's mouth, slipped a hand grenade down its throat and blown it apart.

Typhoid Mary was in her element. For two days her kitchen belched steam and smoke and food emerged vaguely recognisable as cooked meat, but the tropical heat and flies did their work, so by the third day she was trying unsuccessfully to conceal the extreme deterioration of her ingredients with a doughty mincing machine and dirty handfuls of chilli peppers.

Napoleon was right to say an army marches on its stomach. All we had to drink was the cheapest Colombian coffee and I was the only person with teabags, so by the third day, the British were desperate. Dean Shelley came crawling over the verandah on his belly towards me, gasping out, 'A teabag! A teabag! Anything for a teabag.'

Eventually, all the fifty Colombians and our stores had been brought down the river and I tried to start up training again, with weapon handling and fire and movement drills.

I sat them all down in a circle and described, through Ricardo, how to do a camp attack, and that night we did an approach march in the jungle area behind the river and walked through the whole sequence. Of course we were tired after that, but a cockerel behind the kitchen kept me awake all the following night. At two o'clock in the morning I lost my temper. I sneaked over the sandy earth to its cage and battered the wire with a stick. The bird stopped crowing and eyed me suspiciously. I went back to our hut and lay down on my bed again and, just as I passed into deep sleep, I distinctly heard a strangled squawk. The following day, Typhoid Mary gave me a very reproachful look as she passed me on the way to the river with the dead cock in her hands, to throw it in the water. It was her prize fighting cock! I looked round the guys, who all looked quite innocent, except Shelley. He must have been watching me in the shadows when I thumped the cage and nipped over to administer the stretched neck treatment.

We were in one of the remotest parts of the world, stuck on the bank of a jungle river, feeling very cut off and living in a degree of squalor made bearable only by an increasingly strained sense of humour. Then, I suddenly discovered that Mungo had a radio telephone. In broken English, he started talking about our contract in such a way that I was suspicious. Through Ricardo, I pressed him and he showed me the radio-telephone which linked onto the International Direct Dialling network. He had been using it to call our backers in Bogota and elsewhere. He did not discuss our contracts any more and a day later he said, 'We must move again.'

'Why?' I wanted to know, fast losing patience.

'*Communistas!* They are close by,' he said excitedly, grinning.

'Tell me where, and we'll go and attack them!' I retorted in exasperation.

He wouldn't have it. I argued but he insisted that we move again. To my annoyance, we only moved twenty minutes down river, which hardly seemed sufficient if they were really afraid of a threat from a large group of FARC. I was convinced there was another reason. Worse, Typhoid Mary came too.

Stuck in such a remote place, our original purpose to attack the communist secretariat at Sumapaz was losing its immediacy. However, I was determined to stick to the plan and went for a walk to find a place to train. Mungo led me across a large open grass field, which had been cleared back from the river for cattle, and we entered the jungle on a track. I had never seen such a path design before, but it made sense. Thick tree bark had been laid on the ground, supported by wood stakes driven into the earth, to form a walkway which lots of men could use time and again without churning the track into a mud bath, which is inevitable when rain and flooding make a jungle track impassable. At the end of this track, in the gloom of the jungle about a hundred yards from the open grass field, was a camp.

The place was unoccupied, but all the huts were extremely well made, of wood and roofed with palm fronds, and it had not been allowed to get overgrown by the encroaching jungle. 'What's this place?' I asked Mungo.

Off-hand, he replied, '*Communistas!*'

'Yeah,' I answered coolly. I pointed at the largest hut in the centre of the camp and said knowledgeably, 'That must be where the commissar gripped them all with his political lectures.' You couldn't tell me anything about communist camps, not after Borneo and Africa.

Mungo looked puzzled but nodded politely.

On reflection, he must have thought I was very thick. The right-wing and the communists do fight each other, but in Colombia this classic power struggle is not for the hearts and minds of the people, but, quite simply, to control these remote jungle areas where *Erythroxylum coca novagranatense* is grown. So, while Mungo visualised coca leaves being processed and the warm air filled with the sweet smell of kerosene, I imagined a circle of keen sweating faces being harangued about Karl Marx.

I poked about the huts some more and realised my mistake. In one hut I found powerful electric heat lamps, in another there were microwave ovens for the laboratory, in a third, mixing machines like large dishwashers, probably for breaking up the leaves, and finally in a fourth was a stack of hundreds of polythene bags. None of this was anything to do with Karl Marx.

Back in our camp by the river, where the lads were settling in to several more wooden huts on stilts, I confronted Ricardo. 'What the hell is going on?' I demanded crossly.

'The communists were here,' he said blandly. 'And they were driven out.'

I gave him a long look and left it at that. None of these Colombians ever mentioned drugs, cocaine or any other, at any stage during the whole time we were there. Which in itself was odd. Some of the Colombians with us disappeared off in the boats every day and came back in the evening, or they went off in groups into the jungle, but there was never any explanation. Even on reflection, I have no idea what they were doing (though I can make a suspicious guess, of course), nor can I decide what they thought we were supposed to be doing for them. I concluded there was nothing for it but to give our training one last attempt.

I started lectures again, using one of these large wooden huts as a lecture room, and Ricardo translated. All the Colombians squatted on the floor and listened attentively to my fiery presentation of a camp attack. At intervals I stopped and they turned to Ricardo for the translation. The impact was lost at once. Ricardo was gently swinging back and forth in a hammock slung across between two windows in the corner of the room. This was South America, but not the conditions for good lectures as recommended by the British Army *Methods of Instruction* manual.

There was a streak of madness in the place. No one got any sleep inside the huts, because all the Colombians liked hammocks. They slung them beneath our hut, between the stilts, and all night long the whole hut shook back and forth, squeaking with the sibilant hiss of stretched cord.

Another time, a Colombian called Mia Farrow (literally) caused uproar. He had been a communist in the FARC before switching allegiance to the DEA and was typically self-important, full of South American machismo. The FARC had sent him to Russia where he had trained as a medic but he preferred to call himself a doctor. I suppose a trip to Russia was quite something to these young Colombians. They were so impressed with Mia Farrow's stories, that they agreed to let him circumcise them. For a fee. He said it was good for their love life! The first we knew was the camp echoing with screams all one morning and for several days young men minced about in agony, swearing they were going to kill him. Of course, my medic had to fix them up with penicillin injections to stop the inevitable infections.

Another night, we were all woken by the sound of firing. Everyone tumbled out of bed and started shooting into the darkness, only to find two of the Colombians had gone off drinking in a little shack further down the river bank and, returning drunk, decided to fire off the contents of their magazines to see how alert we were. We calmed them down and I came back to find Ricardo standing by our hut and staring at a grenade he was holding uncertainly in his hand. He said to me, 'I'm not cut out for this, Mr Peter!'

He was right. We had had enough. The food was terrible, we

couldn't sleep, and the training was constantly interrupted. Far from training drug cartel 'hit squads', we weren't getting any training done at all, and the plan to attack Sumapaz seemed more distant every day. I couldn't see the point of being in the jungle. I became convinced that we were being kept out of the way, just to have us handy if they did eventually decide what they really wanted us to do for them.

I needed to talk to the men in charge in Bogota. Ricardo and I used Mungo's radio-telephone to make the arrangements and we left. The guys were fed up. They thought I was leaving them and I went to some trouble to explain before they understood I had to speak personally to the men in Bogota. The fact is they had never served in command positions in the army, and couldn't easily see the officer's, or management's, side of the coin.

Of course, Ricardo was overjoyed. He was fast losing weight and was dying to get away from Typhoid Mary. He was a genial man, an army officer who hated living like a 'jungle Indian'. We took a boat back up river and flew from the airstrip to Bogota.

In Bogota my suspicions were confirmed. Ricardo set up meetings with the army officers I had met before and we thrashed over the whole business.

I was still prepared to attack the communist secretariat if they could get their act together. I wanted to put pressure on them, because I made up my mind that if we had to call a halt to the whole business, it would be their fault for failing to produce the logistics and support, not ours for lacking the guts or determination. I had discovered that there had been an Israeli connection, as I had suspected in Paradise Island. My 'made in Israel' slippers had belonged to one of a team like ours, but, unlike us, the Israelis had refused to go into the jungle.

I said, 'We need helicopters.' To drop us off short in Sumapaz and make the final approach to the target on foot.

'It's too high. The altitude is too much for choppers,' they said.

This was nonsense. During the talk, it became obvious that the whole problem was simply that they could not make up their minds what they wanted us to do. I made up their minds for them and insisted they fly all my guys back to Bogota.

We stayed in the Hotel Dan and during these few days in Bogota, Roy Kaulback chatted up a female journalist only to discover she had photographs of the *Casa Verde*. Unknowingly, she showed him an article in a glossy magazine with pictures of the Green House in Sumapaz. It was nothing more than an attractive little green-painted mountain farm house. Roy, who had studied Sociology at Cambridge

University, did not require his 'A' grade on a South African Army intelligence course to realise that our plan to attack the *Casa Verde* had been a bait to hook us in the first place.

I told the Colombians they must make up their minds what they wanted us to do. Finally, they admitted there was no real plan and advised us to go home.

Back in the hotel, there was some muttering about pay. I hate this, but it's an inescapable facet of civilian life. From being soldiers of fortune in the jungle camp, they had instantly turned back into civilians in the luxury of the hotel. Actually, Dave Tomkins was excellent over this, dealing with the Colombians who paid up all that was due very fairly.

At my last meeting with the Colombian Army officers, I said, 'Please, next time, let me come out here to set up everything myself, and then, when I'm sure the job is ready, I'll bring over the men. That way there'll be no confusion, which is bad for the team, and you won't be paying men to hang about.'

They agreed.

On Friday 18 November, Dave and I flew back to England.

When I got home, the first thing I did was to send Murray Davies £500, to repay his loan which got me to Rhodesia all those years ago in 1976, with a bit of interest.

12

The Colombian Adventure, Part Two

He began to decipher the instant that he was living, deciphering it as he lived it, prophesying himself in the act of deciphering the last page of the parchments, as if he were looking into a speaking mirror.

GABRIEL GARCIA MARQUEZ, *One Hundred Years of Solitude*

I am pleased to say that there was no security leak by any of the team on their return home. We all felt there was more to do in the future and they kept quiet. A breach of security to the Press or any of the secret services, of Britain or the United States, would certainly have blown the operation apart at that stage.

So, on Tuesday 21 February the following year, 1989, I was sitting in the Booth Hall at lunchtime wondering why British security firms would not employ me. I had more soldiering experience than most and I had successfully managed the whole spectrum of civilian security operations, for COIN in South Africa: static guards, cash-in-transit, and keypoint armed militia operations, all of which covered a region of South Africa bigger than England. My brooding was rudely interrupted when the swing doors of the bar crashed open and Dave Tomkins burst in.

'Here we are, fellers!' he shouted, posing theatrically at the door. He looked typically debonair, in fashionable clothes, gold watch, bracelet, neck chain, coiffured grey hair and his expensive Cartier sunglasses for which I had paid half as a present on our way home three months before. In his right hand he held a wad of dollars.

He sat down and I said quietly, 'Dave, what the hell is going on?'

'They want us back,' he replied, slipping into a conspiratorial whisper to match my tone, 'and there's a real job to do.'

Three days later, on Friday, we left England's cold winter and flew to Panama, where we spent two days in sweltering heat sightseeing the Canal, which surprised me by its narrowness, and waiting for our connection to Colombia. We were going to Cali, Colombia's third-largest town after Medellin, in the Rio Cauca valley where a pleasant combination of tropical warmth and altitude among the high sierras produces a rich and beautiful agricultural region, principally noted for its sugar cane.

On Sunday 26 February we landed at Cali airport where we were met by our gallant Colonel Ricardo.

He was delighted to see us and, after many heart-warming handshakes and greetings, he ushered us smoothly through the usual police checks. Later, when we were on our own in an enormous apartment in the smart part of Cali, he announced dramatically, 'Mr Peter, they've made up their minds. They want you to kill Pablo Escobar.'

This was a task!

'And you'll get all the backing you need.' He gestured round the spacious flat and went on, 'You will be based here. Treat it as your own. I shall be your liaison officer and interpreter as before, and they want you to start the planning at once.'

Of course there was the usual *manana* to cater for, with Ricardo going off for several days at a time, but it was soon obvious to me that they were serious. Pablo Escobar, perhaps the most important cocaine drug baron in the world, was our target.

I have no doubt that the idea of employing a team of ex-soldiers to assassinate someone is repugnant to many people. They may be offended by the savagery and illegality, but I imagine they will be reading this in the comfort of their homes in more civilised places than Colombia. Instead of being outraged by people like me, let the moralists think of Escobar's guilt in the cocaine and crack drug trade, and the misery he has caused millions of addicts and their families. He has consistently evaded justice and perhaps men like me offer the only realistic way in which men like Escobar can be dealt with in places like Colombia.

This won't satisfy some. They will call the argument superficial, the first step onto the slippery slope to a lawless society, totalitarianism and corruption. George Bernanos was right, they will shout. 'Beware "the end justifies the means".' All I can say is that Escobar was a big enough villain for me, and the twelve of us were prepared to take the risk.

He was closely protected by seventy guards and lived in a heavily defended villa called Hacienda Napoles on the road between Puerto

Triumpho and Medellin. Puerto Triumpho was about ten kilometres from Puerto Boyacar where we had been the year before and Ricardo arranged for me to fly over the place in a twin-engined Caravan airplane on a normal flightpath. Armed with a Canon and 70–210mm lens with a fast film setting to avoid camera shake, I took hundreds of photographs and made notes. The house was enormous, ring-fenced, guarded by towers and barrack buildings and I knew from the previous year how all the road junctions and approaches in the whole area around would be covered by a network of lookouts and mobile patrols all linked by radio. This was not going to be easy and the thing fascinated me!

While I set about working up a plan in our apartment, Dave Tomkins flew out to collect the team. They arrived as before on different flights via various countries so that operational security was maintained. There had been one or two changes. Four men were unable to come back; Gerry O'Brien, Roy Kaulback, Mark Griffiths and Gordon Brinley. In their place were two ex-22 SAS men, Don Milton and Stuart McVicar, an ex-21 SAS Territorial called Andy Gibson, an ex-British Para called Ned Owen, and two men from the South African special forces Recce Commando called Pete Donnelly (also ex-Scots Guards and Rhodesian Light Infantry) and Billy Potts (also ex-Royal Marine and Rhodesian Light Infantry). All together we were twelve. They joined me in our comfortable apartment in Cali, which was a great change from the filthy conditions of the jungle, and I gave them a briefing. 'We shall be moving on to another place soon, where we can start our workup training,' I said, 'but while we're here, don't go round in more than twos or draw attention to yourselves. Behave in a touristy manner.'

Two of them let me down. I was well ahead with my plans, so I went for a walk in the middle of Cali, to have a look at the shops. The town was less busy than Bogota, more provincial, but the streets were still noisy with traffic, hectic Spanish pop music and poorly dressed people selling cheap shoes, plastic buckets and little gold trinkets of frogs and Inca gods. There is a strong religious under-current in Colombia, the rich gold-leaf of Catholicism beaten over the hard wood of older beliefs, and I nipped inside a couple of big churches to absorb a little good homely Catholic atmosphere. On my way back through the main square, I glanced through the window of a bar and recognised a distinctive yellow tracksuit one of the guys had been wearing. I went inside, to join them. Two of them were slumped, nearly unconscious, at a table on which there stood not just one but two empty Black Label whisky bottles. I thought they were joking, to wind me up. They were not joking, for they were totally blitzed, but they did wind me up. I was furious, especially as one was ex-SAS and the other ex-44 Para Brigade. They were jeopardising the whole operation. I got them back to the apartment, and next morning when they sobered up, I fined the two men $200 each and left everyone in no doubt that drink was out. The two culprits were not bad men. In fact they were good soldiers, but idiots with drink. It is one thing being good on operations out in the bush where there is no drink, but quite a different self-discipline is required in a civilian environment when there are bars all round. I enjoy my drink, but when I am working, on a job, I do not drink. However, the lesson was learned. From then on we drank crates of Coca-Cola and I had nothing but 100 per cent commitment from them all.

I prompted Ricardo to move us to our training base immediately. Actually, if I had hoped for something spartan, in sympathy with our training, I was in for a surprising disappointment. Our flat had been very comfortable, but our new quarters were exceptional. We were housed in a really beautiful white villa roofed by acres of terracotta tiles in the hills behind Cali, surrounded by landscaped gardens, mown grass lawns, ornamental trees, a swimming pool, a tennis court, a football pitch which served as a heli-pad, a running track round the perimeter, forests of security lights and fencing, and the largest satellite dish I have ever seen. Inside, the rooms were enormous and luxuriously appointed, we were very well catered for by a few discreet resident staff, there was a weight training room downstairs, and the place was empty, all for us. What a contrast to the year before.

I did four flights in the Caravan past Escobar's house and accumulated plenty of information. I briefed the guys on the job, but I gave no names, nor the location of the target at that time. I said I would wait until we had all the kit together. There were weeks of training ahead and the last thing I wanted was someone to produce an excuse to bottle out and find some scoop-hungry journalist with a loose hand on his chequebook.

I had good reason to be cautious. Only two weeks after arriving, Terry Tagney came to me to say he really could not face the sort of attack I had told them we were going to do. This was the kind of weakness which might destroy the team, but, as I could not hold him in Colombia, I covered up for him by telling the others that his wife was threatening to leave him and sent him home sworn to secrecy. I am sorry to say that once he was home, he went on television and described his reasons for leaving in a rather different light, by saying he had had 'a sudden attack of common sense' which obliged him to return home.

The rest of the team stayed solid. I gave them enough information for our training to begin even without the weapons which Ricardo was still organising for us. I must say that I tried to put all my experience of years into this training. We started with the usual but necessary and I may say terribly satisfying programme of fitness. As a result of spending so much time in a wheelchair and on crutches, and drinking too much during those two frustrating years without being able to exercise, I was still carrying too much weight, but my leg bones had set firm, for better or worse, and, while I was no longer as fast as I had been, I was strong and became very fit. We warmed up running round the track, then worked out on a speed circuit in the weights room and soon pulled into shape. I lost a lot of weight and built up muscle to the point where I was no longer embarrassed to take off my shirt!

We also saved time by working on our military skills, dry, without weapons. We practised our immediate action contact drills on the football pitch, where we also worked on helicopter emplaning and deplaning drills. I set out chairs in the same configuration as the seats inside a helicopter and we practised covering each other getting 'in' and 'out'. This was going to be a vital part of my plan.

When the weapons arrived, I really knew our backers meant business this time. A shiny aluminium box van, like a refrigeration unit, drove up the paved driveway to our villa. Almaro, a thin wiry paratroop Major who was another interpreter and liaison officer, hopped out and, with a flourish, unlocked the bars at the back to reveal an Aladdin's cave of brand spanking new weapons, ammunition and explosives. These were not the shabby German G3s we had been given at Paradise Island, which had been cast-offs from the militia. This was the *crème de la crème*. There were American M16s, pistols, plenty of magazines, pouches, gleaming ammunition in boxes, grenades, M72 66mm Light Anti-Tank rockets, pounds and pounds of PE4 plastic explosive, time pencils, detonators, safety fuses, primers, detonating cord, switches and so on. Everything was in excellent condition.

My training programme was progressive, building one thing on another, because I wanted no mistakes on the attack. Rather than rush off to fire our new weapons on the range, I made everyone practise weapon handling in the villa first. For a week among other subjects, we concentrated on stripping and assembly, handling and stoppages, and we got very slick.

I was very pleased with the men. The atmosphere was excellent and a complete contrast to the previous trip. Everyone was committed and enthusiastic. They could all see that we were getting the equipment and support I was asking for, and everyone worked hard.

Actually, we had so much good equipment, some of the guys began to complain they wanted more. This is typical of soldiers, and I suppose people in general. As ex-soldiers in the British, Rhodesian or South African armies, all these men had been used to getting the job done with what was available, or as they used to say in the British SAS, 'Just a length of para-cord and a piece of masking tape.' Now, faced with a veritable hamper of goodies, they wanted more.

All special forces units risk falling into this trap and it leads swiftly to operational castration. A unit's success brings attention, which brings finance, which pays for new equipment, which is when the rot sets in. Like children, soldiers ask for more and their expectations rise for more expensive and complicated equipment. Just having the best personal weapon is not good enough. They want all the other things too, which would be nice to have, just in case, like SatComs for everyone. Of course, special forces soldiers will say they need equipment variety to meet all the demands put on them. However, swamped with fancy gear, soldiers lose the skills of basic soldiering and become dependent instead on exotic technological equipment. Finally, they begin to think the job cannot be done without it. And that's the kiss of death to any unit.

My team had ten 30-round magazines each, pistols, grenades, LAW rockets, plastic explosive, machine guns and I called a halt to their demands. I said, 'There are only seventy or eighty enemy guards on our target and you've got enough ammunition between you to kill over three thousand people!'

We started firing live ammunition in a secluded spot in the scrub hills beyond Cali. My programme was similar to our previous one in the woods at Paradise Island, except now we had a definite target which I had seen from the air and we could tailor our range practices to suit.

We were well supported now but we could never relax. On the way to the range one day, we stopped at a little café beside the road, the Café Sello Rojo, a long, whitewashed concrete shed, with the usual terracotta tiled roof and several shuttered doorways which were rolled up for ventilation. The weather was hot but overcast and humid and we were always thirsty. We parked our red and white Toyota Landcruisers and the aluminium weapons truck and stood about drinking Coke when a policeman passed on a Harley Davidson motorbike.

He was straight from Hollywood, dressed in black leathers patched with fancy badges, a holstered revolver, gleaming black sunglasses, and a white helmet. My heart sank when I saw him checking us out.

Our boots had caught his eye. We were all in T-shirts and jeans but trying to wear in our army boots, and that single uniformity looked decidedly strange in Colombia. Sure enough the cop turned round and cruised back. He got off his bike, propped it up, straightened his black leather jacket, adjusted his sunglasses and sauntered over with an unpleasant expression on his face. When he found we could speak no Spanish, he was at once suspicious. The atmosphere became tense, he became aggressive, probably because he knew the police station was only a hundred yards away in the village, and the guys began to edge towards the aluminium weapons truck. Almaro strode up and waved his major's identity card in the policeman's face. This produced a vicious clash of Colombian machismo. The traffic cop had no intention of being bullied by an army officer and spat out a torrent of Spanish, the gist of which was clearly, 'Get fucked!'

Dave Tomkins floated round the two, smoking and smiling genially, trying to pour oil on the troubled waters, saying, 'Everything okay then?'

Almaro glared at him. He was furious that in spite of all our backing, he was helpless faced with this obstinate small-time traffic policeman. The story is the same the world over.

Almaro's response was also a world beater. He bribed the cop. He walked out of earshot round the side of the café and made a call on his radio to our base station. Then he ignored the policeman's demands for an explanation with dismissive gestures till, about twenty minutes later, another man on a motorbike roared down the road and pulled in. This was one of ours, the 7th Cavalry, but more subtle. The rider handed a small bag to the major who handed it to the traffic cop who took it with ill grace as his due. He swaggered back to his Harley and motored off. Such is South American life, but I wish I could have been bribed to stop every bit of trouble I've ever been in.

A cement Virgin Mary and Child watched over this corrupt little scene from a stone plinth. Garishly painted blue, pink and yellow, with her concrete child balanced fantastically on one hand, the Virgin stared blandly over our heads at the fields of sugar cane. The more violent a society, the more it parades its religion.

Our helicopters arrived. A glass bubble Hughes 500, which I wanted to use as a command K-car over the target, was flown by Tiger, a really keen police pilot. A troop-carrying Bell 204, the Huey of Vietnam fame, was flown by a very experienced and sober Colombian called Pablo.

Our villa was an excellent base, but I wanted a larger training area where we could fire without restrictions. They had already prepared something for us. We flew in the helicopters over the 10,000-foot peaks of the Western Cordilleras behind Cali and dropped down the other side over the thick flat jungle plain north of Buenaventura, which is a large port on the Pacific coast.

Our training camp was at La Gagua which was nothing more than a wide bend in the Rio Manguido. The river provided us with an important training ground. On the bend were several hundred yards of flat, firm pebble and sandbanks which we could use for rangework, to build models of our target and to land the helicopters. When the helicopters were not being used, we pushed them on their slides along hardwood slats into hides built under cover of the jungle trees. They were covered with tarpaulins and camouflaged with atap leaves to cut down the reflection of the glass and wet tarpaulins. The technique reminded me of the one we had found on the hillside near Boyacar the year before. Our reason for doing this was 'Opsec'. These helicopters were sterile in that, although the Bell was painted in Colombian police green and white colours and the Hughes was painted Colombian Army plain green, they did not come from any government or police department. Although our backers certainly had the clout, taking away an aircraft from an official source might have provoked unwelcome questions. Our choppers had been flown into the country specially for this job. We hid them in case real police or army flying over our jungle camp saw them by sheer bad luck.

We lived in a solidly built wooden cabin painted ochre red with a verandah overlooking the river. There was a good clean kitchen and we were well looked after by several cheerful Colombian Indians. These men had been preparing this place specifically for our operation, laying out the helicopter slats, building up the hut, and the aircraft mechanic was the hardest-working grease monkey I have ever seen.

There was as much room to rehearse here as I needed. We built a scaled-down model of Escobar's house with wood poles cut from the jungle and hessian for walls and the ex-SAS men were in their element. Their training on 'house-clearance' learned in the SAS anti-terrorist team combined well with my own experience of fighting real enemy through bunkers in Angola. We built up in stages, first on dry practices, then firing live ammunition, from one man entering a single room, through two men, to a group of four working through several rooms one after the other. The weapons handling was good from our earlier work, and the guys' confidence increased as they improved with each element of my plan. Though we were only twelve men against eighty, we all felt increasingly bullish about our chances.

Our training continued through March and into April. We went back and forth between our villa in Cali and our training camp at La Gagua. Day after day, we practised so that the guys became fluent with every detail of the skills they would need, building on room clearance, firing the 66mm anti-tank rockets, throwing grenades and blowing satchel charges. All the time Colonel Ricardo kept me informed about the likely date of our attack. Obviously, they did not want us to attack until they were 100 per cent sure Escobar was at home, and equally I told Ricardo that I did not want to commit the team until I was 100 per cent sure we were ready. Ricardo, and our sponsors, completely understood and I began to tie in our skills to my plan of attack.

Back at La Gagua, I briefed them on each phase of the whole plan: how we would fly onto the target, how both choppers would suppress two guard towers each with machine-gun fire, the hover-landing to off-load the assault team, the order of taking out the guard positions, attacking the guard accommodation, clearing the villa itself and so on. We began to practise each phase of the plan over and over, firing thousands of rounds, blowing pounds of plastic, and throwing dozens of grenades until everyone knew their own tasks so well that I made them change round. I was determined everyone would carry a clear picture of the whole attack plan in their minds so they would understand what was happening around them while they were busy on their own tasks. This also meant everyone could react flexibly if things went wrong. Each man had a personal radio with an earpiece and I would command them from above in the Hughes helicopter K-car where I could see the action, direct them and be in touch with every man on the ground.

The programme was going too smoothly. One day early in May we were back in the villa in Cali and Dave Tomkins phoned his home in England to chase up some more equipment we needed. His wife, who was helping, said, 'James Adams of *The Sunday Times* has been trying to contact you.'

This was the last thing we wanted to hear. If details of our plans hit the newspapers, the operation would be cancelled. Simple as that.

Dave's wife gave us Adams's home telephone number. He had guessed that the story was extremely sensitive, if he knew little else, and preferred to keep any conversations away from *The Sunday Times'* offices. Dave called him at home.

'I would like to talk to you about your recent trips to Colombia,' said Adams, coming straight to the point. Dave had been going back and forth to buy equipment such as radios and webbing, and had probably clocked up six trips by then.

'What are you talking about?' Dave replied guardedly.

Bluntly, Adams then detailed Dave's flight numbers and dates, one by one. He said, 'I know you're in Colombia now and that Alec Lennox, Peter McAleese and Dean Shelley are there.' He finished by saying, 'I'm about to print the story tomorrow morning. D'you want to make a comment?'

With hindsight, I believe we should have called his bluff and said, 'Go ahead and print.' Adams did not know enough of the facts to have damaged the operation. I think he told us all he knew, to create the maximum impact, but we had no control over his speculations. We had no idea then how he had come by the information or who his source was and we felt vulnerable. Perhaps we should have had a PR front, someone briefed by us, in England, to handle people like Adams, to keep them at arm's length and issue statements as necessary, but, as soldiers, we were head down in our training and were taken off-balance. We were at a disadvantage and he knew it.

With difficulty, Dave persuaded Adams not to publish but only on condition we met him in Panama.

On Thursday 11 May, Dave and I flew from Cali to Panama City, the day after a riot in which General Noriega's paramilitaries brutally hospitalised opposition leader Guilliermo Endara with iron bars and beat up his supporters who were demonstrating against vote-rigging. Panama was very unstable in the build-up to the American invasion.

We went to our rendezvous with James Adams in the Hotel Continental in the evening, as the sun was setting. We found the patio bar by the swimming pool and sat down at one of the tables with a beer each to enjoy the last of the sun with other guests. We were in casual shirts and trousers, Dave his usual suave self with sunglasses and gold chain. Adams was late. He may even have been watching us from somewhere in the shadows, but he appeared on the patio with the studied elegance of a seasoned world traveller. Tipping a rolled-up copy of *The Times* at us in recognition, he walked over at a stylish pace between the other tables and sat down. He was in his mid-forties but deliberately cultivated a youthful image, with smoothly coiffured blond hair, à la Jason Donovan, and a trim figure. He was wearing a carefully crumpled fawn cotton suit with the cuffs turned back on his wrists, *Miami Vice* style, which he probably thought appropriate in Panama City at that time, a pale yellow open-neck shirt and comfortable slip-on shoes with no socks. After introductions, he called over a waiter with a flick of his hand, allowed us to order another couple of beers, and then asked for a long drink I had never heard of, which turned out to be filled with fruit, topped with a small paper umbrella, and strongly alcoholic.

There ensued a few minutes of verbal strutting while we metaphorically circled each other like rival dogs. Dave Tomkins had learned his tricks at a rather different school to James Adams but they both put in a lot of mirror time and I was treated to the sight of two professionals at battle. Dave toyed with the gold Krugerand on the end of his chain and talked about the important arms deals he had done while Adams swanked about Frederick Forsyth using his material for his books. Adams's trump was his threat to print a story about us and he set about softening us up.

'What you're doing is an open secret in Whitehall,' he said in a hard, knowledgeable way, hoping to frighten us.

This did not have the impact he wanted. I felt quite sure people in Whitehall in the secret services and narcotics departments would be only too delighted if Pablo Escobar was off the scene. Besides, the fact is that the CIA and the DEA have more clout in Colombia than Whitehall and we had already been in touch with a contact in the CIA, to test their reaction to what we were doing. Unofficially, the CIA response was, 'Do the job as soon as possible and get out.'

Actually, I very much doubt that anyone in Whitehall had any idea what we were doing in Colombia at that time.

However, Dave and I were on a damage-limitation mission. We were not sure how much he knew. The last thing we wanted was Adams to print a story which would blow the security of our operation, so we felt somewhat at his mercy. He took full advantage. He suggested we all had dinner together and we went to a seafood restaurant where he continued a barrage of questions for more than an hour. His technique was relentless and, in retrospect, not very subtle. He taxed us about Dave's arms deals and my soldiering life, typically concentrating on the short mercenary period in Angola rather than the years of my regular service in Rhodesia and South Africa, and every few moments suddenly switched back to our 'job' in Colombia. He could tell we were on to something really big, but we gave nothing away. It was clear he felt very much in control and, though he finally agreed to hold back his story on condition that we gave him an exclusive on our operation, his cool and rather arrogant bonhomie got me down. I decided to go on the attack myself.

'James,' I said, leaning forward over the table and looking him straight in the eyes, 'why don't you come with us?'

'What d'you mean?' he asked, startled.

'Come with us. On the operation. With me. You'll see the whole business first hand.' Non-combatants get in the way, but here was a chance to take a journalist with me into the fighting, really involve him in what we were doing and be correctly reported for once in my life. I felt quite enthusiastic. 'I'll fit you into the team,' I told him encouragingly. 'Then you'll be able to write a real story!'

He declined.

His attitude changed abruptly after that. Altogether more cautious, our conversation continued on more equal terms. He had lost his opportunity to be part of the action, and relegated himself to reporting it second-hand.

We met him the following day but nothing further emerged. We flew back to Cali on 14 May reasonably satisfied that he would not blow the story until we had finished the job.

However, our trip to Panama made me realise how delicate our security might be. We had been so involved in our training in our villa and in the jungle at La Gagua, where security was excellent, that I had lost sight of what was going on elsewhere and plainly more people knew about us than needed to.

Outside Colombia, we were confident Adams would not publish for the time being, but how long would he hold off, for fear someone else might steal his scoop? Would his source who had betrayed Dave go to someone else? On our return, Dave made numerous calls back to England and finally pinned down this Opsec leak to a man who had supplied radios to us. This charmer had bugged and taped his telephone calls with Dave and bubbled us for a handful of filthy lucre, carelessly putting our lives at risk. Knowing we were in Colombia, it had been easy for Adams to find out Dave's flight details after that. The circle of people in the know would have spread wider if Adams had told anyone else himself, because people love sounding important by talking about stories like this. The circle would have spread still wider if our contact in the CIA had told anyone. I guessed he had made a report to cover his own back (and enjoy the kudos) and who knows what circulation of readers such a report might have?

There was reason to think that the CIA knew more about our operation than they let on. The concept of 'decapitating' drug cartels, which means removing the leaders, was gaining favour in Washington over the more resource-draining effort of stopping the thousands of little men in the lower echelons of the drug trade. That year, the US Attorney General Dick Thornburgh said, 'You take an Ochoa, an Escobar, a Gacha or a top money launderer out of the operation, it disrupts them.'

There was reason to worry about security inside Colombia too. Our contact in the CIA had been quite blunt. He warned us not to speak to anyone in the DEA (the US Drug Enforcement Administration). The DEA are very active in Colombia but they use a good many local undercover agents and the CIA man told us they would be as liable to corruption by drug money as anyone else in Colombia. Actually, I do not think the DEA knew, but I had no control of our backers or who they might tell.

For certain, the more people who knew, the greater the chance of a catastrophic leak to Pablo Escobar himself, in which case we might fly in to an enemy ready and waiting. The bottom line was that our lives were forfeit and the risk increased day by day.

I told Ricardo we wanted to attack as soon as possible and set about the final dress rehearsals with full equipment and live ammunition.

We flew down to La Gagua and gathered in the cabin for the full orders' briefing I had prepared for the attack, with our pilots, Ricardo and all the team dressed up, tooled up and ready to go. I set out my models of the target house, aerial photographs which I had fitted together in a panorama, sketches, diagrams and variously scaled maps and painstakingly took them through every detail. For the technically minded, I have included these orders as Appendix E.

'This is Operation Phoenix,' I told them, calling it after the South African 44 Parachute Brigade arising from its own ashes. 'And our mission is to kill Pablo Escobar.' Several photographs of him stared down at us from the wall.

After my orders, I questioned them on details, to make sure they understood precisely what each and every man was to do and we went out to the helicopters for a full-scale dress rehearsal. We wore camouflage uniform, boots and combat waistcoats which contained ammunition pouches stitched across our chests and other pouches for extra equipment, grenades and ammunition round the back. Every man wore a thin black balaclava helmet with a large phosphorescent yellow cross sewn on the top so I could identify our men from my K-car in the air. This was a trick I had learned in Rhodesia. Anyone else on the ground would be fair game. They also carried extra bags of grenades, 66mm anti-tank rockets and explosives.

I climbed into the Hughes helicopter. Dave Tomkins, Almaro the army major and Ramon, another interpreter, sat in the back. Our pilot Tiger gunned the engines and we lifted off the river bed, up and over the jungle canopy. With the beat of the blades, I could feel the excitement building. We had trained so hard, perfecting every detail, for weeks, and I was supremely confident. Below, the other pilot, Pablo, pulled the larger Bell 204 off the sand banks and we began our simulated flight to the target. This was not merely a question of wasting time. From this moment on we were totally engaged.

Operation Phoenix Two only had four phases. I have always believed a plan of attack should be simple, direct and aggressive. There was Phase One, the flight from La Gagua in the jungle to our refuel point at San Diego, codenamed Kiko; Phase Two, the Assault; Phase Three, the Reorganisation; and Phase Four, the Withdrawal.

On this rehearsal we practised everything from Phase Two on.

As we flew over the jungle canopy, Dave Tomkins behind me was busy sorting out the big satchel charges we were going to use to bomb the guard houses. He needed them ready to hand. He checked the safety fuse igniters on each short length of three-second-delay safety fuse and pinched the splayed tines of the safety pin ready for pulling. By trial and error, we had found that when we dropped the charges, the safety fuse trailed behind and acted as a stabiliser which kept the charge upright. Then we found that if we packed the charge with a bag of air at the bottom, the air-bag burst on landing, cushioning the charge and stopping it from breaking up.

Flying above us and to one side, the men in the Bell were going through in their minds the important features we expected to see on our fly-in towards the target. I had detailed simulated points to maximise the realism of our attack.

They started with the terracotta roofs of the small village of Dora Dal, which told them there was only six minutes' flying time left. Tiger took our Hughes frighteningly low above the trees on the final run-in. We saw the Akatamia airstrip, the San Diego refuelling point codenamed Kiko, then Escobar's own airstrip which he could not use because it had been cratered by the Colombian Army, then the target villa, Hacienda Napoles, then we were over the wire perimeter fences round the football pitch and over the villa complex itself.

I opened up with my pintle-mounted GPMG at two wooden guard towers on the perimeter fence, one after the other, to neutralise them, while the men in the Bell fired on the other two towers.

Then Tiger swung the Hughes round to bomb the buildings. As we flew over the guards' quarters and along the length of the target villa, Dave leaned out, pulled the pins from his charges, yanked out the extractor handle to ignite the three-second fuses and dropped three 6-lb explosive charges on the side of the villa furthest from the Bell, which was swinging round over the football pitch firing and checking there were no obstacles to landing.

The Hughes rocked as the charges went off one after the other beneath us and we flew on to drop a further two big 10-lb charges on the other guard billet at the main entrance. The helicopter shook as Tiger swung round out of the blast. We pulled into a higher orbit over the house and gave covering fire while Pablo took the Bell down to hover-land over the football pitch and all the guys tumbled out with their equipment.

As soon as Pablo's Bell banked away, the assault team split into the Support Group and the House Clearance Group. Stuart McVicar's support fire team opened up at once on the guards' quarters with a 7.62mm G3 on automatic and with 66mm anti-tank rockets. The building disappeared in flames.

The House Clearance team began to move towards the villa, each of the two call-signs leap-frogging each other with fire and movement.

Covered by the men on the ground, Tiger dropped in to hover-land too. Almaro, Dave and Ramon leaped out to join Stuart's support fire team. Tiger and I lifted off to orbit over the villa and suppress any guards we saw on the other, or 'black' side of the villa.

For ease of description, I had designated each side of Escobar's villa with colours. We had dropped the teams on the front which I called the white side, black was the back, red was the right and blue was the left, the end nearest the guards' quarters. The three main parts of the villa were numbered; 1 (the blue or left wing), 2 (the centre) and 3 (the red or right wing).

'Moving to red side, to start point for white 1,' said Billy Potts, the assault team leader, his voice crackling in my earphone. I looked down and saw the dark figures with the distinctive yellow crosses on their heads running forward through the trees to begin the house clearance from the right-hand end, opposite the guards' quarters, at the red end.

'Entering white 1!' panted the assault group commander beneath me as his team lobbed grenades inside the building. They waited for the explosion and then burst through the door. This was no hostage saving situation, when assault teams use stun grenades and aim to save lives. We were attacking an enemy stronghold where we expected every man we met to be armed and we were using high explosive military grenades.

As the assault team worked its way through the rooms of the villa beneath us, Tiger kept the Hughes swinging round over the target area, on the black and blue corner of the villa, furthest from the teams, where I could fire the GPMG at any guards trying to escape or reinforce those in the villa.

Our backers had given us good intelligence about Escobar's guards. There were seventy of them and they were well armed with a variety of useful weapons such as the GPMG and M60 machine guns, AR15s, Israeli Uzis and American Ingrams. However, they did not expect to be attacked so no one carried more than three magazines. Like all bullies, they were used to throwing their weight about, their morale was high and they drank heavily all day. They wore civilian clothes. This is why the yellow crosses on the guys' black balaclavas were vital, so I could see in the smoke where they had got to and fire at everyone else with my machine gun in the Hughes.

With the support team on the white side of the villa, and the assault groups working their way through inside from red to blue, my job in the Hughes was to use my GPMG to eliminate anyone I saw outside the villa on the black and blue sides. Between us, we had all sides of the villa covered and no one could escape.

While Tiger kept the Hughes moving back and forth above so we couldn't be hit by ground fire below, the explosions of grenades and firing were almost continuous. The support group by the LZ were firing 66mm anti-tank rockets, the G3s on automatic fire and rifle grenades fired from G3s.

The assault team's breathless voices marked their relentless, explosive progress through the villa. 'White 1 cleared, moving to white 2!'

They advanced in two smoothly practised four-man groups, under Billy Potts and Don Milton, taking each room in turns, throwing grenades, waiting for the explosions, running inside firing their M16s at anyone left alive, reforming while the second group followed through to attack the next room without pause.

'Guards trying to enter at black 3,' I called on the radio, to warn the men inside the villa and at the same time opening up with my GPMG at the new targets. The assault teams knew the black side was a free fire zone for me in the Hughes flying above them and let me get on with it. 'Guards suppressed at black 3,' I radioed after several minutes firing.

'White 3 cleared,' crackled Billy Potts' voice. 'Jose killed and mission complete.'

'Phase Three,' I ordered.

The assault team ran back through the shattered house and re-grouped with the support group while I called in Pablo with the Bell. He had been to check an airstrip about four kilometres away which we were going to use on the withdrawal and I wanted him to make sure there were no barbed-wire obstacles across it.

When he arrived Tiger dropped down to hover-land and we picked up Dave, Almaro and Ramon. Then Tiger pulled the Hughes back into orbit so we could maintain suppressive fire at opportunity targets while Pablo swooped in to hover-land and pick up the ground teams. I fired a last long burst and pulled away after them.

We landed and I debriefed the men. I was delighted with the dress rehearsal. The weeks of making them practise over and over and over again had produced a viciously efficient assault. The men really worked hard, they fought through with the confidence of knowing they had everything tuned to a degree they had never experienced before in their army lives and now it was all coming together.

Every morning when we started work I went through the whole plan. I tested them over and again, firing questions at one after the other as we practised,

'What callsign is the support group?'

'What callsign is assault group 2?'

'What side of the door are you?'

'Who's the entry man?'

'Who's the bomber?'

'Who's the lookout?'

'Stop!' I would say and switch my questions to another man, 'You take over, what happens next?'

We did that live rehearsal five times and by the end I can tell you that after eleven weeks of training these men knew every answer to every possibility we might meet on the attack, every single drill, action and emergency. We had the Principles of War tuned to a fine pitch. This was no bunch of mercenary idiots. Whatever stupid-ities these men may have committed elsewhere in their lives, whatever foolishness they may be accused of in the future, they had become excellent, highly motivated fighting men on that task in Colombia. They were all rearing to go, and I was proud of them.

Then Ricardo, who as our intelligence officer had been keeping in touch with our backers in Bogota, told me that Escobar was at the villa. The attack was on!

I started the attack sequence, warning the men, our support and the pilots that we were ready to go the following morning. Our

Colombian helicopter mechanic worried me by saying there was something wrong with the Bell 204 engine but he grafted hard for several hours up to his elbows in oil and cured the problem.

That last evening in the cabin at La Gagua, the fury of our recent live rehearsals gave way to calm, deliberate preparations for the fight. Outside in the darkness of the jungle, we could hear the soft rustle of the river beyond the sandbank, the endless call of night insects and see the glowing trails of fireflies. Inside the cabin, the men moved about singly in their rooms or on the verandah making their final adjustments to their equipment. They were quiet because they knew the next morning they were going to risk their lives. They were thinking of the seventy guards, not in panic, but calmly going through in their minds the way our attack plan would eliminate them from the contest, in the towers, in the guard house, the other side of the fences, in the guards' quarters. They looked at Escobar's photographs. They cleaned their weapons for the last time, minutely checking them so there would be no malfunctions. They examined the grenades, the 66mm rockets and Dave Tomkins checked over his explosives. There was the occasional joke, which showed bravado and the fire of confidence, and then we went to bed early. I slept well.

We were up at five o'clock. I stepped off the verandah out onto the sandbank to look at the weather. The sky above was brilliant blue and promised a perfect day. Immensely cheered, I went back into the cabin for a cup of tea. After breakfast, we dressed and loaded the helicopters, making a few small adjustments to equipment. Ricardo called on our radio net from Cali, and, using coded language, told me to hold on until he had received definite confirmation that Escobar was at home. We waited tensely for several hours, and then the radio crackled again with Ricardo's voice.

'He's there! Go!'

I checked my watch. Eleven o'clock. We all paraded by the helicopters, weapons to hand and ready to board. After so much time together training, there was an unspoken bond between us which prompted me to say something to them before we set out. 'Good luck' seemed insufficient. The words sounded too much like a weak English understatement which did nothing to match the excitement boiling inside me. I have always been fascinated by military history, famous generals, their battles and leadership, and I tried to recall the lines from *Julius Caesar*, when Marcus Brutus leaves Cassius before the Battle of Philippi, knowing he might never survive. In tones which rang with my own feelings of total commitment, I told them, 'Whether we shall meet again I know not. Therefore our everlasting farewell take. For ever and ever farewell. If we do meet again, why, we shall smile! If not, why then, this parting was well made!'

Some of you may think this was pretentious, but we were a close band of men at that moment, with fire in our bellies and gladness in our hearts for the fight, and that sensation is the finest drug in the world.

The adrenalin rushed again as the rotors began thumping round before take-off and then we were airborne, swinging over the green jungle towards our target. I was convinced we had done everything possible to make this operation work, I had been given everything I asked for and we had trained like never before. There was nothing to stop us.

Tiger flew our Hughes low over the trees, swinging back and forth up the curving valleys, northeastwards into the foothills, while Pablo kept the Bell slightly higher on our left, so we could both see each other in case anything went wrong. We had two high mountain ranges to cross, between peaks rising to 15,000 feet, the first to cross back into the Rio Cauca valley and then the second beyond that into the Rio Magdalena valley to our final refuel point at Kiko just short of the target.

I looked round at the guys squashed in the back and I could see morale was high. Tiger was piloting us with élan, sitting cheerfully on a tiger skin I had given him for good luck, Almaro passed sweets around from the back next to Dave Tomkins and Ramon. Once again I felt that great sense of closeness which is only experienced among men about to risk their lives. I really felt a surge of delight, like the last of the great adventurers.

We crossed the first mountain range without incident, though I was concerned to notice wisps of cloud thickening over the peaks.

We left Manizales in the Cauca Valley on our right and began to gain altitude to cross the last range. I looked ahead through the Hughes' glass bubble and could see cloud hanging round the peaks on all sides. It was not encouraging.

I asked Tiger if he had contact with the other air support. Three other aircraft were vital to my plan. They were flying to join us from Cali and a secret airstrip near Bogota. Soon, precisely on cue, we heard the pilots answering calls crackling on our earphones. Everyone was on station. One of the newcomers was a Bell Jetranger helicopter-ambulance flying low, which would hold off the target ready to fly in if there were wounded or dead, or to ferry us out if the Hughes or the Bell 204 were shot down. The second plane was a small Cessna flying high above us with Ricardo aboard which was loaded with

Telstar radio rebroadcast equipment. All the men on the ground had a radio, earpiece and mike. They were on Channel 1 to me in my Hughes. All the aircraft were on Channel 2 also linked to me, through the other side of my headphones. The Cessna Telstar had rebroadcast equipment to boost the signals to make sure we would all get through to each other. On tests, it had punched through loud and clear from as far away as forty miles. I could listen and control both channels through my earpiece and mike in the Hughes, switching from one to the other to speak, though most conversation was going to be with the men on the ground. Ricardo was on hand in the Cessna to translate my commands for the Colombian pilots if required. Lastly, an empty fixed-wing Caravan was circling further away ready to pick us all up from an airstrip about four kilometres away from the target after the attack.

Everything was in place. The operation was set to go. We had one range to cross, then refuel at Kiko, and then attack!

We flew up towards Cuchilla del Tigre, the last obstacle before the target. The clouds swirled round the peaks above us and hung thickly on the dense trees covering the steep mountain slopes below. The sun occasionally burst through with a flash of light on the white clouds. Tiger followed the valley up to the top, hugging the contours. Our Hughes was sandwiched between the white clouds and green slopes as he searched for a way through, while Pablo circled higher in the Bell on our left.

Tiger pointed at his fuel gauge. We were running low, with less than 100 lbs of fuel in the tanks.

I glanced at the altimeter: 8,900 feet.

Suddenly Tiger pointed to a bright shining gap in the clouds ahead, where the sun lit the pass and the way through. I was confident we could make it. Kiko was only a couple of minutes' flying time away. Tiger tilted the Hughes forward and headed fast for the bright hole in the clouds.

Suddenly the sunlight vanished, the gap disappeared like the reflection it was, we flew into the clouds and straight at the trees. Tiger shouted and pulled at the controls but it was too late. The Hughes smashed into the green canopy, the perspex bubble shattered and the whole aircraft twisted upside down with the power of the rotor blades caught in the branches. I felt a terrible wrenching pain in my back. The noise of the screaming engine, breaking metal and splintering branches filled my ears. Disorientated, I remember falling, the momentum of the helicopter plunging it through the trees towards the steep slope beneath. Eventually, we stopped moving. I was hanging head down, held in my seat by my safety belt. I looked around. The Hughes was wedged near the ground between jungle trees, broken palms and thick undergrowth, creaking as it settled. The engine stopped. Almaro and Ramon clambered out past me and dropped to the ground beneath. Tiger was hanging beside me in his seat, covered in blood, mortally wounded by one rotor blade which had half severed his left arm and cut off his leg at the hip. He was alive, but grey-faced with shock and hardly conscious.

I unclipped myself and fell painfully to the ground which sloped away steeply. I stood with difficulty and searched in the upside-down Hughes for the emergency shock packs we had prepared. Dave and Almaro lifted Tiger from his seat and laid him on the ground, but when I tried to give him a drip, I could not find a vein strong enough to take the needle of the giving set. Instead, I jabbed him with morphine. Dave too tried to get a drip in Tiger's remaining arm but he was too far gone.

My own pain washed over me and I began to suffer shock myself, losing balance. Dave, Almaro and Ramon had survived the crash better in the back and they sat me down among the leaves and undergrowth on a small ledge on the steep slope. Dave made me drink from another drip. Pain seemed to well up in every part of my body. It was worst in my back and chest. I had severely wrenched my spine and broken five ribs, and we had all sustained superficial cuts and bruises from the chunks of metal and perspex flying round when the Hughes broke up on impact.

I knew Tiger was dying and I tried to persuade the others to give him the last rites, but they did not know how. Maybe they felt it was pointless, but I felt bad about leaving him alone as he died. Perhaps in retrospect, the extreme disappointment at being stopped dead in our tracks was beginning to affect me. We had been only eight minutes' flying time from the target. However, regret was a luxury for later. For the moment our problems of survival were paramount.

We could hear the other helicopter still above us, out of sight, circling over the canopy and, when Dave and Almaro found two personal radios from the wrecked Hughes which still worked, we called up Pablo. Our flares had been smashed in the crash but they found a red airmarker panel which they hung out on the trees and Pablo announced he could see it.

He radioed that there was a landing site about seven hundred metres away to the east and that we should make for that, but I was in agony. I had stiffened up fast and found I simply could not move at all.

I told Dave to set out on the bearing Pablo had given and try to find the landing site where he could be picked up by the Bell. He left with his weapon and one radio. Meanwhile Almaro found another jacket to cover me and keep me warm against the dangers of shock.

'D'you want an Uzi?' he asked. 'There's one in the chopper.'

I shook my head, confused.

Then he set out too, with Ramon and the other radio.

As I heard him sliding down the steep slope below me after Dave, I realised that in my confusion I had broken the rules. I had let both radios go and had no weapon handy either. I felt no anger about it but, as the day passed and I lay cocooned in pain, unable to move, I knew I was in for a hard time.

We had crashed at 8,900 feet and the mountain was cold. The wind got up at dusk, buffeting the trees round me and making the wreck of the Hughes grind on the tree trunks. Painfully, I wrapped myself in my jackets, but I could not help shivering. The grey light faded quickly under the dripping leaves of the canopy and the temperature dropped. I lay in total darkness, cold, filthy, covered with Tiger's blood and exhausted, while images drifted through my consciousness, of Jane looking clean and beautiful at home, of the men during our training and the tough figure of my grandfather, Old Miles. It was a long, miserable and sleepless night.

Eventually, thankful, I glimpsed the first translucent grey light of dawn through the trees above me and I decided it was no good just lying there and freezing to death. I was struck by the idea that I might be on my own for days. We had been flying over a very remote part of the mountains and I knew from my map study that it might take a long time for a search party to find me.

Meantime, I had to survive. I struggled to my hands and knees, which I think took more than half an hour, and crawled my way by inches over to the wreck, holding on to roots and trees, desperate not to slip on the steep slope and trying to keep my breathing shallow against the pain of my broken ribs and back.

Like a modern-day Robinson Crusoe, I wanted to find what might be useful in the shattered ship. I tried to ignore Tiger's stiffened corpse under the broken Hughes and the terrible grey pallor of his blood-spattered face. Maybe my own problems made me over-sensitive, but he had been a Catholic and I still felt badly about his lonely death without the comfort of the last rites. For the living, debris was scattered all round. I picked up the Uzi Almaro had offered me, with three full magazines, Almaro's sweets, several drip bags to drink and plastic explosives which I burned to warm my hands. Most irritating, my watch had come off in the crash and I could not find Tiger's. It had probably been flung off his wrist into the jungle somewhere when the rotor blade ripped into his arm.

Later in the morning, I heard a fixed-wing plane, probably the Cessna, circling above and it was intensely frustrating not being able to speak to them on a radio. However, at least they were there to encourage me. After the Cessna left, some time passed till I heard a helicopter which I thought landed not far away. Soon afterwards I was sure I heard two shots. I fired several times in reply but the sounds of the low-velocity rounds seemed to be absorbed in the cloud and the wet foliage of the trees. No human noise disturbed the damp silent jungle around me. I guessed I had imagined it.

The clouds filled the trees with mist and it began to drizzle. I realised the planes would be unable to fly any more that day.

'The game is on!' I said to myself fiercely. I was on my own. The fight was on for my life.

I made another slow, painful trip to the helicopter, concentrating hard not to slip on the steep wet earth. This time I found a packet of biscuits, two tins of tuna, part of the escape rations we had prepared, some shell dressings, plastic bags and a torn flak jacket.

Back on my shelf, I tried to warm myself up as the shivering wrenched my broken ribs. I wrapped the torn flak jacket and the shell dressings round me as best I could, and stuck my legs in a plastic bag. My feet had gone numb and felt as though I had broken bones there too, but I dared not take off the boots to see. They had swollen badly and I was sure I would never be able to pull them on again. This was Escobar's territory and I could not shake off the fear that his men might find me before my own. I had to keep on my boots in case I was forced to fight.

Darkness fell again and I began to dream, visualising extraordinarily real scenes against the black jungle night. I found myself on a brightly lit stage and dreamed all my pain and injuries were drug-induced. The drugs had somehow caused me to make up the crash in my mind. I began to float deliciously free of my painful body and relegated the whole plan of attack on Escobar's house to a dream. I sat comfortably on the roof of a railway building and observed that the jungle had shrunk to a number of small theatrical bushes dotted around on the stage.

'I'm just going to change the videos,' announced Dean Shelley helpfully, appearing with extraordinary realism right in front of me. At this, I noticed I was being filmed and Shelley explained that I was not in the jungle at all, but in a railway station and the bushes were props. 'All your actions and words are being taped,' he added and vanished into the shadows behind the stage.

The dark night and shivering took over for a moment but my mind was soon away again and this time I was standing in a very luxurious apartment surrounded by be-medalled and moustachioed Colombian generals in splendid uniforms, who were saying, '*Bueno! Bueno!* The experiment was excellent. *Mucho gusto. Bueno!*'

I was puzzling over what the experiment might be, when another man, wearing a suit, butted in to say that no one was really concerned about the two hostages still being held under a bridge in Cali. The generals took no notice of this at all.

The inconsistencies seemed quite normal. Nor was I in the slightest surprised to see Frederick Forsyth walk over in a bright, shiny, white mackintosh. Rather casually, he said the generals had taken my watch and added that he intended to use the material for his new book.

'But what about the hostages?' I demanded furiously.

He turned up his mackintosh collar, stuck his hands in his pockets so that he looked like something out of *The Third Man*, and declared throatily, 'Don't worry! There'll be no problems any more!'

They say dreams are a release, and I suppose for a short while mine gave me respite from the cold and the painful sleeplessness. I shifted position in the dark, unsuccessfully trying to find a comfortable position on the wet leaves. I was so tired I drifted off again.

I heard Dave Tomkins speaking in a seductive voice, saying, 'Walk to the railway lines, Peter, and when you've crossed them, the drug will wear off. One of the other guys who is injured will come and pick you up in a truck and it'll all be okay.'

I walked to the railway in broad daylight and waited, looking up and down the empty track which disappeared down straight lines into the distance in both directions, but no one came for me. The daylight of my dream faded.

I opened my eyes and was enveloped in the black jungle night. Water dripped on me from the unseen leaves above, cold seeped round my aching back and shivering tremors racked my ribs. Half-conscious, I swore out loud, 'Dave, if this is your idea of a joke, it's gone a bit too fucking far!'

Dawn gradually lightened the tall trees over my hide on the steep slope and I set my mind to another day. I crawled again to the helicopter and found some more plastic explosive from Dave's satchel bombs which I burned for a little warmth. I also hoped the smoke would filter up through the trees and show the others where I was.

I heard a plane above me, but the grey mist was still thick in the trees and I doubted they could see anything through the clouds over the mountain.

I crawled back to my ledge, made a fire with plastic explosive and heated a tin of sausages I had found. I had little appetite but forced myself to eat. I began to wonder if I could get out myself. Maybe I could drag myself to Kiko, our refuelling point. We had been so nearly there. I had only three drips left, of one and a half litres each, but I reckoned I could catch water dripping from the trees using the plastic bag. The trouble was that I had not found my compass and had no idea which direction to take. I told myself that at least if I stayed where I was, the others knew where to look. I spent the rest of the day shivering painfully, and drifted exhausted in and out of fitful sleep during my third, long, cold night on the mountain.

I dreamed again that night, that I lived in a graveyard and I had a friend. His name was Death.

In the morning, I was terribly stiff and cold, but I crawled again to the helicopter, more for something to do than in the hope of finding anything. I saw Tiger's dead body again, lying under the wreck. He was a ghastly grey-blue colour and his awful wounds looked glazed and unreal. I guessed the altitude and cold were delaying his decomposition as I saw no flies on him. I felt no anger that he had crashed the chopper and stopped us reaching our target. He had been a good pilot and he had paid the final price for his mistake. It was small satisfaction that we had at least softened the pain of his death with the morphine, though there was nothing we could have done to save him.

Scrabbling about on my hands and knees in the undergrowth beneath the chopper, I found a drip, which I drank at once, and some more of Almaro's sweets among the dead leaves. I suppose all that took up most of the morning, as I only moved for short moments before having to rest and stop the surges of pain round my chest. Later, I dragged myself back to my ledge and prepared to wait out the rest of another day.

Suddenly I heard the sharp hard sounds of a machete chopping wood below me. Voices speaking Spanish carried clearly up the slope.

I came fully alert with a jolt of terror, like Robinson Crusoe finding the footprint in the sand. I pulled myself round to the edge of my hide, rolled on my stomach and held my Interdynamic ready. We had crashed only eight minutes' flying time from Hacienda Napoles, in the centre of Escobar's territory and for all I knew these were his men. I gripped myself and prepared to fight.

Like most people in a tight corner, I prayed. Fervently and urgently, I asked God to guide me and to let me give a good final account of myself before departing this world.

I tried to ignore the pains in my chest and back and concentrate on the men advancing steadily up the slope towards me. Determined to 'die with honour', I waited, gripping my Uzi tensely, as the chatter of Spanish voices and the steady clipping of machetes drew closer and closer.

I peered carefully over my ledge and could just see the black hair of the nearest man. As he topped the rise, I shouted hoarsely to release my own fear, and thrust my Uzi forward, ready to fire.

'*Amigo! Amigo!*' screamed the man, staring terrified into the muzzle of the Uzi. '*Colonelo* Ricardo, Ricardo!'

Even in the state I was, I recognised Colonel Ricardo's name which the man was using as a codeword.

The rescue party had arrived.

There were two men and three *campesinos* whom they had employed to cut a path through the thick jungle. None of them spoke English, but one gave me a can of Pepsi which I poured straight down my throat. Another cut off my boots and my trousers, to see the extent of my injuries. I lay back for a moment with the sheer relief of being found and then painfully pulled on some civilian trousers and running shoes which one of them brought from the helicopter. Then I asked, 'How far have we got to go?'

One of the Colombians shrugged and replied, 'Five hours' walk.'

I stared at him. It took all my energy and resolve just to crawl to the helicopter, let alone 'walk' for five hours.

I had no option. We were nearly 9,000 feet up at the top of a mountain and thick clouds meant they could not winch me out by chopper. I had to walk down. Leaning on a succession of men in the rescue party for support, I set out down the slope, tottering and sliding downhill terribly slowly, like an old, old man. Each step was agony. I thought that once I got moving, the pain would ease off or soften to a dull ache. It did not. I could hear my ribs grind and stab my chest every step of the way down the endless slope.

The *campesinos* did their best to cut away the undergrowth, leaves, hanging vines, lianas, and clinging, spiny fronds, but I have never seen such thick, overgrown and dirty jungle. We followed the same stream bed they had walked up to find me and I lost count of the waterfalls we had to descend. The ground was so steep the only way down was to climb the rocks beside the tumbling water. When they realised I couldn't climb, they cut down a tree, skinned off the leaves and lowered me down by a rope tied round my chest as I hung onto the pole, gasping and speechless, gritting my teeth.

When I had recovered, the men below me stepped confidently down the slope again, while I followed, hanging on to one of the *campesinos*, slithering uncertainly on wet leaves and stones, afraid to hurt myself by slipping, and hurting anyway. Every time I heard another waterfall below, my morale sank.

Hours later, it seemed to me, I asked in desperation, 'How much longer?'

'About one hour,' called back the man in front of me, turning round and looking up the slope.

Looking at the watch of the man helping me, I asked an hour later, 'How far?'

'Maybe two hours,' the man called up casually, ignoring the shock in my face, and carried on slashing right and left at the lianas hanging in our way.

The light faded, dusk turned into night and the *campesinos* never stopped. In utter darkness, lit only by the swinging, flashing beams of their torches turned back to light my path, I slithered on downhill. I have never felt so sorry for myself, or so desperate and helpless.

I made a pact with my God not to complain of the pain. I kept my side of this unequal bargain and I guess he kept his because eventually they stopped walking on a sandy island in the middle of the stream.

They had sheets of polythene which they wrapped round me and we settled down to sleep, one on each side of me to keep me warm. At least, I think that's what they were doing, because in the darkness I heard them rootling through my small zip bag, and whispering to each other as they divided up my goods. I felt disappointed as they had been so helpful. Next morning I found they had stolen all my 30,000 pesos escape money.

I slept fitfully, unable to turn properly against the hurt in my chest and was awake as the grey light of dawn filtered through the trees hanging over us. Gesticulating at their watches and pointing downhill, I asked them, 'How far to go?'

'One hour,' they said. 'One hour.'

Cheered, I gritted my teeth and we set off down the slope again. Fighting every step of the way, I became obsessed with time, looking at their watches as we walked. Five hours later we were still going.

The jungle canopy was thinning in places overhead and when I saw a hosepipe running out of the stream, I asked again, 'How far?'

'One kilometre.'

This took another hour. I was totally exhausted. The last several hundred yards towards a small wood and atap leaf hut seemed to last for ever. They took me inside, laid me down to rest on the floor and covered me with hessian sacking. I passed out at once.

Only an hour later, they shook me awake from deep sleep to say the helicopter was coming. Needless to say, the landing site was not right outside the hut. They patiently dragged me to the top of a hill further away where I sat in long coarse grass, drugged by exhaustion and the warmth of the late afternoon sun.

I heard the steady beat of a helicopter. A Bell 204 swung round above the hilltop and came in to land. I stood up, swaying on my feet. As its skids touched the grass, the down-drought from the rotors washed over me and I collapsed flat on my back, like a puppet without strings. Several of the *campesinos* helped me to my feet and into the helicopter.

After a short flight to an airstrip, they transferred me to a light Cessna and we took off at last light. An hour later, we circled over the lights of Cali spread out in darkness below, and landed. A Landcruiser came onto the airfield to take me straight from the Cessna into Cali, to the apartment block we had used weeks before when we had first arrived.

Four days had passed since I had seen the guys. We had all been fully committed to the attack, we had trained like brothers, as close-knit a team as any I have prepared in all my experience, but when I walked in, filthy, bruised and exhausted, I found them all there, showered and changed, arguing with each other about money.

***

We tried to go again. We assessed that security was not so badly breached by our crash that Escobar knew, so I moved the men out of the way to Panama while our backers found another helicopter and a new pilot. I stayed in Cali, recovering from my injuries, planning a new attack, and liaising with Almaro and Ricardo. However, the momentum of the operation had gone. I had wound up the men over weeks of detailed, intensive training and they had willingly followed me over the top. Only crashing into a mountain had stopped us killing Escobar. The galling anti-climax was too much for them. The fire in their bellies had died.

Ned Owen skipped off of his own accord. He flew back to England from Panama and promptly sold his story to television.

On 13 August, James Adams published his story, telling us on the phone that he had to do it because our mission was virtually public knowledge. He said Washington knew all about us, which was true enough because we had told the CIA ourselves, but our assessment in Colombia, with Ricardo, was that Escobar had no inkling. Adams may have been sensitive about this as his article was headlined that our plans were 'known – even to their enemy'. He rather condescendingly described me as a 'simple soldier' and then proceeded to blow the whole plan with an artist's impression of our attack and plenty of speculation to fill in the gaps.

Terry Tagney added his two pennyworth by going on television from South Africa.

Security was in shreds, our backers agreed it was pointless to continue and I disbanded the team after a farewell dinner in Panama.

Epilogue

In England, I went back to Birmingham and took over the Gunmaker's Arms. I enjoyed running this red brick Victorian pub in Smallheath and produced an impressive turnover, so much so that over the next two years the brewery persuaded me to take on another thirteen other pubs in the area. I know they thought I was ideal, as poacher turned gamekeeper, but I have never come across so much unprincipled lying, begging and stealing in my life. Once, I walked into one of my bars to find that every man there owed me money, and they were all drunk.

However, I set up all the memorabilia of my military life in the Gunmaker's, in the snug bar on the first floor, and numerous friends visited.

One cold spring day in April 1992, I was sitting in the snug when Liz in the bar phoned up to say there were two men to see me.

'Who are they?' I asked.

'They look like toffs, Peter,' she said in her strong Brum accent.

'Send them up,' I told her, puzzled. I was not expecting any trade visitors.

I met them at the top of the stairs and saw at once Liz was right. These two were definitely out of place in Smallheath.

One was tanned, in his mid-forties, wearing a grey suit and highly polished brown brogues. He was of medium build and fit-looking, his jaw was strong, with a small dimple in the chin, and he had the air of one who spends a lot of time abroad.

The older man was in his fifties, of medium height with grey hair brushed straight back. He wore glasses, a white shirt with a silver club tie, and a long black Melton overcoat over a dark pin-striped suit and expensive black brogue shoes. I rather thought his outfit lacked a red carnation in the lapel of his coat. He was the very image of a man who works in the City of London, but he was certainly no stockbroker.

There was something about the manner of both these men, concerned, benign, but with eyes that were implacably hard, and I was suspicious at once.

'Are you Mr McAleese?' the older man asked politely.

'I am,' I nodded.

'May we talk with you in private, please?' It was more a command than a request.

I invited them into my snug bar and noticed them both looking round my photographs and badges which I had mounted on the walls.

'What can I do for you?' I asked. Plainly, they were not paying a social call but I offered them drinks. The older man chose a half-pint of Black Label lager, while the younger man in the grey suit opted for a safe glass of Perrier water. Oh dear, is there no style any more? James Bond, where are you?

We sat at one of the round tables and the older man began with, 'You don't know who we are, but we know who you are.'

His voice rang with all the righteous conviction I recognised from the past, when my actions have been so often prejudged by men who have never met me or even bothered to ask for my side of events. I watched them, I listened carefully, but I said nothing.

He went on, 'We know all about your recent trips to South America, and we feel we should advise you of the following.' At this, a tiny smirk appeared on his face.

I looked up at the wall beside our table. We were sitting between a framed copy of the McAleese family motto written in calligraphic style, 'Touch not the cat but a glove,' and a photograph of fearless Old Miles in his Argyll kilt. I looked back at my two suave visitors and said nothing.

The knowing smirk again. He said, 'You've been out there again, to set up another operation to kill Escobar, haven't you?'

I said, 'Yes.'

'You were told to recruit your own pilots, weren't you?'

'Yes.'

'Do you realise you were going to be shot down, after the job?'

I said nothing. Did he take me for a fool? Did he not wonder how I had survived so far? Plainly, these men had read a file on me in their office in London, an incomplete file in all likelihood, as the Security Services never trouble to ask us for an interview when they make up a file on us, and there was nothing I could say. Plainly, their view of me stemmed more from my time as a wild young trooper in the British SAS and from lurid nonsense about me in the tabloid press, always thirsty for talk of 'mercenaries', rather than any knowledge of my time in Africa. I was certain they had not read my Confidential Reports as a sergeant major in the South African Army. They had come with their minds made up. There was nothing I could say which would make any difference and I did not want to upset them. They were powerful, because they represented the establishment, and I did not want to buck the system.

I have had plenty of fights in my time, I've been in jail, but I have never fought the system, because I believe in it. Through years of service and operations for three governments and in three regular armies, I rose to the rank of sergeant major, and I did my best to uphold in that rank all the traditions of the finest airborne regiments anywhere in the world: the British Army, the Rhodesian Army and the South African Army. If these men saw nothing of that in me, then there was no point talking.

They spoke to me for a few more minutes while I politely answered, 'Yes' or 'No', and then they stood up to go. The older man paused a little theatrically at the door and said, 'My final piece of advice to you, Mr McAleese, is don't do it!'

The younger man gave me a hard look and then they stamped downstairs and out into the street.

I expect they thought they had done rather well, and it was nice of them to take the trouble.

But who knows what I might do next?

Appendix A

List of Mercenaries, Angola 1976

Name	Home Town	Notes on Outcome
Name	*Home Town*	*Notes on Outcome*

A. Recruiters

Aspin, Leslie	London	Main interest in controlling pay. Never went to Angola.
Banks, John	London	Ex-Para. Contacted by Hall/Belford after earlier publicity.
Belford, Donald	Leeds	Original FNLA contact in UK, after medical mission in Angola.
Taylor, Colin	London	FNLA's 'European Advisor'. Made only brief visits to Africa.

B. First group to Angola, arriving in Kinshasa on 5 January

Callan, 'Colonel'	London	Taken prisoner, tried and executed in Luanda.
Christodoulou, Charley		Killed in ambush.
Hall, Nick	London	Self-styled 'Major'. Spent most time in Kinshasa. Came home.
Wainhouse, Mick	London	Self-styled 'Captain'. Sick with dysentery in Kinshasa. Came home.

C. Second 'Advance' party which arrived in Kinshasa on 20 January

Aves, Paul		Wounded.
Barker, 'Brummy'		POW, tried and executed in Luanda.
Boddy, Tony		Killed in action on 3 February.
Copeland, Sam	London	RSM to 'Col' Callan. Ex-Para, executed for murders.
Dempster, Chris		Came home, with Hussey.
Freeman, Barry	Germany	Wounded. Flew to Kinshasa in Fokker on 3 February.
Griffiths, 'Stars'		Came home.

Name	Home Town	Notes on Outcome
Hussey, 'Fuzz'		Ex-SAS. Came home, with Dempster.
Johnson, Mike		Ex-Legion. Killed on withdrawal from San Antonio di Zaire.
Lewis, Brian		Flew to Kinshasa in Fokker on 3 February.
McAleese, Peter	Glasgow	Ex-SAS. Came home on 23 March after some time in Kinshasa working with British Embassy sorting out names.
McCandless, Jamie		Ex-SAS. Killed in action in FAPLA ambush.
McKenzie, Andy		POW, tried and executed in Luanda.
McPhearson, Pat		Wounded. Flew to Kinshasa in Fokker on 3 February.
McPherson, Stuart		Came home.
Rennie, Mick		Came home.
Saunders, Dougie		Came home.
Tilsey, Bert		Joined Jonas Savimbi's UNITA.
Tomkins, Dave		Came home. Later, with Peter McAleese in Colombia 1988–92.

D. The men in this section arrived in two groups, in Maquela on 31 January and in Kinshasa on 9 February. (This list was derived from a handwritten list prepared by Peter McAleese and staff at the British Embassy in Kinshasa at the time, together with names from other sources. This list is probably incomplete but gives an idea of the chaos of the campaign.) Many of those named here were only in Angola for a few days, and twenty-four of them only in Africa for four days before being sent home.

Note that the fighting stopped on 17 February, when the last mercenaries crossed from Angola into Zaire.

Name	Home Town	Notes on Outcome
Acker, Gary	USA	Ex-corporal US Army. Sentenced to sixteen years in Luanda prison.
Aiken, Danny	Edinburgh	Ex-RN diver. Came home with Peter McAleese on 23 March.
Aimann, Richard	UK	Came home.
Aitken, Ken	London	Ex-Rhodesian SAS. Left with Butcher and came home.
Arnold, S.	London	Killed in action?
Bacon III, George	USA	Ex-US Special Forces. Good soldier. Killed in ambush on 15 February.
Baldwin, Andrew	London	Came home.

APPENDIX A

Name	Home Town	Notes on Outcome
Bayliss, Ray	Chippenham	Ex-Royal Marine. Came home.
Birtwhistle, ?	Leicester	Wounded. Came home.
Black, Andrew	London	Pilot. Came home.
Blackmore, Robin	Watford	Ex-Para. Murdered at Maquela on 2 February.
Brooks, Billy	Borehamwood	Murdered at Maquela on 2 February.
Bufkin, Dave	USA	Pilot. Flew Peter McAleese about on several occasions. Came home.
Butcher, Ray	Bournemouth	Ex-Para. Left with Aitken and came home.
Canes, Sid	Bradford	Not known.
Canning, ?	Ealing	Came home.
Carroll, P. T.	Islington	Came home.
Carter, Sid	Bradford	Killed in action.
Cashmore, John	England	Killed in ambush on 15 February.
Cassidy, ?	U.K.	Ex-Para. REME. Very good mechanic. Came home.
Chambers, Jim	Rushden	Came home.
Coleman, Patrick	London	Came home.
Davies, Phil	Birmingham	Murdered on parade by 'Colonel' Callan on 2 February.
Deacon, ?	Plymouth	Came home.
Dickens, ?	England	Killed in ambush on 15 February.
Dimmock, Malcolm	England	Killed in ambush on 15 February.
Elford, Lewis	Plymouth	Wounded. Came home.
Ellis, Allen	Leeds	Came home.
Evans, Colin	UK	POW. Tried and sentenced to twenty-four years in Luanda prison.
Fortuin, 'Satch'	London	POW. Tried and sentenced to twenty-four years in Luanda prison.
Friery, John	Kettering	Came home.
Gawthrop, Brian	Cambridge	Came home.
Gawthrop, Vic	Cambridge	Died of a heart attack (weighed seventeen stones).
Gearheart, Daniel	USA	POW. Captured with Soldier of Fortune ID card. Tried and executed in Luanda.
Geary, Terry	Romford	Came home.
Grillo, Gus	USA	POW. Tried and sentenced to thirty years in Luanda prison.

Name	Home Town	Notes on Outcome
Grundy, ?	Wirral	Came home.
Hammond, Paul	Bury St E.	Came home.
Harris, ?	UK	Left Sao Salvador, jailed in Zaire, came home.
Hart, Dave	UK	Came home.
Heaton, David	Plymouth	Murdered at Maquela on 2 February.
Heaton, ?	Pontefract	Killed in action.
Henderson, Keith	UK	Came home.
Hill, ?	Rochdale	Wounded. Came home.
Hillaney, Morgan		Jailed 12 February.
Holland, Andy	UK	Killed in ambush on 14 February.
James, ?	Peterlee	Came home.
Jarman, ?	UK	Left Sao Salvador, jailed in Zaire, came home.
Jenkinson, Roger		Not known.
Jones, F.	Andover	Wounded. Came home.
Kay, John	Bradford	Ex-RDG. Murdered at Maquela on 2 February.
Kelly, John		'Spider'. Came home.
Keray, Vic	Windsor	Wounded. Came home.
Kesterton, Tony	Barnard	Came home.
Kildunne, ?	Bury, Lancs	Came home.
Kovacz, Lazlo	UK	Came home.
Lawlor, John		POW. Sentenced to twenty-four years in prison in Luanda.
Leach, ?	Humberside	Came home.
Lobo do Sol, ?	USA	Came home. Enjoyed US Vietnam 'Vet' hippy appearance.
Lockyer, John	UK	Came home.
Lynch, ?	Bradford	Came home.
Madison, Barry		Probably never actually went out to Africa.
Mahoney, ?	Penarth	Came home. Possibly man who did the impressive escape and evasion.
Malone, John	Glasgow	Left Callan to get help. Came home.
Marchant, Kevin	Borehamwood	Ex-Para. POW. Sentenced to thirty years in prison in Luanda.
Marczynski, James T.	Bradford	Ex-CG. Murdered in Maquela on 2 February.
Maynard, ?	Slough	Not known.
McAleese, Tom	Corby	Came home. Peter's cousin.

APPENDIX A

Name	Home Town	Notes on Outcome
McCartney, Andrew	Perth	Murdered at Maquela on 2 February.
McCulloch, ?	Corby	Came home. Friend of Tom McAleese.
McIntyre, Malcolm		POW. Tried and sentenced to sixteen years in Luanda prison.
McKeown, Mike	Clwyd	Narrowly escaped being massacred at Maquela. Came home.
Mellstrom, ?	North Shields	Not known.
Molyneaux, K.	Widnes	Came home.
Morris, M.	Fareham	Came home.
Morrison, Hugh	Bournemouth	Ex-Legion, wounded in Land Rover accident. Came home.
Moss, Charlie		Ex-Anglian. Came home. Career soldier. Always very smooth.
Mott, Malcolm	Northwood	Came home.
Munday, ?	Kettering	Killed in action?
Myers, J.	Leeds	Came home.
Nammock, John	London	POW. Tried, sentenced to sixteen years in Luanda. Now released.
Newby, 'Canada'	Canada	Killed in ambush on 15 February.
Newton, ?	Ilford	Came home.
Nilbor, Barry		Wounded. Internal injuries. Came home.
O'Brien, Dennis		Wounded. Jailed 11 February. Came home.
O'Connor, John	Warrington	Suffered a heart attack but came home.
Oates, Tom	USA	Ex-LAPD. Self-styled 'Captain'.
Oram, Clifford	Stockton	Murdered at Maquela on 2 February.
Paden, Dave	Preston	Narrowly escaped being massacred at Maquela. Came home.
Patay, Laszlo	UK	Hungarian origin. Went to South Africa.
Randall, Barry	Hertfordshire	Ex-Para. Murdered at Maquela on 2 February.
Ranson, ?	Braintree	Came home.
Rennick, ?	Leamington	Came home.
Richmond, R.	Luton	Came home.
Risbridger, Max	Hove	Ex-Legion. Murdered at Maquela on 2 February.
Roden, Frank		Came home.
Rolls, Peter	London	Wounded. Came home.

Name	*Home Town*	*Notes on Outcome*
Ryan, Fred	Wakefield	Wounded. Right arm severed in action.
Saunders, R. H.	Sittingbourne	Came home.
Scaley, Eugene	USA	Arrived and at once took refuge in US Embassy in Kinshasa.
Serivenis, ?	Marlow	Killed in action?
Sharpley, ?	UK	Ex-Para. Came home.
Sloggett, Ben	Clacton	Not known.
Smith, Brian	Warrington	Ex-RGJ. Murdered at Maquela on 2 February.
Smith, David	Leyton	Came home.
Souter, ?	Glamorgan	Came home.
Spence, ?	Plymouth	Came home.
Stanley, Dave	W. Didsbury	Came home.
Talbot, A.	Ruislip	Came home.
Ward, Andrew	Leicester	Murdered at Maquela on 2 February.
Webb, Harry	Leeds	Murdered at Maquela on 2 February.
Whirity, Kevin	Coniston	Ex-Para. Narrowly escaped massacre at Maquela. Came home.
White, Terry	Farnborough	Pilot. Came home.
White, Max	Luton	Not known.
Wild, B. G.	South Africa	Killed in action.
Wileman, Michael	London	Murdered at Maquela on 2 February.
Wilson, Terry		Wounded. Came home.
Wiseman, Michael	Cheshunt	POW. Tried and sentenced to thirty years in Luanda prison.
Wright, M. F. J.	Basildon	Not known.
Young, ?	UK	Ex-Para. Came home.

E. Summary of Statistics

   Total on the above lists actually in Angola   143

1. Taken prisoner by Marxist Angolan Army and tried and executed in Luanda: 4
       Tried and sentenced to prison in Luanda: 9

2. Executed after FNLA court martial, Holden Roberto present, for murders at Maquela on 2 February (Sam Copeland):   1

3. Killed in action or died: 17

4. Wounded in action (including a couple in Luanda):   17
   Note: This figure was probably higher.

5. Murdered at Maquela on 2 February (by Sam Copeland, Chris Dempster, Paul Aves, Barry Freeman, Andy McKenzie, Tony Boddy and Portuguese called Uzio). This figure also includes Davies, murdered by Callan: 14

6. Suffered a fate not known: 7

So, the final casualty figures make grim reading. Nearly half (60 of 143) were either killed (36) and wounded (17) or are missing (7).

Appendix B

Chart Showing Rhodesian Counter-Insurgency Command and Control Structure

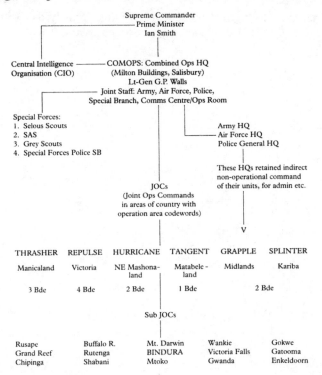

Supreme Commander
Prime Minister
Ian Smith

Central Intelligence ——— COMOPS: Combined Ops HQ
Organisation (CIO)   (Milton Buildings, Salisbury)
                            Lt-Gen G.P. Walls
                 — Joint Staff: Army, Air Force, Police,
                   Special Branch, Comms Centre/Ops Room

Special Forces:
1. Selous Scouts
2. SAS   Army HQ
3. Grey Scouts   — Air Force HQ
4. Special Forces Police SB   Police General HQ

                                          These HQs retained indirect
                                          non-operational command
                        JOCs   of their units, for admin etc.
                 (Joint Ops Commands
                 in areas of country with
                 operation area codewords)

                                          V

THRASHER	REPULSE	HURRICANE	TANGENT	GRAPPLE	SPLINTER
Manicaland	Victoria	NE Mashona-land	Matabele-land	Midlands	Kariba
3 Bde	4 Bde	2 Bde	1 Bde	2 Bde	

Sub JOCs

Rusape	Buffalo R.	Mt. Darwin	Wankie	Gokwe
Grand Reef	Rutenga	BINDURA	Victoria Falls	Gatooma
Chipinga	Shabani	Mtoko	Gwanda	Enkeldoorn

Notes:

1. Three Fire Forces were operated, in Hurricane, Thrasher and Repulse and allocated to other areas when required.

2. The principal elements necessary for success in counter-terrorist campaigns are present (regular army and police; special forces and Special Branch; airforce; and Combined Ops) but there are others not shown, for example:

   a. Funds for all the necessary resources, bribing the enemy to change sides and offering inducements to the people, are essential and Rhodesia was always short.

   b. Propaganda is also important and was attempted, but as Rhodesia was up against such total world antipathy, this was serious uphill work.

270

Appendix C

Confidential Report by 44 Parachute Brigade of South African Defence Force

CONFIDENTIAL

Confidential Report 80021355PP A02 P. McAleese

1. *Responsibilities* A02 McAleese is at all times prepared to accept responsibility for all tasks he undertakes and for all those working under him.

2. *Leadership* This soldier is an excellent leader of men which arises from a thoroughly adult outlook and an impressive military background.

3. *Initiative* He always uses his initiative and always commits himself completely to everything he is required to do.

4. *Trustworthiness* We would not hesitate to inform him of the most classified material, including all operational matters. He is thoroughly trustworthy.

5. *Personality* He has an agreeable personality and gets on well with everyone.

6. *Discipline* A02 McAleese is self-disciplined, and administers good discipline to his subordinates.

7. *Dress and Behaviour* He behaves like a professional soldier and is outstandingly smart.

8. *Loyalty* He is completely loyal towards the South African Army, to his superiors and his subordinates.

9. *Knowledge of Current Tasks* As a result of his wide experience and his continuing enthusiasm to learn, his military knowledge is of the highest standard.

10. *Recommendation* It is recommended that A02 McAleese is made substantive in his rank and begins his duties as such after 1 January 1982.

Signed: (Jap van Swart)

Appointment: So1

Notes by the Commander

The Commanders are in agreement with the proposal that T/A02 McAleese is made substantive in his rank with effect from 1 January 1982.

(Signed)

F. J. BESTBIER
Colonel
Commander, 44 Parachute Brigade

VERTROULIKE VERSLAG : 80021355PP AO2 P. MC ALEESE

1. **Verantwoordelikheid.** AO2 McAleese is ten alle tye bereid om verantwoordelikheid te aanvaar vir take en ook die optrede van sy ondergeskiktes.

2. **Leierskap.** Die lid het uitstekende leierskapsienskappe wat spruit uit sy volwasse benadering en goeie militêre agtergrond.

3. **Inisiatief.** Hy pas altyd inisiatief toe en bly altyd besig al het hy nie spesifieke toegekende take nie.

4. **Betroubaarheid.** h Mens skroom nie om uiters verantwoordelike take aan hom toe te vertrou nie en hy het hom ook al onder operasionele omstandighede as h betroubare leier bewys.

5. **Persoonlikheid.** Die lid het h aangename persoonlikheid en almal kommunikeer goed met hom.

6. **Dissipline.** AO2 McAleese is h gedissiplineerde soldaat en dwing ook dissipline af by sy ondergeskiktes.

7. **Netheid en Houding.** Hy is h professionele soldaat en hierdie eienskappe van hom is, soos te wagte, uitstekend.

8. **Lojaliteit.** Hy is lojaal teenoor die SAW, sy meerderes en ook sy ondergeskiktes.

9. **Kennis van sy Huidige Taak.** As gevolg van sy ondervinding en entoesiasme om te leer, is sy militêre kennis van h hoogstaande gehalte.

10. **Aanbevelings.** Dit word aanbeveel dat AO2 McAleese bevorder word na substantiewe AO2, terugwerkend na 1 Jan 82.

(C. DE SMART)
SGT OPLEIDING : KMDT

OPMERKINGS DEUR BEVELVOERDER :

Bevelvoeder gaan akkoord — m aanbeveling dat T/AO11 m'a na substantiewe AO11 bevorder word, terugwerkend na 1 Jan

(F.J. BESTBIER)
BEVELVOERDER 44 VALSKERMBRIGADE : KOL

(In opdrag)

VERTROULIK

Appendix D

Colombia's Drug Export Trade

The figures here are extraordinary. They detail the essential structure of Colombia's drug trade and show how cultivating a small glossy-leafed shrub produces black-market exports which dwarf the country's official export trade. These figures demonstrate the colossal impact drugs must have on all strata of Colombian society. (Figures and calculations are courtesy of the US Drug Enforcement Agency and were prepared with the assistance of the British Narcotics Control Dept.).

A. *Marijuana*

After a fairly successful eradication programme, Colombia is no longer such a large producer of marijuana, growing only some 2,000 hectares compared with Mexico's estimated 28,710 hectares. So, in Colombia, its export value will be ignored for the purposes of this study. Actually, for drug dealers, marijuana's problems are simply that its volume to value ratio is not as commercially attractive as cocaine.

B. *Heroin*

Increasingly, heroin poppies are grown in Colombia. Current production is estimated at some 2,500 hectares, and the profit margins are greater even than for cocaine.

C. *Cocaine*

1. The Plant There are principally two varieties of coca plant, *Erithroxylum coca hortense*, which is benign and not used for drugs, and *Erithroxylum coca novagranatense* which is, and is grown widely in Colombia.

2. Colombia's Position in the League Colombia produces 10 per cent of the world's cocaine, with the rest coming from countries to the south: 30 per cent from Bolivia and 60 per cent from Peru. Ecuador's production is negligible by comparison. However, Colombia's geographical position at the top of the Andes makes it necessary for these other countries to export nearly all their cocaine through Colombia. For example, Peruvian drug producers and traders give 82 per cent of the street value of their production to Colombian traffickers. The value of this trade to the Colombian drug cartels may be imagined by looking at the study of Colombian home-grown cocaine which follows.

3. *Growing Conditions* A cocaine shrub looks something like a tea bush and grows very easily in the hot, tropical dampness of the Colombian jungle even though it flourishes best at altitude. So, for example, 200 lbs of good Bolivian dried coca leaves, grown at altitude, are required to make 1 lb of paste, whereas 400 lbs are required from the Colombian llanos.

4. *Area under Cultivation in Colombia* The Colombians grow plenty. The United States Drug Enforcement Agency estimates that some 37,500 hectares are used to grow coca plants in Colombia, most of it in the llanos.

5. *Factors of Production* In pure agricultural terms, what factors reduce the total yield and so affect the amount of total saleable cocaine?

	Factors	*Assumptions*
a.	Leaf yield per shrub, average shrub 1.2 m high:	125 gms
b.	Locals eat leaves while they pick them.	
c.	Plant density, per square metre:	1.1
d.	Harvests per year (sometimes as many as 5 or 6 have been known):	4
e.	Alkaloid content in plant. This is the useful content of the plant. 'Free-basing' is the process of freeing cocaine alkaloid from all impurities.	0.32%
f.	Losses: (1) Laboratory inefficiencies during processing (2) Rodent and insect damage (3) Law enforcement action Total:	30%
g.	Weight losses during drying process of leaves:	60%
h.	Area of Colombia under cultivation:	37,500 ha

6. *Calculation of Production*

One hectare produces ($10,000 \times a \times c$)	1,375 kgs
less losses due to drying process of leaves (% factor *g*)	825 kgs
which leaves	550 kgs/ha
Then take into account the useful alkaloid content of the plant (% factor *e*), which leaves useful weight of cocaine of (kgs/ha × factor *e*)	1.76 kgs/ha
Multiplied by the number of harvests (factor *d*)	7.04 kgs/ha

Multiplied by the number of hectares cultivated in the
whole country (factor h)   264,000 kgs/yr

less all losses, of damage, laboratory inefficiencies and law
enforcement (factor f) which leaves   184,800 kgs/yr

Now, given that ratio of base coca to cocaine hydrochloride
is 1:1, this leaves us with an average production of cocaine
from Colombia per year of   184,800 kgs/yr

7. *Valuations*

a.	At trade price to a dealer with his own network	$2,800 US/kg
	So, value of all cocaine at trade prices is	$517 million
b.	At street price for a dealer with his own network,	$60 US/gm
	So, value of all cocaine at street price is	$11,088 million
c.	At street price cut four ways to sell to user	$240 US/gm
	So, value of Colombia's cocaine on street to users is	$44,352 million

8. *Official Colombian Exports*

Official exports cannot compete with such drug traffick.
The value of official Colombian trade exports in 1989, such as coffee,
bananas, cut flowers, clothing, ferro-nickel and coal, produced only $5,739
million (Source of figures: World Bank).

9. *Summary*

Colombia's cocaine trade at street prices $44,352 million US

Add:

Colombia's share of Peruvian and Bolivian cocaine
(82%, see para C2 above) $327,318 million US

From which the final comparison between legal and
illegal money can be made:

Total black market cash controlled by Colombia's
drug cartels (in cocaine alone) $371,670 million US

Value of Colombia's legal exports $5,739 million US

Therefore it can be imagined what impact the illegal drug trade has on all
aspects of Colombian life.

Appendix E

Operation Phoenix

Set all participants down in their groups, in order within their groups, pilots and assault team:

Hughes 500 K-Car Pilot: Tiger Command Group c/s 0 McAleese (Commander) Tomkins (Dems 2ic) Almaro (Interpreter) Ramon (Interpreter)	*Bell 'Huey' 204* Assault Team Carrier Pilot: Pablo		
	House Clearance Groups		Support Group
	c/s 1	c/s 2	c/s 3
	Potts ic	Milton ic	McVicar ic
	Donnelly 2ic	Shelley 2ic	Gibson 2ic
	Moore	Lennox	(Tomkins)
			(Almaro)
	Bormann	Owen	(Ramon)

INTRODUCTION

Operation Phoenix is so called as the symbol of the rebirth of the Pathfinders.

The task is an attack on Hacienda Napoles, the villa of Pablo Escobar, one of Colombia's most important cocaine barons. The purpose is to kill him.

APPENDIX E

A. *GROUND*

1. *Aids*

Photographs taken from the air laid out in a mosaic.
Sketch plan of the target villa,
a. showing coloured codes for each side: Red, Blue, White and Black sides, and
b. showing codes for rooms inside, White 1, 2 and 3.
Model of the target villa.
Photographs of Escobar.

2. *Maps*

1:50,000
1:250,000

3. *Salient Features*

Bend in east–west road between Puerto Triumpho and Medellin (ERV)
San Diego, or Kiko refuelling point.
Akatamia airstrip.
Dora Dal village. Striking white stucco buildings and church.
Escobar's airstrip alongside Hacienda Napoles (earlier cratered by Colombian Army).
The target villa, Hacienda Napoles.

4. *The Target Area*

Football pitch, rising up slightly. 1st Option Landing Site.
Sandbank on flooded area by football pitch. 2nd Option Landing Site.
Security fences round villa.
Four wooden guard towers.
Tennis court (prisoner handling site).
Target villa.
Swimming pool.
Patio by swimming pool (white tables and chairs).
Carpark on red side of villa.
Main gate on red end of villa. (Estimate 7 guards).
Guards' quarters 'stable block' 200 metres on blue side of villa.

5. *Inside Target Villa*

White 1, large lounge with swimming pool outside.
White 2, sleeping and living quarters of Escobar.
White 3, his close protection bodyguards.

B. *SITUATION*

1. Enemy

   a. *Guards* Estimated total of 80, split up on following tasks:
   (1) static guards in ones and twos on road,
   (2) group of 7 occupying main gate of villa,
   (3) group of 18 on mobile patrol outside villa grounds,
   (4) group of 8 in guards' quarters – stables,
   (5) group of 8 in white 3,
   (6) group of 8 in white 1 area of villa.
   Estimate no group inside villa area bigger than 7 or 8.

   b. *Dress* Civvies: jeans, shirts, belt webbing.

   c. *Weapons* AR15s, pistols, Uzis, Ingrams, GPMG or M60. Never seem
   to carry more than 3 mags.

   d. *Morale* Think they're untouchable. Heavy boozing. Bullies. Said to
   be fairly lax attitude because the whole area in Escobar's payroll,
   including the local police.

   e. *Enemy leadership* Pablo Escobar.

2. Own Forces

See breakdown above for groupings.

   a. *Command Group*
   c/s 0: GPMG on a pintle in Hughes. M16s and 9 mm Interdynamic
   SMG. PE charges.

   b. *Assault Team*

   (1) House Clearance c/s 1:
      (a) Composition: 2 × entry men, 1 × bomber, 1 × lookout.
      (b) Weapons: M16s, 9 mm pistols, grenades, white phosphorus,
      coloured smoke, bunker bombs.

   (2) House Clearance c/s 2: ditto.

APPENDIX E

(3) Support Group c/s 3: G3 on auto, G3 rifle grenades, 66 mm LAW rockets, grenades, 9 mm pistols.

c. *Dress*

(1) Military: all to wear assault vests, combat camouflage uniform, boots, black balaclava with phosphorescent yellow cross on top for ID from air.

(2) Civilian: change of civvies, escape money, day's rations, water bottle, in small bags.

d. *Comms*
Each man carries personal radio with earpiece and mike.

3. *Atts and Dets*

a. *Command and Assault Teams.* The following are attached to these groups:

(1) Helicopters: 1 x Hughes 500 and 1 x Bell 'Huey' 204 fitted with a Bell 205 engine which gives it greater lift capacity.

(2) Personnel: 2 x heli pilots, Pablo and Tiger; 2 x interpreters, Almaro and Ramon.

b. *Air Support* The following extra air support is required:

(1) 1 x Caravan fixed-wing.

(2) 1 x Cessna fixed-wing, with Telstar radio rebroadcast equipment with Colonel Ricardo as interpreter.

(3) 1 x Bell 214 Jetranger helicopter ambulance.

Notes: All rotary-wing and fixed-wing lift capacity, fuel-weight ratios, range calculations, take-off times from different airfields, and rendezvous time are pre-planned.

C. *MISSION*

To kill Pablo Escobar (twice).

D. *EXECUTION*

1. *General Outline* The operation to be carried out in four phases

a. Phase One: Flight from La Gagua to Kiko.

    b. Phase Two: Assault.

    c. Phase Three: Reorganisation.

    d. Phase Four: Withdrawal.

2. *Phase One*: Flight from La Gagua to Kiko

    a. Bell 204 slightly ahead of Hughes 500, so men in each heli can see what the others are doing.

    b. Groupings in helis as per list above.

    c. On arrival at Kiko refuelling point, helis land, everyone debuss, into all-round defence, refuel helis, doors taken off Bell 204.

    d. Final check of equipment.

3. *Phase Two*: Assault

    a. Take off from Kiko.

    b. Fly north towards Dora Dal village, passing to its east.

    c. Locate target villa, Hacienda Napoles, on our right.

    d. Swing east over top of villa. Hughes on northern side and Bell 204 on southern side.

    e. Both helis fire on guard towers, two each.

    f. Bell 204 also check football pitch landing site for wires.

    g. Hughes fly over length of villa dropping 3 charges of 6 lbs PE, and 2 charges of 10 lbs PE on main gate house. Hughes then up in orbit to dominate area, using pintle-mounted GPMG to suppress enemy guards from guards' quarters, or villa or elsewhere.

    h. Bell 204 flying round till Hughes in orbit when it lands on football pitch, covered by Hughes.

    i. Assault team debuss.

    j. Bell 204 take off, fly to northeast to check airstrip for wires and report clear to Caravan above.

    k. Assault team on landing site to cover the hover-landing of Hughes which lets off 3 men (Tomkins, Almaro and Ramon to join Support Group).

    l. Hughes back into orbit over the blue/black corner of villa to suppress all enemy movement on blue side and black side, and give any other support necessary, e.g. suppress reinforcements of enemy guards from other directions.

m. Detailed groupings and tasks.

   (1) Support Group

      (a) Stay in area of football pitch landing site.

      (b) Neutralise and isolate guards' quarters in stable block.

      (c) Cover House Clearance Groups to villa.

   (2) House Clearance Groups

      (a) Move across patio and swimming pool area to white 1 at red side of villa.

      (b) Assault of villa by leap-frogging of c/s 1 and c/s 2 through inside rooms white 1, 2 and 3, as follows in detail:

        (i) c/s 1 assaults white 1, covered inside by c/s 2 which neutralises any other enemy guards seen from direction of main gate area on red side of villa.

        (ii) c/s 2 assaults white 2, passing through c/s 1 which covers rear of c/s 2. Lookout men remain to cover rear of assault groups.

        (iii) c/s 1 assaults white 3, passing through c/2.

        (iv) Limit of exploitation to be black side of villa.

   (3) Support Group

      (a) Assault guards' quarters in stable block once House Clearance Group controls the villa and radios it is ready to cover them across.

   (4) Caravan holds off away from target area.

   (5) Cessna Telstar circles high as rebro station.

   (6) Bell 214 Jetranger heli-ambulance holds off low in case of injuries/death.

4. *Phase Three*: Reorganisation.

a. Confirm Escobar killed, by going back through rooms as necessary. Photograph him.

b. Collect all prisoners (servants etc.) on tennis court.

c. House Clearance Groups and Support Group reorganise together in all-round defence on football pitch landing site.

5. *Phase Four*: Withdrawal.

    a. Hughes K-car calls in Bell 204.

    b. Hughes warns Caravan to land at airstrip.

    c. House Clearance Groups Assault Team covers area of landing site on football pitch for Hughes to land.

    d. Hughes hover-lands and takes off Tomkins, Almaro and Ramon.

    e. Hughes covers Bell 204 to land on football pitch. All assault team boards heli and Bell takes off.

Note: Bell 214 Jetranger available in case other helis damaged.

    f. Both Hughes and Bell 204 helis fly to landing strip, land and all personnel board Caravan.

    g. Caravan takes off towards Ibaque.

    h. Exfil.

6. *Coordinating Instructions*

    a. Timings.

(1) Phase One	11.20 hrs	2 × Assault Team helis dep La Gagua
	12.10	Cessna 'Telstar' rebro dep Cali.
	12.45	Jetranger heli-ambulance dep Bogota.
	13.30	Caravan fixed-wing dep Cali.
	13.50	2 × Assault Team helis ETA at Kiko to refuel.
(2) Phases Two	14.50	2 × Assault Team helis dep Kiko.
and Three	14.55	Cessna 'Telstar' rebro arr over target.
	15.00	2 × Assault Team helis arr target.
		Jetranger heli-ambulance arr target.
		Caravan arr over target.
	15.30	2 × Assault Team helis dep target.
(3) Phase Four	15.35	2 × Assault Team helis arr airstrip.
		Caravan arr airstrip. Transfer to Caravan.
		Caravan dep airstrip.
		All aircraft dep target area.
	18.10	Arr exfil RV.

b. Actions on.

(1) Heli crash before target	Abort Operation.
(2) Heli crash on target	Carry on. Use Jetranger to ferry team to airstrip for lift out by Caravan.
(3) Heli lost during assault	Carry on. Use Jetranger as above.
(4) If lost/separated	Proceed to junction of bend in road and road bridge over river and lie back in cover. This is ERV.
(5) If wounded	Wait for first aid and heli-ambulance.
(6) Counter-attack	As per rehearsals.
(7) At ERV	Adopt LUP drills. Use fire-fly lights with colour coded filter which rescue party could ID with IR binos.

E. *SERVICE AND SUPPORT*

1. *Dress*

   a. Combat uniforms, boots, flak vests.

   b. Balaclavas with phosphorescent yellow cross.

   c. Belt kit, 2 water bottles, escape kit, mag pouches for 10 mags.

   d. Spare civvy clothes and light shoes and 30,000 pesos escape money.

2. *Weapons*

   a. Personal weapons. M16s with 10 x 30-round mags, 9 mm pistols, 9 mm Interdynamic SMG, 7.62 mm GPMG pintle-mounted.

   b. Special. HE grens, Phos grens, smoke grens, M72 66 mm LAWs, G3 rifle grens, PE charges. Bullhorn loudspeaker (tell non-coms to lie down).

3. *Medical*

   a. Each person carries own 'Shock' pack made up with drip bag, giving set (needle), penicillin and Reverin (for stomach wounds) in sack sealed with 3 x tapes for attaching drip and giving set to arm.

   b. Each group in Assault Team has a medic.

   c. Doctor in heli-ambulance Jetranger.

   d. Surgical team on standby in Cali.

F. *COMMAND AND SIGNAL*

1. *Comms Net* All ground call signs are on the same channel and wavelength, to speak to Hughes 500 K-car, but the air support is on another channel, to avoid confusion, as follows:

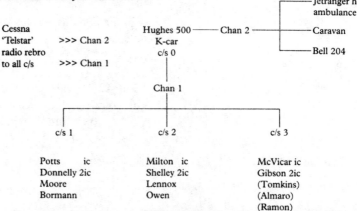

2. *Radios* All ground personnel have radio, earpiece and mike. Peter McAleese in Hughes has radio with both channels coming in to his earpiece and a switch to speak to either Channel 1 or Channel 2.

   (*Note:* there was not much traffic on Channel 2 between a/c).

3. *Codenames*

Peter McAleese	– Papa Mike
Bell 204 pilot	– Pablo
Hughes 500 pilot	– Tiger
British personnel	– Lions
Colombian personnel	– Cyclists
Caravan a/c	– Mustang
Cessna 'Telstar' rebro a/c	– Telstar
Heli-ambulance, Jetranger	– Red Cross

4. In event comms break down, throw smoke to bring in helicopters:
   Green: come in and safe to land.
   Red: unsafe to land.

Red on green: someone wounded but safe to land.
(*Note:* only red and green smoke available).

5. Password: Question: Pesos?
               Answer: Dollars.

Synchronise watches. Questions.

Index

INDEX

Hartful, Steve, 126
'Henry' (in Colombia), 215–16, 217
Hereford, and SAS, 50–1
Hesse, Hermann, quoted, 60, 205
'Hilton Assignment', 56–7
Hind, Lance Corporal Chuck, 35–6, 90, 95
Holt, Tim, MM, 56
Hopton, Major, 53, 54
Hussey, 'Fuzz', 76
Hutton, Sgt Major Jock, 122, 123

Ihaka, 'Kingie', 40
Indonesian attack on Malaya, 35
Intelligence, 39, 127
IRA protection rackets, 134
Israeli link with Colombia operation, 216, 229

Johnson, WOII, 18
Johnson, Andy, 107
Johnson, Mike, 71
Joliffe, Baz, 97
'Julio' (in Colombia), 215–16, 219, 220, 221

Kampala, 201–2
Karlen, Rt Revd Henry, 98
Kaulback, Roy, 155, 213, 229–30, 233
Kaunda, Kenneth, 146
Kavalamanja operation, 115–16
'Keep' system in Rhodesia, 136
Kgabo, Michael, 192
Kirk, Dr Sandy, 138, 146–7
Kissinger, Dr Henry, 91
de Klerk, Lt Peter, 171
Kluzniak, Steve, 103, 104–5, 106, 108–9, 113, 122
KMS in Uganda, 200–7
Kruger, Colour Sergeant, 93

Langley, Sgt Andy, 120–1
Large, Sgt Don 'Lofty', 24, 26
Lennox, Alec, 151, 213, 240
Letts, Capt Robin, 23, 24, 26, 29, 31
Libya, 'Hilton Assignment', 56–7
Lillico, Sgt Geordie, 37, 42, 46
Lima, Commandante, 72–3, 75
Lock, Joe, 199
Lottering, Yvonne, 179, 188, 195, 196
Loyola, Sister, 12–14, 15
Lule, Yusef, 202

Lutz, Sergeant Major, 120

McAleese, Alexander 'Sanny', 12
McAleese, Billy (uncle), 9, 10, 15
McAleese, Billy (brother), 13, 17
McAleese, Billy (son), 158, 184, 187, 196
McAleese, Catherine (daughter), 196
McAleese, Jane, née Crist (wife), 95–6, 98, 110, 111, 133
    daughter Emelda, 95
    medical work with blacks, 124, 137
    pregnant, leaves Zimbabwe, 153
    to South Africa, 154, 178, 179
    birth of Billy, 158
    neglected, 182
    and the injured PM, 184–8, 189
    marriage under pressure, 193
    pregnant with Catherine, 193
    back to Britain, 196
    problems of finding work, 198–9
McAleese, Jason (son), 56
McAleese, 'Kiter' (father), 8, 9, 10, 11, 19
McAleese, Marlene, née Good (first wife), 52, 56, 57
McAleese, Miles (grandfather), 10, 11–12, 162, 261
McAleese, Tom (cousin), 79
McCandless, Jamie, 76
McCormack, Capt Scotty, 101
McGuinness, Chief Superintendent Mac, 123, 124, 125, 128, 129, 133, 141, 152
McGuire, Jim, 122, 132–3
McKenzie, Major Alistair, 166, 167
McKenzie, Andy, 79, 88
McKenzie, Capt Bob, 98–9, 105, 106, 115, 120
McPherson, Stuart, 71
McVicar, Stuart, 233, 245
Malayan emergency, 34, 35, 127, 136
Malloch, Jack, 103
Malteo, Johnny, 16
Mandela, Nelson, 179
Manuera, Lieutenant, MC, 40
Maquela (Angola), 73, 74, 75, 77
    massacre at, 78–84, 88
Marquez, Gabriel Garcia, quoted, 208, 231
Mayne, Col Paddy, DSO, 61
Measham, Dougie, 200
Mercenaries, in Angola, 88–9, 263–9
    see also Banks, John

INDEX